WITHDRAWN

ETHNIC IDENTIFICATION:
THE GREEK AMERICANS OF HOUSTON, TEXAS

IMMIGRANT COMMUNITIES & ETHNIC MINORITIES IN THE UNITED STATES & CANADA: No. 68

Series Editor: Robert J. Theodoratus
Department of Anthropology, Colorado State University

Continued at back of book

ETHNIC IDENTIFICATION:
THE GREEK AMERICANS OF HOUSTON, TEXAS

Donna Misner Collins

AMS Press
New York

Library of Congress Cataloging-in-Publication Data

Collins, Donna Misner.
    Ethnic identification : the Greek Americans of Houston, Texas /
by Donna Misner Collins.
      — (Immigrant communities & ethnic minorities in the
United States & Canada ; no. 68)
    Includes bibliographical references.
    ISBN 0-404-19478-8
    1. Greek Americans—Texas—Houston—Cultural assimilation.
    2. Greek Americans—Texas—Houston—Ethnic identity.
    3. Houston (Tex.)—Social conditions. I. Title. II. Series: Immigrant
communities & ethnic minorities in the United States & Canada; 68.
    F394.H89G73   1991
    305.8'8907641411—dc20

                                    89-48334
                                          CIP

All AMS books are printed on acid-free paper that meets the
guidelines for performance and durability of the Committee on
Production Guidelines for Book Longevity of the Council on Library Resources.

AMS PRESS
56 East 13th Street
New York, N.Y. 10003, U.S.A.

MANUFACTURED IN THE UNITED STATES OF AMERICA

ACKNOWLEDGEMENTS

Thanking all those who helped in this project is a very pleasant task. First I would like to thank the Southwest Center for Urban Research, the National Science Foundation, and the National Institute of Mental Health for the grants which made it possible to undertake the research project.

A number of people gave invaluable guidance. Particular thanks go to Drs. Stephen Klinebert and Ken Leiter for helping me make the research project and dissertation much better than I ever thought they could be, and to Drs. Bill Characklis, Ron Provencher, and Edward Norbeck for providing the moral support which was at times badly needed. Thanks to Barbara Podratz for her administrative guidance, typing, and years of friendship.

Many people who are very close to me deserve my deep appreciation for their fantastic help and patience with this project—my parents, parents-in-law, and particularly my sister and husband, who provided not only emotional support, but also hundreds of hours of work. I cannot thank them enough for all they have done.

I would also like to thank Father Nicholas Triantafilou and the Board of Trustees of Annunciation Church for their permission to conduct this study. The last group I must acknowledge is of course my good friends of Houston's Greek community. If I were to thank people presonally for their help, the list of names would go on for many pages. I hope that a heartfelt Σάς εύχαριστῶ will convey my appreciation for the help of so many wonderful people. Everything that is of value in this work, I dedicate to them, and to my husband.

TABLE OF CONTENTS

PHOTOGRAPHS: Community Activities

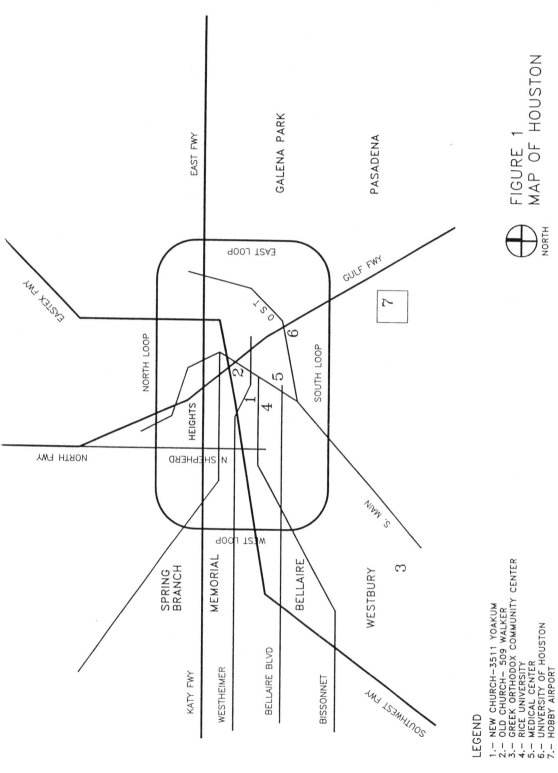

FIGURE 1
MAP OF HOUSTON

NORTH

LEGEND

1.– NEW CHURCH–3511 YOAKUM
2.– OLD CHURCH– 509 WALKER
3.– GREEK ORTHODOX COMMUNITY CENTER
4.– RICE UNIVERSITY
5.– MEDICAL CENTER
6.– UNIVERSITY OF HOUSTON
7.– HOBBY AIRPORT

FIGURE 2
MAP OF GREECE

PART I

INTRODUCTION, HISTORY, AND ETHNOGRAPHY

CHAPTER 1

INTRODUCTION

This study examines ethnic identification among the Greek Americans
of Houston, Texas. Its major focus is on the forces which enable the
ethnic group to continue as a viable entity. Of particular interest in
this analysis are the social boundaries of the ethnic group, i.e., those
elements which define group membership.

Within the American sociological tradition, much attention has been
concentrated on the nature of "assimilation," the process by which
immigrants become Americanized. In general, the assumption has been
that through assimilation group differences will disappear and ethnic
groups will actually cease to exist. Recent evidence that this predicted
process has in fact not occurred has renewed interest in the possibility
that America may remain a culturally-pluralistic society. It is too
early to state with assurance which of these views describes the ultimate
form of American society, but a good case could be made for either
assimilation or pluralism as the predominant response of ethnics to
contact with American culture. The fact is that, in a sense, both
assimilation and pluralism are occurring. Immigrants and their traditions
have changed (and still do change) significantly after living in America
a short time, but they and their descendants have also in many cases
remained loyal to the ethnic group and retained their membership in it.
Because of this seemingly conflicting evidence, sociologists who have
examined the phenomenon of ethnic groups have stressed the view--
assimilationist or pluralist--which best fits their own conception of

1

the nature of social life and of the most appropriate outcome of immigration to America.

The cause of this confusion is the failure of sociologists to adequately explore the significance of boundary maintenance for assimilation/pluralism. How does the ethnic group remain separate from the surrounding society? How are its members kept within the group? These are the questions which are important to ask, rather than whether a group's old-world customs are maintained intact in America, for example. The essential, basic meaning of assimilation is the disintegration and eventual disappearance of the ethnic group as its members one by one leave the group, i.e., become "assimilated" into American society. Therefore, the researcher must examine those forces which keep the individual within the group or draw him away. Thus ethnic identification plays a significant role in the future of ethnicity in America, for it is through the individual identificational choices of its members that a group flourishes or dies. Unfortunately, ethnic identification has been a neglected area of research, and the few direct examinations have been characterized by a simplistic view of the nature of this phenomenon.

This chapter will develop more fully the theoretical perspective which has been described here in a very sketchy manner. A rather detailed examination of the concept of "assimilation" will be followed by a discussion of previous work in the area of ethnic identification, which points to a somewhat more complex concept of ethnic identification than is presently found in the literature on ethnic groups. An alternative way of viewing ethnic groups—in terms of their social boundaries—will be presented in an effort to clarify many of the problems associated

with the current concept of "assimilation". These theoretical sections
are purposely presented rather autobiographically to enable the reader
to see how the theoretical orientation developed, through interaction
with both my research data and the literature on ethnic groups. This
admittedly makes for a rather lengthy exposition, but I feel that the
theoretical perspective and its relationship to the field of ethnic
groups may be understood most fully in this way. A brief discussion
of the research methods and setting will conclude the chapter.

I. The Concept of Assimilation

Ethnic groups--groups possessing distinctive cultural traditions
whose members share a sense of common history and destiny, of 'peoplehood'
--have throughout history come into contact in many ways, including
military conquest, the redrawing of national boundaries, and migration.
The last of these has been the most significant in the history of America;
indeed it is not exaggerating to say that the United States has been
created by the migration of millions of people from virtually every
continent of the world. Whereas this migration was in some cases in-
voluntary, with the importation of slaves providing the obvious example,
in most cases people voluntarily immigrated to America, hoping for a
better life in this "new world" than they had left in the old.

Situations in which culturally distinct groups come into extended
contact are of great interest to social scientists. Numerous theories
have been proposed to explain and predict the varying modes of adjustment resulting from differing situations of contact (Lieberson 1961).
"Acculturation" and "assimilation" are the terms most commonly used to

denote the results of group contact, and their definitions warrant

examination.

Although "acculturation" and "assimilation" are closely related

and are concerned with similar phenomena, there are important differ-

ences between the two concepts. "Acculturation", as the term is used

by anthropologists, has a very specific meaning, and its most widely-

accepted definiton is that proposed by Redfield, Linton, and Herskovits.

> Acculturation comprehends those phenomena which result when
> groups of individuals having different cultures come into
> continuous first-hand contact, with subsequent changes in
> the original cultural patterns of either or both groups
> (1936:149).

Two specific dimensions of this definition, as well as of the "assimi-

lation" definitions which are to follow, are of particular interest.

"Acculturation" implies that the cultural patterns of either or both

of the groups involved may be modified by the contact, and does not

specify any amount of "change"--i.e., the changes in a situation of

acculturation may be many or few. The anthropological concept of

acculturation in general presents fewer problems than the term "assimi-

lation", which has been used primarily by sociologists. This is partly

due to the fact that a single definition of the concept has been commonly

accepted, and this definition has the virtue of vagueness, of not address-

ing such conceptual problems as varying degrees of acculturation.

On the other hand, there are myriad definitions of assimilation,

and most specify the way in which assimilation occurs, the types and

degrees of adjustment which constitute assimilation, and so on. Further-

more, American sociologists have examined this process only within the

context of the American situation, in which many immigrant ethnic groups

have been expected to "fit into" what has been presumed to be a rather
firmly-established society. Thus the comparative viewpoint from which
anthropologists examine acculturation is largely lacking in sociological
discussions of assimilation. For this reason, definitions of "assimilation" either obliquely or directly refer to the American situation.

"Assimilation" has not been adequately and consistently defined.
Discrepancies are evident in the several definitions which are given
here by way of example.

> Social assimilation is the name given to the process or pro-
> cesses by which peoples of diverse racial origins and different
> cultural heritages, occupying a common territory, achieve a
> cultural solidarity sufficient at least to sustain a national
> existence... In the United States an immigrant is ordinarily
> considered assimilated as soon as he has acquired the language
> and the social ritual of the native community and can parti-
> cipate, without encountering prejudice, in the common life,
> economic and political. The common sense view of the matter
> is that an immigrant is assimilated as soon as he has shown
> that he can "get on in the country" (Park 1930:281).

Here "assimilation" is viewed as a process involving rather limited
cultural change; the individual is assimilated if he has sufficiently
mastered certain basic cultural elements of the host society, at least
to the extent that he can "get on in the country." Although this definition technically allows for changes in either of the groups involved
in achieving "cultural solidarity", it specifically states that in the
American case, the immigrant is assimilated when he has adjusted to the
"native community".

> By assimilation we mean the process whereby groups with differ-
> ent cultures come to have a common culture. This means, of
> course, not merely such items of the culture as dress, knives
> and forks, language, food, sports, and automobiles, which are
> relatively easy to appreciate and acquire, but also those less
> tangible items such as values, memories, sentiments, ideas,
> and attitudes. Assimilation refers thus to the fusion of
> cultural heritages (Berry 1951:217).

Like the definition of "acculturation" this definition allows for changes

in either group, but it suggests that assimilation is not complete until

no cultural differences remain between the groups involved. Park and

Burgess take this concept one step farther and explain the way in which

this process occurs.

> Assimilation is a process of interpenetration and fusion in
> which persons and groups acquire the memories, sentiments,
> and attitudes of other persons or groups, and by sharing their
> experience and history, are incorporated with them in a common
> cultural life... As social contact initiates interaction,
> assimilation is its final perfect product. The nature of the
> social contacts is decisive in the process. Assimilation
> naturally takes place most rapidly where contacts are primary,
> that is where they are the most intimate and intense, as in
> the area of touch relationship, in the family circle, and in
> intimate congenial groups (Park and Burgess 1921:735).

This definition explains assimilation as a process whereby groups come

to have a common culture, but it also delineates the way in which this

occurs--through extensive social relationships between groups. Assimila-

tion is not specified as a one-way process, but the connotation of this

definition is that one group is incorporated into the society and culture

of another. A fourth and final definition:

> Social assimilation is the process by which different cultures,
> or individuals or groups representing different cultures, are
> merged into a homogeneous unit. The analogy is with the bio-
> logical process whereby a living body ingests external matter
> of various different kinds, and transforms it into body cells
> of harmonious types. It is important to note that this physio-
> logical assimilation does not result in identical body cells,
> but in various types of cells that are adapted to, and normal
> in, the entire organism no matter how complex it may be. Like-
> wise, social assimilation does not require the complete identi-
> fication of all the units, but such modifications as eliminate
> the characteristics of foreign origin, and enable them all to
> fit smoothly into the typical structure and functioning of the
> new cultural unit... In essence, assimilation is the substitu-
> tion of one nationality pattern for another. Ordinarily, the
> modifications must be made by the weaker or numerically inferior
> group (Fairchild 1944:276-7).

Fairchild's definition raises several questions. E.g., what degree of homogeneity is required before one could say assimilation has occurred? What is meant by "complete identification of all units?" Despite these problems, this definition is included as representative of a fairly common view of assimilation. Another work by Fairchild (1926) indicates that "assimilation" signifies the disappearance of immigrant groups as individual ethnics become Americans. This does not mean that all members of American society must become carbon copies of one another--individual personality differences will of course remain--but all ethnic differences must inevitably vanish. Thus the end result of assimilation is seen as "the substitution of one nationality pattern for another", and one group, the "weaker", is expected to conform to the patterns of the other.

These four definitions demonstrate the confusion associated with the concept of "assimilation". Few sociologists agree on even the two elements discussed here. Is assimilation a one-way process, in which the immigrant makes all the concessions, or does the receiving society modify some of its patterns as a result of contact with immigrant groups? One of the most significant points of difficulty with the concept of "assimilation" is its end result. Some sociologists, such as Fairchild, have characterized assimilation as a process which results in a homo-geneous unit having no traces of the individual "foreign" groups. Others declare that an individual is assimilated if he is conversant with a few very basic cultural elements of the receiving society. There is of course a significant difference in these two conceptions of assimi-lation. One requires that the individual make a few concessions, only those necessary "to sustain a national existence," whereas the other insists that the "foreign" individual drop all previous cultural, social, and identificational ties; in other words, he must become invisible, and his group must cease to exist.

In these two conceptions of assimilation--more or less representing the extreme poles between which other conceptions lie--one senses that the sociologist's view of assimilation is in many cases not so much an objective description of "what is" as an assertion of "what ought to be." The three main "theories" of assimilation in American society--Americanization, the melting pot, and cultural pluralism--are so well known that there is little point in discussing them in detail. Each represents a different philosophy about the nature of America, and the advocates of each insist that the essence of "America" will be fulfilled if immigrants conform to their conception. The Americanization movement was based on the idea of the inherent superiority of the American culture, and its proponents contend that immigrants should dissolve all ties to their traditional culture and society, thereby becoming 100% American. The melting-pot conception (Zangwill 1909) stated that America, as a "nation of nations" whose populace encompasses every nationality, is "God's Crucible, the great Melting Pot"; the many immigrant groups should, through intermarriage, blend together, thereby becoming one new and almost superhuman group--Americans. In both the Americanization and melting-pot conceptions, it is assumed that immigrant groups must disappear, an assumption which is challenged by cultural pluralists. They stress that American democracy will be enriched by the presence of culturally distinct groups, and thus the immigrant should retain his culture and ethnic community, while being socially and politically integrated into American life (Kallen 1924).

In general sociologists have responded to the realities of modern American society by casting their theories after the form of one of these three prevailing philosophies. E.g., Park (1950) proposed a model in which contact, competition, accomodation, and finally, assimilation were outlined as the four stages in the "natural history of race and ethnic relations." Park's model is based on a major theme of classical sociology--the dramatic change brought about by the pressures of industrialization and urbanization, i.e., the transition from Gemeinschaft to Gesellschaft--and therefore assumes that ethnic groups, being communal, must disintegrate as a result of the progressive force of assimilation (Etzioni 1959). This emphasis on assimilation as a "natural" force is also grounded in conceptions of the nature of American society, as Metzger pointed out in his discussion of the theoretical framework from which American sociologists have viewed ethnic and race relations.

> This framework, it is believed, rests essentially on the image
> of American society which has been set forth by American
> liberalism, wherein the minority problem is defined in the
> narrow sense of providing adequate, if not equal, opportunity
> for members of minority groups to ascend as individuals into
> the mainstream culture. America, in this view, is the land of
> opportunity through competitive struggle in the marketplace;
> it can, and will, provide opportunities for all to gain just
> rewards for individual merit..."opportunity," in this system,
> is the opportunity to discard one's ethnicity and to partake
> fully in the "American Way of Life"; in this sense, assimila-
> tion is viewed as the embodiment of the democratic ethos
> (1971:628-9).

Park's theory has been criticized on several points (see Etzioni 1959 as well as Metzger 1971), but it has nevertheless provided the general framework for later discussion of the position and future of ethnic groups in the United States. Many classical studies of American ethnicity have used his assimilationist view as a guiding light (e.g., Wirth 1928, Warner and Srole 1945, Sherman 1961). The controversies in this tradition do not question the inevitability of assimilation so much as the details of the assimilation process. Is the process unilinear, with each generation more assimilated than the last, as Park and Wirth suggest? Or is it a cyclical process in which the second generation—psychically scarred by the trauma of marginal status—rejects its group and heritage, while the third generation, which has not suffered the pains of association with a "foreign" group, "returns" with intellectual interest to examine its immigrant roots (Hansen 1952)? The debate on Hansen's principle—"What the son wishes to forget, the grandson wishes to remember"—and on the nature of ethnicity in the second and third generations has continued (Lazerwitz and Rowitz 1964, Herberg 1955, Nahirny and Fishman 1965, Bender and Kagiwada 1968, Glazer 1954).

The melting-pot philosophy, in a modified form, has also had several advocates among American sociologists. The most notable have been Kennedy (1944) and Herberg (1955), who argue that American society is a "triple melting pot" composed of the three major religious groupings—Protestant, Catholic, and Jew—within which nationality groupings are breaking down. These variations differ from the original melting-pot theory in one important respect, however: they stress that assimilation has resulted in a "transmuting pot" in which foreign elements are modified to fit an Anglo-Saxon model. Herberg makes this observation:

> The "national type" as ideal has always been, and remains, pretty well fixed. It is the Mayflower, John Smith, Davy Crockett, George Washington, and Abraham Lincoln that define

the American's self-image, and this is true whether the American
in question is a descendant of the Pilgrims or the grandson of
an immigrant from southeastern Europe... Our cultural assimilation has proceeded in essentially the same way as has our
linguistic development--a few foreign words here and there, a
few modifications of form, but still thoroughly and unquestion-
ably English. The "Anglo-Saxon" type remains the American ideal
to which all other elements are transmuted in order to become
American (1955:21).

Recent events have made sociologists question the validity of the

assimilationist and melting pot theories. The 1960's saw the rise of

"black power" and similar movements among Indians and Chicanos. Encour-

aged by these minority movements, others began to see their ethnicity

as a special source of identity and pride; it was (and is) "in" to be

ethnic. These events challenged two generally-held assumptions: (1)

that ethnics have gladly, and in great numbers, assimilated, abandoning

their group associations and traditional cultures to take on "American"

identities and values; and (2) that American culture is monolithic and

essentially WASP, with ethnic deviations from it merely representing

temporary way stations on the road to assimilation. Each of these will

be discussed in turn.

Faced with the reality of pluralism which became so evident in the

1960's, many have reconsidered the value of cultural pluralism in a

democratic society (again, see Etzioni and Metzger). Correspondingly,

social scientists are beginning to assert that American ethnic groups

have in many cases retained their traditional forms. Greeley, a leading

advocate of the reality of cultural pluralism in America, has suggested

that the emphasis on the rationalization of modern society has in the

past blinded many sociologists to the vast range of social phenomena

based on the bonds of kinship, common religion, and consciousness of

kind which are still vitally important in today's urban industrial society.
On the other hand, Gordon (1964) has taken issue with the cultural-
pluralist model, asserting that virtually all members of ethnic groups
have become culturally American--i.e., are "culturally assimilated"--
despite the fact of their continued group association and identification.[1]
He views cultural assimilation as the first step toward total assimilation,
and "structural assimilation", the entrance of ethnics into "American"
primary groups and institutions, as the keystone of the assimilation
process. Thus he suggests that the term "structural pluralism" is a more
accurate description of contemporary American society. Nevertheless,
Greeley (1964, 1971) and Parenti (1967) contend not only that structural
assimilation is not inevitable, and that feelings of ethnic identification are still of great importance to many individuals, but also that
cultural variations continue to exist among different ethnic groups.
There is some evidence to uphold this viewpoint. E.g., research on the
responses of members of different American ethnic groups to pain and
illness (Zborowski 1969, Suchman 1964) demonstrates that distinctive
cultural resonses continue to exist, despite cries of "cultural assimilation" from all sides.

The developments of the 1960's also called into question the assumption that America is essentially WASP. WASPs have been considered the
majority, "the" Americans, but--now representing only 1/3 of the popula-
tion--they have become a numerical minority. Schrag has dismissed the
accompanying cultural "decline of the WASP" which has become evident.

> They--the WASPs--never thought of themselves as anything but
> Americans, nor did it occur to others to label them as anything
> special until, about twenty-five years ago, their influence began
> to decline and they started to lose their cultural initiative and

preeminence. There were, to be sure, regional distinctions, but whatever was "American" was WASP... For most WASPs, their complaints were proprietary. That is, the old place was going down because the tenants weren't keeping it up properly. They were the landlords of our culture, and their values, with rare exceptions, were those that defined it: hard work, perseverance, self-reliance, puritanism, the missionary spirit, and the abstract rule of law... Who and what has replaced them, then, in the invention and production of our culture? Jews and Negroes, Catholics and immigrants... The spokesmen of American literature and culture tend increasingly to represent the pluralistic residues of a melting pot that--for better or worse--never worked as well as some Americans had hoped (1972:182-3).

In reality, America has never had a monolithic society or culture. It would be difficult to answer de Crevecoeur's question, "What, then, is the American, this new man?" "The American" does not exist, for "American" is too amorphous a category. Americans are Midwesterners or Southerners; lower or upper middle class; Episcopal or Jewish; rural or urban dwellers; of Irish or German heritage; white or black--all of these dimensions, and many others, contribute to the tremendous cultural and social diversity of America and provide important sources of distinctive identity for individual Americans. Ethnicity has always been an aspect of American life, overlooked because it was assumed to be on the way out.

This raises a further important question about assimilation: if America is characterized by such diversity, to what does the immigrant assimilate in becoming "American"? The fact that there is no homogeneous culture and value system means that there is in fact no standard "American." Rather, there are many different types of Americans. Nevertheless, one can visualize the process of assimilation as not so much "moving toward" some standard version of "the American" as moving away from one's ethnic group. The point is not so much that the individual becomes more American in any specified way, as that he becomes less Greek, for example. Indeed, the research reported in this volume has found that individuals who may be classified as "assimilating" are not really attempting to become "American" (because they see much to criticize in aspects of American culture) so much as trying to become less involved in the Greek American community. The force which draws them away is not the siren call of "Americanism", but the opportunity to escape from certain aspects of the Greek community, such as perceived narrow-mindedness and provincialism. This idea will of course be discussed in greater detail in the pages which follow.

Thus ethnicity, which has always been assumed to be on the wane, has proven to be a more tenacious aspect of American life than early theorists had expected. Recent evidence (Veidemanis 1963, Gans 1958, Abramson 1973) seems to suggest that some form of the pluralist, rather than the assimilationist, model presents a more accurate view of the realities of American society. Nevertheless, one must be as cautious of those who have recently begun to assume cultural pluralism as of those who have assumed assimilation in the past, for each theory has been greatly influenced by the values prevailing at the time of its ascendancy. When assimilation was considered "right", social scientists saw evidence of this process all around them, and now that cultural pluralism is in vogue, they are increasingly sensitive to evidence of ethnicity.

In short, the concept of "assimilation" presents numerous problems. It has not been consistently defined; sociologists frequently use the term to denote varying degrees or types of adjustment to American society. Furthermore, many models of assimilation have been based not on objective analysis, but on preconceived notions about the rationalization of modern social life and about America's purpose. These many difficulties with

the concept have led some social scientists to suggest alternative terms

such as "absorption", "integration", and "adaptation". E.g., Goldlust

and Richmond comment:

> The term "adaptation" has the advantage of not involving a
> priori value judgments concerning desirable outcomes or
> conveying the same ideological overtones that have come to
> be associated with the notion of "assimilation". The conver-
> gence of an immigrant population, in time, to a state of
> assimilation with the indigenous population, may be a special
> case of a certain type of adaptation, while the convergence of
> the members of a receiving society toward the characteristics
> of the migrant group may be another... In practice, both
> processes may be at work simultaneously and other changes,
> including the greater differentiation and diversification of
> the social system as a consequence of migration, may also
> occur (1974:195).

Their discussion allows for the assumption of immigrant characteristics

by the receiving population, as well as the reverse case, but insists on

neither outcome, thus providing a badly-needed sense of objectivity which

the term "assimilation" lacks. Nevertheless, a proliferation of terms

will not solve the problems which face the sociologist who examines the

nature of ethnicity in America. The concept of assimilation has been

around a long time, and is no doubt here to stay; furthermore, "assimila-

tion", in its most strict and far-reaching sense (in which an ethnic

group disappears) represents a very real possibility in America, and

placed together with the other end of the implied continuum--pluralism--

the complex of assimilation/pluralism represents a viable description of

the continuum of alternatives available to ethnic groups. Sociologists,

rather than creating more terms, should examine the conflicting tendencies

of assimilation and pluralism in an attempt to uncover the forces in

American society which encourage each, as well as to delineate the varying dimensions of the adaptation process.

"Assimilation" in this work refers to both an end result and the process by which it occurs. An ethnic group is assimilated when it ceases to exist; this result occurs by its individual members' having become "assimilated", i.e., having left the group. This definition raises a further question. How does an ethnic group "disappear", and when can it be said to exist no longer? If an ethnic group is defined as a community of interacting individuals who define themselves as holding in common certain central values and perspectives which differentiate them from others, then that ethnic group disappears when the differential inter- action among community members which is necessary for the maintenance of group distinctiveness no longer exists. In other words, this view stresses the group aspect of ethnic phenomena: a group which no longer has any members by definition ceases to exist. The significance of "assimilation" is not whether Greeks or Italians or Poles become culturally "American", but whether people will continue to identify themselves with, and participate in, the ethnic group. The main concern of this research project was precisely this: the forces which enable the group to continue as a viable entity, i.e., to resist assimilation. Of course assimilation, as evidenced in the disappearance of an ethnic group, is determined by many personal decisions of individual ethnics to either remain within the group or to leave it. What are the forces--from American society, and within the ethnic group itself--which affect this decision?

Several factors within American society serve to encourage assimila- tion (or, alternatively, to discourage pluralism), and each acts with persistent force to make the individual less "ethnic". Participation in the economic sphere, public education, political activity, and the mass media (the press, television, radio, and movies)--each of these brings the ethnic into contact with people who are not group members, and with ideas, values, and practices which may not be consistent with those of his group. There is little doubt that these homogenizing forces are pervasive in contemporary American society, or that their ethnic versions --such as ethnic businesses and the foreign language press (Fishman 1966) --which have acted as a buffer between ethnics and "American" culture are in general disappearing. Thus the continued existence, and in some cases flourishing, of ethnic groups demonstrates that there must be equally powerful forces which encourage a pluralistic response. With the obvious exception of prejudice and the barriers to "American" society which members of certain groups find, there has been little attention specifically paid to these factors. Not all groups are objects of prejudice, and so there must be internal and positive factors--as well as external, negative ones --which encourage maintenance of the ethnic group; a major purpose of this project was to explore these factors.

In addition to examining the forces which encourage either of the alternatives of assimilation and pluralism, the aspects of the process by which an individual or group becomes assimilated or chooses a pluralistic response are in great need of delineation and further study. Gordon has begun this procedure by attempting to analyze the components of this process. He has outlined seven basic aspects of assimilation, which are reported in the following chart (1964:71):

1. cultural assimilation--change of cultural patterns to those of host society

2. structural assimilation--large-scale entrance into cliques and institutions of host society, on primary group level

3. marital assimilation--large-scale intermarriage

4. identificational assimilation--development of sense of peoplehood based exclusively on host society

5. attitude receptional assimilation--absence of prejudice

6. behavior receptional assimilation--absence of discrimination

7. civic assimilation--absence of value and power conflict

Although one may question the validity of some aspects of Gordon's scheme (for example, his insistence that assimilation is a one-way process in which immigrants adopt patterns of the "host society"), it provides a basic framework with which to work. This scheme supplies a systematic way in which social scientists may examine assimilation versus pluralism among different ethnic groups, as well as delineating the subprocesses of assimilation, which themselves require further study. Thus in the present study I chose to examine particularly the role of identification (#4) in the assimilation/pluralism complex.

II. Theoretical Orientation

A. Current views of ethnic identification

A review of the literature on ethnic identification shows that social scientists have not dealt adequately with this phenomenon, and that the concept itself is, to quote Nahirny and Fishman, quite "murky". Early theories (e.g., Wirth 1928) imply that the identificational choice posed for the 'ethnic' is clear: total identification either with America or with one's ethnic group. Later theories pointed out that this either-or view is oversimplified, for an individual's identity is not indivisible, and identity choices are not mutually exclusive, as Gordon (1964:25-8) so clearly indicated in his discussion of personal identity in America. He visualized the ethnic identity of an American as a series of "memberships" --based on national origin ("Irish"), religion ("Jewish"), race ("black"), and nationality ("American")--arranged in concentric rings, "each a step farther removed from the core of personality and self-identification." The order in which these rings are arranged varies from one individual to the next. Gordon does not discuss the relationship of these self-identifications to others--such as self-attributes (intelligent, lazy, good-natured), or roles (a mother, a teacher)--within the individual's self-conception, but one may assume that all these identifications may vary in their centrality to his self-conception. For example, being a lawyer may play a more central role in one person's self-conception than being Italian; in another's, being white may be more significant than being Catholic, which in turn may be more important than being a father or a pipefitter.

Based on this model of an individual's self-conception, the currently prevailing view of ethnic identification conceives of a continuum from "more ethnic" to "less ethnic" (or, in some cases, "more American").[2] By analyzing certain responses, the researcher attempts to estimate the centrality of a person's "ethnicity" to his self-conception. The individual whose answers are less traditionally "Jewish" than those of his co-religionists is seen to lie on the "less Jewish" (or "more American") end of this continuum, because his responses imply that "Jewishness" is less central to his own self-conception than it is to the self-conceptions of other members of his group. Recent studies (Geismar 1954, Lazerwitz 1953, Uyeki 1960, Sandberg 1974), despite a more accurate conception of the nature of ethnic identification as a continuum, narrowly conceive of this phenomenon as reflected in social and cultural behavior, rather than considering it directly. E.g., Lazerwitz (1953) developed an index of Jewish identification which was based on the individual's responses concerning his activities in the Jewish community and his religious behavior, and responses to a social distance scale. Of these, the behavioral items received twice the value of the attitudinal items when the identification index was computed. Although ethnic identification may well be correlated with social and cultural behavior, to assume that the one factor has been isolated by measuring the other is a mistake. This becomes obvious if one examines the only study which has seriously attempted to measure ethnic identity independently of cultural and social attitudes and behavior (Sengstock 1969). An individual's identification of himself as a Chaldean was determined by his use of "we" to refer to Chaldeans and "they" to refer to non-Chaldeans, and Sengstock found that American-reared Chaldeans continue to personally identify themselves as Chaldeans after they have dropped other aspects of the ethnic socio-cultural pattern, such as language, food preferences, attendance at Chaldean church, and preference for Chaldean religious services.

Furthermore, the nature of the "ethnic" element in one's self-conceptions has not been the object of serious study; if someone's reply on a "Who am I?" test is "a Greek", what does this signify? Neither have researchers directly examined the forces which encourage the individual to develop and maintain ethnicity as a central element of his self-conception. Thus the original concern of this study was to examine these two questions--the components of "Greekness" in the self-conceptions of individual Greek Americans and the ways in which such "Greekness" is developed and maintained. These topics are discussed in Chapter 5.

B. Reconsideration of ethnic identification

My original assumption was that those who had a strong sense of identity as "Greeks", i.e., for whom "Greekness" was a prominent element of their self-conception, would more readily resist assimilation into "American" society and culture, and conversely, that those for whom "Greekness" was of little importance would tend to be the more easily assimilated. As my research proceeded, however, I began to realize that "ethnic identification" does not actually represent a single phenomenon; rather, there are two distinct facets of identification. The first is "identification" in the sense I have discussed the concept so far--the centrality of Greekness in one's self-conception, i.e., his sense of identity as a person "of Greek blood" who takes great pride in his heritage; whereas the second represents the individual's identification of himself as a member of the Greek community. This important distinction has not been clearly delineated, but has remained implicit in the literature on ethnic groups. Through careful reading one realizes that some authors in discussing "ethnic identification" are actually referring to one's identification as a member of the ethnic group, his active participation in the group. E.g., Rinder defines ethnic identification in this way:

> Our focus is on the tie which binds the individual to the group--
> defined here as the social psychological bond of identification.
> We conceive the individual's identificatory (reference group)
> decision as being determined, in Homans' terms, by the balance
> of costs and rewards accruing to the available alternatives. ...
> Between groups there lies a boundary. Forces which hold a
> minority member within that group through the retention of his
> identification are designated as centipetal; forces which spin-off

or separate a minority group member by moving his identity across the boundary and toward the superordinate group are designated as centrifugal (1965:6-7).

On the other hand, in an examination of ethnic identification among Japanese Americans who had been placed in relocation camps, Uyeki comments:

> The experiences of the Nisei...struck at the very core of their self-conceptions, especially ethnic identification. Probably each evacuated Nisei had to face consciously and/or unconsciously the disruption of his ethnic identification, and each had to decide on his conception of self in national and ethnic terms (1960:468).

The implicit assumption (although it has apparently never been stated) is that these two aspects of identification, an "ethnic" self-conception and group membership and participation, follow one from the other, and thus there is really no need to make a conceptual distinction between them. In fact, it is not uncommon in a single passage to see these two types of identification referred to as one concept, "identification". E.g., Goldstein and Goldscheider make the following comments in their discussion of Jewish identification:

> Even if the social exclusion of the Jew is declining, the fear of discrimination, and concomitant insecurity, may be a powerful factor in the identification of Jews with their own group. ... Since the Jew knows that his quest for status within the general community has predefined limits, he turns to the Jewish social structure for a sense of identification. The need for identification is most pronounced in a society characterized by anonymity and alienation. "American" is not a sufficient label for identification, and members of subsocieties in the United States seek more narrowly circumscribed identities. The American Jew, unlike most other Americans, does not identify himself ethnically, as a Russian or Pole or German. Consequently, he has no alternative but identification as a Jew (1968:10-11).

At the beginning of this passage, the authors are discussing "identification" in terms of group membership, whereas at the end they are concerned with self-conception.

The fact that these two facets of ethnic identification are generally considered to be inseparable perhaps explains the common dependence on behavioral factors such as group participation to measure the level of an individual's identification. This assumption is understandable, for one type of identification is in many cases accompanied by the other: a person for whom Greekness is a central element of self-conception will likely be predisposed to remain a member of the Greek group through participation in the local Greek community. Nevertheless, the conceptual distinction between the two should be made to help clarify the nature of ethnic identification, and the processes by which such identification (in both its aspects) is developed, maintained, or changed. For example, it may be that in the assimilating individual, a change in the salience of ethnicity in one's self-conception consistently precedes loss of social identification with the Greek group through severing ties with the local Greek community, or vice versa. In general, the former alternative seems to be the more common occurrence, as the following chapters demonstrate.

My research experience showed me that each facet can exist independently of the other, for the forces which generate and maintain the one may still continue to operate when those which affect the other have ceased. E.g., an individual can sever his ties with the local Greek community and still maintain a strong Greek self-conception; on the other hand, many non-Greeks--having of course no personal identification as "Greek"--are, by virtue of their marriage to Greeks, very active community members who strongly identify with the community. Despite these changes in personnel, the Greeks still exist as a strong ethnic group; members strictly hold the dichotomy between themselves and outsiders, οἱ ξένοι (i xeni), "strangers". Thus the presence of a number of non-Greeks in the Greek community and the absence of many individuals of Greek descent brings into question the nature of the ethnic group--in what sense is it the "Greek" community? I will return to this question shortly.

Of the two types of Greek identification, the individual's identification of himself as a participating member of the group is the more crucial for the maintenance of the ethnic group. Individuals may continue to identify themselves as "Greeks" outside the context of the ethnic group, but in doing so, they contribute little or nothing to the continuation of the group as a viable entity. Furthermore, even if a "Greek" self-conception can be maintained independently of group membership and without the confirming contacts with other Greeks, it is unlikely that such a sense of "Greek" identity can be passed on to one's children; the odds are that this form of ethnic identification cannot continue indefinitely through several generations. This is primarily because a child cannot observe concrete manifestations of Greekness in group behavior without active involvement with other Greeks. Even though one or both of his parents may be Greek, if he seldom sees them interact with other group members, there will no doubt be a large question in his mind--"Just exactly what is Greekness?" His parents are not Greeks, but Mom and Dad. Not all of their personal qualities, values, and behavior can be attributed to their Greekness, but how is one to tell which represent Greekness in action? Consequently, when one does not have an adequate knowledge of what Greekness really is, it would be quite difficult for him to develop or maintain "Greekness" as a central aspect of his developing self-conception.

Thus the focus of this dissertation is on the role of active

membership in the Greek community as the means for the continued existence
of Greeks as a viable ethnic group. The relative freedom of Greek-
Americans to remain associated with their ethnic group or to assimilate
into the larger society makes them an excellent group in which to examine
this facet of ethnic identification. Such freedom of choice is less
available to many other groups--e.g., persistent discrimination has
excluded many groups from full participation in the larger society, and
other groups lack a sufficient number of members to provide a local
community within which the individual can participate. Rinder (1965)
has suggested a model of intergroup relations which delineates two
boundaries between the ethnic group and the larger society. The inner
boundary is defined by in-group morale, and the outer, by barriers which
the larger society erects against the group's assimilation. In Rinder's
terms, Houston's Greeks are faced with a low outer boundary in that they
are not objects of prejudice, although this may not be so in other American cities which have larger, more concentrated Greek populations whose
members are not so uniformly middle and upper-middle class as Houston's
Greeks are. The Greek American in Houston is therefore able to make a
choice based on the relative rewards of being a member of the Greek
community, or of leaving the community and participating in non-Greek
social circles. Such a situation allows the researcher to examine in
some detail those forces which encourage and discourage the individual's
participation in the local community.

C. An alternative view of ethnic groups

   Thus the route of analysis was finally chosen: I would concentrate
primarily on the maintenance of the individual's community membership,

the community being the specific local expression of the Greek group in general. One who severs his ties to a specific community is lost to the Greek group as long as he lives in that locality, and the chances are that the same factors which caused his leaving the Greek community in one area would also be present in other areas. Therefore, for all practical purposes, the individual who leaves one local community is no longer socially a part of the ethnic group: he is no longer "Greek" in the sense of group membership. He will no doubt continue to retain "Greekness" as an element in his self-conception, although the salience of ethnicity in his self-conception is likely to diminish when he ceases to interact with other members of his group. In fact, a major reason for leaving the community may be that "Greekness" is (or has become) a more peripheral aspect of the individual's self-conception; perhaps it is less important than his image of himself as a professional, for example. Thus, because the two facets of ethnic identification are closely related, the development of Greekness in self-conceptions would also be an area of interest in this project. In particular, I chose to explore the two aspects of ethnic identification in terms of the Houston Greek community as a group, by examining the ways in which the group and its members act to maintain both the group itself and the salience of Greekness in the self-conceptions of its members. This emphasis on the continuation of the Greek group was prompted by the orientation I sensed in Houston's Greek community, for, as the reader will see in the following chapters, the central meaning of being "Greek" for these individuals is being a group member, and much individual and collective energy is spent in maintaining the group. This orientation sent me back to the literature on ethnic groups to see if anyone had developed the line of thinking toward which the research data were leading me.

I found my answer in Barth's Ethnic Groups and Boundaries. In this essay, Barth takes issue with the prevailing view of ethnic groups which gives central significance to the sharing of a common culture within the group. He gives an alternate definition of the ethnic group, as a form of social organization whose continuity depends on the maintenance of a boundary. Noting the fact that boundaries between ethnic groups persist despite a flow of personnel across them, he comments:

> The critical focus of investigation from this point of view becomes the ethnic boundary that defines the group, not the cultural stuff that it encloses. The boundaries to which we must give our attention are of course social boundaries, though they may have territorial counterparts. If a group maintains its identity when members interact with others, this entails criteria for determining membership and ways of signalling membership and exclusion. Ethnic groups are not merely or necessarily based on the occupation of exclusive territories; and the different ways in which they are maintained, not only by a once-and-for-all recruitment but by continual expression and validation, need to be analysed (1969:15).

This "boundary" which is diagnostic of group membership is determined not by those overt, "objective" cultural differences one might notice between groups, but by factors which are socially relevant within the context of the group. Barth further contends that

> most of the cultural matter that at any time is associated with a human population is not constrained by this boundary; it can vary, be learnt, and change without any critical relation to the boundary maintenance of the ethnic group. So when one traces the history of a ethnic group through time, one is not simultaneously, in the same sense, tracing the history of "a culture": the elements of the present culture of that ethnic group have not sprung from the particular set that constituted the group's culture at a previous time, whereas the group has a continual organizational existence with boundaries (criteria of membership) that despite modifications have marked off a continuing unit (1969:38).

The adoption of this perspective gives the researcher a clearer understanding of the nature of ethnicity in America. The persistence of social and identificational ethnicity despite numerous changes in ethnic cultural patterns no longer must appear to be an unexplainable delay in the "inevitable" course of assimilation. Rather, the ethnic group can be viewed as a continuing form of social organization which provides the individual with certain rewards for maintaining his identification with the group. In this view, cultural changes are not the harbinger of eventual group dissolution (assimilation); they actually indicate only that some of the cultural elements of the group are undergoing modification.

The theoretical orientation of this work is basically that formulated by Barth, and it may be summarized in the following manner: An ethnic group represents a form of social organization which is set apart by a social boundary. This boundary determines group membership, whether one is a group member or an outsider, and it is comprised of factors which are relevant to group members. (E.g., in his research on the Pathans of Afghanistan and Pakistan, Barth [1969a] found that the Pashto language was not of central importance for group membership. The Pathan saying "He is Pathan who does Pashto, not [merely] who speaks Pashto" makes explicit the fact that membership is predicated on living by a body of customs, which revolve around the male's honor.) Other aspects of the group's culture may change, perhaps because of ecological factors or contact with other cultural groups, without significant effect on the group. Furthermore, individuals may cross the group's boundaries--members may leave, and non-members may enter--without threatening the group's boundary or its existence. Based on this theoretical orientation, the following chapters

will discuss the central elements of Greekness which are considered
necessary for group membership; how individuals cross the social boundaries
of Greekness, thereby entering or leaving the group; the forces which
encourage one to remain a member; and the standards of proper "Greek"
performance which are imposed upon group members.

D. Other areas of interest

In addition to the main focus on "group" identification, I was
interested in several other aspects of American ethnicity which have
been previously neglected as areas of research, or little understood.

1. Second and third generations

The bulk of the recent sociological work on ethnic groups has examined
recent immigrants to Israel and World War II refugees (e.g., Weinstock 1969,
Eisenstadt 1955, Shuval 1963). The future of the ethnic group depends not
so much on immigrants, who in most cases retain the important aspects of
their traditional culture and identity as a matter of course, as on members
of the second and third generations, who are to a greater extent able
to choose their cultural patterns and loyalties. As discussed in a
previous section, the nature of ethnicity in these later generations has
continued to be a topic of heated debate, and for this reason, the way in
which members of the second and third generations orient themselves toward
their ethnic status is of particular interest. The basic question which
has interested sociologists--is each generation less traditionally "ethnic"
than that which preceded it, or is there a resurgence of ethnicity in the
third generation after the second has drawn away from the group and its
customs?--is actually beside the point when ethnic groups are viewed from
the theoretical perspective indicated by the present research. On the

basis of this theory, one must hypothesize that there is no change in the ethnicity of group members across the three generations. Between the first and third generations there may be great alterations in the cultural content of "Greekness", but the basis of group membership, of identity with the group, remains.

2. The family

The maintenance of the ethnic group as a viable entity depends in large part on the successful transmission of its distinctive patterns to each new generation (Rossi and Rossi 1961, Fishman 1961), and only a small part of the family's role in the transmission of cultural, social, and identificational patterns among American ethnic groups has been discussed. In most cases, it is through one's family that the individual becomes a member of the ethnic group--he is born a Greek--and the family also plays a significant part in introducing him to the meanings (and social boundaries) of his ethnic membership. The chapters which follow outline in some detail the impact one's family has on his ethnicity and the ways in which his family acts to ensure his remaining in the ethnic group.

3. Intermarriage

The consequences of intermarriage for ethnic group membership, and consequently for the continuation of ethnic groups, have remained almost totally unexplored. Most studies (Kennedy 1944, Abramson 1973) have concentrated on the rates of ethnic intermarriage, and in many cases claimed that increases in these rates indicate widespread assimilation and eventual disappearance of ethnic groups. This is based on the assumption that the ethnic who intermarries necessarily severs his ties with the group, and that the children of such marriages are no longer "ethnic" but "American". Thus intermarriage is viewed as the melting pot at work.

Undeniably, intermarriage is a serious threat to any ethnic group, through

intimate contact with outsiders and especially through the mixing of

"blood".   Chapter 6 will report the ways in which Houston's Greek

community acts to impede marriage to outsiders. There is admittedly a

correlation between marriage to an "outsider" and leaving the ethnic group,

but the existence of such a correlation does not tell much about the

mechanisms involved in entering or leaving the group, or about how inter-

marriage affects the individuals, families, and ethnic groups involved.

Furthermore, one should not automatically assume that every ethnic who

"marries out" leaves the group, for there are powerful forces which act

to keep him associated with his people. In fact, the opposite case--in

which the nonmember joins the ethnic group--is also an alternative which

is frequently chosen. Of particular interest in terms of Barth's theory

is the means by which individuals enter the ethnic group and are social-

ized to become group members. The chapters which follow will consider in

some detail cases in which non-Greeks have entered the Greek community

through marriage, and demonstrate how the children of such marriages,

despite their "mixed blood", can be raised and treated as "true" Greeks.

4. Greek Americans

A fourth objective was to provide ethnographic information on a

little-known group--the Greek Americans. Most of the work on this group

has been historical. Burgess (1913) and Xenides (1922) briefly examined

the social organization and customs of Greeks in their early years in

America, and Saloutos has provided an excellent historical view of Greek

American immigration and life in the United States (1964), a brief volume

on repatriated Greeks (1955), as well as an article (1973) on the recent
transition of the American Greek Orthodox Church from staunch Hellenism
to a position more consistent with the needs of American Greeks.

Sociological research among Greek Americans has unfortunately been
rather limited. Treudley (1949) discussed the role of formal organiza-
tions--businesses, schools, the church, and ethnic organizations--in
helping immigrant groups adjust to American life, and used Boston's
Greek community as an example of this process. In a more recent study,
Nagata (1969) examined the adjustments of newly-arrived working-class
Greek immigrants in Toronto, Canada, and found that they temporarily set
aside Greek values in an "all-out effort" to attain financial security.

> That this is only a temporary expedient, however, ...may be
> inferred from the fact that once social and economic security
> is attained, by the standards of the wider society, the indi-
> vidual will then frequently begin to take part in the associa-
> tional and other institutional life of the Greek settlement
> (1969:67).

For example, the fact that a wife may have to work and send her children
to a day-care center so that her family can survive financially should
not be taken to mean that the family is becoming acculturated because it
has apparently adopted the Canadian pattern and ignored the Greek pattern
(in which the wife does not work, but stays home with her children). Once
the family is financially on its feet, the wife will invariably quit work
and return to her traditional Greek role. Thus Nagata concluded that
behavior which seems oriented toward accomodation to Canadian culture is
frequently a result of the immediate situation in which the individual
finds himself, and therefore should not be interpreted as suggesting the
degree of his acculturation. Although her study is not directly relevant

to the topic at hand because of its concentration on very recent immigrants, Nagata's findings support the view that ethnicity--cultural patterns and group associations--is not an either-or phenomenon, but is contingent on many other factors.

Humphrey and Louis (1973) focused on generational differences in the relationship between ethnic identification and ethnic voting in Norfolk, Virginia, as reflected in voting patterns in the 1968 presidential election (which offered Spiro Agnew as the Republican vice-presidential candidate). The researchers reported that ethnic associational preferences and identification have declined over three generations, but that Agnew as fellow Greek sparked "dormant, if not dying, ethnic sentiments." Indicators of social behavior included knowledge of Greek, subscription to Greek newspapers, ethnicity of spouse, and membership in Greek American organizations. Unfortunately, this study analyzed ethnic identification indirectly by combining responses concerning enjoyment of Greek American companionship, pride in one's Greek heritage, belief in endogamy and "cultural" education, adherence to religious practices, and response to Greek political ceremonies, thereby confounding ethnic identification with cultural elements. The preceding discussion has indicated the problem with using cultural factors such as religious practices, politics, and "cultural" education as a measure of ethnicity: cultural elements associated with the group change over time, or vary according to the ecological circumstances in which the group finds itself, and yet the group may continue to exist as a viable, recognizable entity. Rather than choosing random traditional cultural elements, the researcher should through observation determine which are the salient cultural elements in any one community. Thus this study's conclusion that assimilation is proceeding apace may be unwarranted, since it is based on questionable measurements.

III. The Setting

The Greek population of Houston, Texas probably numbers about 2,500-3,000 individuals,[3] much less than 1% of the city's total population. There is no localized "community" or ghetto settlement, and the Greek population is spread over a very wide geographical area. In 1970 the local Greek Orthodox church, the Annunciation, conducted a census of Houston's Greek population,[4] which reported:

DISTRIBUTION OF HOUSTON AREA'S GREEK POPULATION			
(N=1923)			
southwest	northwest	northeast	southeast
72.4%	10.1%	1.3%	16.2%

Although this table seems to indicate a fairly large concentration in the southwestern area, the reader should bear in mind that Houston's area to its city limits is 503 square miles, and its SMSA covers 6955 square miles and encompasses several counties;[5] thus, 1400 Greeks does not represent a significant concentration in one-quarter of the urban area. The lack of a "little Athens" ghetto makes Houston an excellent city in which to examine the maintenance of both the Greek community and the salience of ethnicity in the self-conceptions of individual Greeks, for much effort must be expended for community members to come together for community affairs, to socialize with one another, to see that their children are acquainted, and so on. For example, it was not unusual to drive 20 or 30 miles in any direction to conduct an interview, and I live very close to the Greek church, which acts as the social center of the community. Under such trying circumstances it would be quite easy for the individual to drop all community participation.

A second factor which makes Houston well-suited to a study of the maintenance of ethnic identification was mentioned earlier: the lack of prejudice against Greeks in the Houston area, which means that they are not forced to associate with their group because of rebuffs by non-Greeks. Furthermore, members of the Greek community are predominantly middle and upper-middle class, and many active members are quite wealthy. This in itself refutes the generally-accepted model of assimilation in which ethnic groups are destroyed by the social mobility of their individual members, who through their economic success leave behind the narrow world of the ethnic group and become "Americans". This traditional sociological view of assimilation, which Metzger (1971) appropriately calls "Horatio Alger in the Melting Pot", is not upheld by the Houston Greek community, and it is of particular interest to examine the nature of ethnicity among such an economically successful group.[6]

The generational composition of the Houston Greek population is also important in terms of ethnic-group theory. To determine this as well as age distribution and household composition, and the areas of Greece represented in this population, I conducted a telephone survey of 175 households. (Information concerning this survey--response rate, how I explained my purpose to respondents, a text of the questions, and detailed results--may be found in Appendix A.) The survey indicated that Houston's Greek

population represents a fairly young community in which recent immigrants
and first-generation individuals each represent 17%, and second-generation people comprise 42%, of the adult Greek population. The predomi-
nance of families with second-generation parents and third-generation
children (whose first-generation grandparents are in most cases still
living) makes the Houston community ideal for examining Hansen's theory
of "third generation return".

Houston's Greek community will be described in greater detail in
the following chapters; this demographic information has been presented
to familiarize the reader with aspects of the community which are of
practical and theoretical significance, and to provide a background against
which to view the ethnographic material which follows.

IV. Methodology

A. Description of methods

The bulk of the research was conducted in a period of 18 months from
April 1973 to September 1974, and the primary research methods included
participant observation in community affairs and semistructured interviews. However, I made preliminary contacts in the Houston Greek community in the fall of 1972, when I discussed the proposed project with
Father Nicholas Triantafilou, the priest at Annunciation. He tentatively
approved the project and later received official approval of the church's
Board of Trustees.

At this time I began to receive weekly bulletins from Annunciation,
and in this way gained some general idea of community activities. I also
began library research on Greek Americans and immediately ran into

problems. The few references to "Greeks" found in indexes invariably referred to passages like "English, Scotch and Welsh, Irish, Germans, Italians and Poles, ...Slovenians, Greeks and Luxembourgers, ...Filipinos and Puerto Ricans have come together to form a nation...", which is not of much help. Even in general tables of information on different nationality groups, Greeks are seldom to be found; they are usually in the category labelled "Other". Similarly, it was not possible to find out much about the American Greek Orthodox church in sociological works, for the four standard religious categories are Protestant, Catholic, Jewish, and "Other".

I also turned to less traditional sources to find information about Greeks and to gain a sense of what being Greek is "about". Throughout the course of the research, I read such things as Greek poetry, novels by Kazantzakis and Greek American Harry Mark Petrakis, and a biography of the composer Mikis Theodorakis, as well as newspaper and magazine articles about Greece and Greek Americans.

My entry into the community began in the weeks preceding Easter, 1973, when I began participant observation in church services and in the church's parochial school. From this point on I participated extensively in church services, since the Orthodox church seemed to play such an important part in the community and in the lives of individual Greeks. I attended as many services as possible, but concentrated particularly on making it to services during major feasts and fasts--saints' days, Christmas, Holy Week, and so on. For two months I visited the several parochial school classes in turn, talking with the children, going with them to Greek language classes, church lessons, and recess, and helping the teachers; during this time I also attended afternoon Greek language classes.

Participant observation began in earnest in June of 1973 when I began going to the Greek Orthodox Community Center (GOCC) to help with Fun Club, a summer program for young children. Shortly thereafter, preparations for the church's annual Greek Festival began, and I spent nearly every day in the church kitchen, helping make dolmades, tiropites, spanakopites, pastitso, and other traditional dishes to be sold at the October Festival. This provided my first introduction to the older-generation women, who are the mainstays of the Festival's cooking work-force. At this time I also started participating in Greek dancing classes and Bible classes, both of which--like most other community activities--are held at the church. In addition to these types of participation, I attended most social functions held at the church, dances, a few weddings and baptisms, adult Greek language classes, an AHEPA (a Greek fraternal organization) convention, Greek restaurants, Lenten retreats, and so on. A family of first-generation parents and their children graciously allowed me to live with them for a week, and this provided my best opportunity for intimate involvement in Greek American life. The fact that the Houston Greek community is not geographically isolated greatly increased the difficulty of involvement since there was no place that I could go and be "in" the Greek community. Anthropologists who conduct fieldwork in small villages do not have this problem, nor do sociologists who study ethnic groups in other urban areas (e.g., Whyte 1943, Gans 1962, Liebow 1967, Suttles 1968, Hannerz 1969). I was, however, in the same position as community members. The geographical dispersion meant that everyone gathered at the church and community center for shared activities, and so I too spent a lot of time at these centers of Greek American life in Houston.

During the research period I also conducted 72 intensive semi-structured interviews with 79 individuals who represented several "types" of community members (i.e., people who participated to different degrees in church, social affairs, organizations, or some combination of these, half-Greeks, Greeks married to non-Greeks, non-Greeks married to Greeks, and people whose participation was marginal) as well as with some people who had severed their ties with the community. Several of the interviews involved more than one respondent, and others were conducted with individuals I had interviewed on previous occasions about different topics. I did not attempt to conduct interviews based on a random sample of any sort because I was interested in talking with those people for whom community membership was not necessarily solidified. The purposive sample included four basic types of people. I interviewed young people who were not yet out of college, or not yet married, because they represent a group which is reaching the critical point. Will they marry Greek? Will they remain in the church? Will they continue to associate with the community? Others whose identification patterns were of interest were Greeks who had married non-Greeks, non-Greeks who had married Greeks, and the children of such marriages. A third group was composed of individuals who had left the church or the community. In each of these cases, I wanted to find out the factors which had influenced their decisions, and the pressures which they felt being brought to bear on them; I was also interested in the place that "Greekness" held in the self-conceptions of these individuals. Those who had already made a firm, more or less permanent commitment to the community were of less interest, although I interviewed a number of people in this category to gain a more balanced picture of community life, and to find out what their hopes and expectations for their own children were.

Since much of the analysis was based upon these interviews, the extent to which my sample differed from the population (as determined by the telephone survey) on certain characteristics such as age, generation, and type of community participation becomes an important question. The survey did not delineate extent of participation but comparisons of age and generation are possible. Because of my special interests, the interviews overrepresent people between the ages of 15-40 (61% of the interviews vs. 41% of the population), the second and third generations (63% of the interviews vs. 49% of the population), and non-Greeks and half-Greeks (31% vs. 17%). I do not believe that these cases of over-representation seriously bias the analysis which is presented here, for two reasons. First, social boundaries and the factors maintaining group membership--the topics with which I was primarily concerned--are matters of common definition which do not vary according to one's age or genera-tion. Second, those who are underrepresented--the first generation and older people--would tend to be even more traditionally Greek in their responses than the individuals I interviewed. Since a major point made throughout this dissertation is that many customary Greek patterns have been maintained, better representation of this group would probably only strengthen this conclusion. A detailed outline of the ages, generation, and types of individuals interviewed may be found in Appendix B, and a comparison of these characteristics of the purposive sample of individuals who were interviewed in depth to the characteristics of the general population as determined by the telephone survey is presented in Appendix D.

Six main "schedules" were used in these interviews; one was for those who had been involved in a situation of intermarriage, another concerned questions of theology and ritual which I wanted to discuss with the clergy, a third involved different ways in which individual Greeks may participate in the community, and the other three were concerned with general aspects of Greek American life--kinship, friends, godparenthood, customs, religion, and identity. These six schedules are presented in Appendix C.

The first interviews were conducted with people I met informally at the GOCC; most were young adults, and women who had brought their children to swim or who were working in the Fun Club. Generally I would introduce myself and explain what I was doing, and then we would chat a while by the pool. Sometimes interviews were conducted on the spot, but usually I asked if they would consent to a later interview. Everyone agreed, after protests of "I'm not the one to talk to--I don't know much about it!", and a time and place were arranged. I encouraged meeting in their houses so they would not be inconvenienced, and so that I could go into some Greek homes. These first acquaintances in most cases provided introductions to their friends and family members, and also suggested the names of others I might want to interview. Gradually my network of acquaintances expanded--particularly after I began participating in Festival preparations--and I was able to choose for myself those individuals whose interviews would be most useful.

As many of the interviews as possible--54 of the 72--were taped to insure an optimal record of the exchange, thereby reducing errors of selective memory. When the interview was about to begin, I asked permission to use a tape recorder. ("Would you mind if I taped this? I find it easier to talk if I don't have to take notes, and later I can listen to the tape and take down some notes from it.") No one ever refused, nor did anyone seem bothered or inhibited by the recorder. I did not even mention recording the conversation to those I thought would be bothered by the recorder, and there were also several other situations in which taping was not feasible; in these cases, I jotted down notes at the scene, if possible, and immediately typed up the interview when I reached home. The same was true after a day of participant observation: field notes were typed as soon as possible after the experience.

At first these notes were placed under very general headings such as Family, Orthodox Church, and Ethnic Identification, but as I gained more information categories began to take shape, and soon there were over 100 folders, each containing notes and interviews. I typed carbons of each interview and placed the sections pertaining to different categories in the appropriate folders, retaining the original. Based on the information in these folders, I wrote a preliminary ethnography analyzing the Greek community in terms of the major categories which had been established --family, networks, the church, dating and marriage, and ethnic identification. Three Greek friends read this ethnography to check for factual errors, and happily found that the descriptions were on the whole accurate. I then studied the original, intact interviews very carefully to discover themes which may have been overlooked in the process of assigning passages to different categories, and finally wrote the analysis in these pages.

B. Critique of methods

1. Observation

Participant observation was chosen as a primary method in this project because little is actually known about ethnic identification or about Greek American life. Moreover, many of the problems which have characterized the field of ethnic groups may perhaps be attributed to the fact that work has been limited primarily to arm-chair theorizing and survey research, with a few notable exceptions. By observing a group and practically becoming a part of it, the researcher can discover the salient features of ethnic identity and culture to an extent which would be impossible through surveys. It was particularly important that I determine those aspects of Greek American culture and society which community members considered significant elements of Greekness, since adherence to these elements helps define who is a member of the group and who is an outsider. It is only after the researcher has a grasp of the situation at hand that he can adequately begin to formulate appropriate questions and hypotheses. Active participation in a group provides this "grasp" by enabling the researcher--through extensively sharing in its experiences--to view the world from the group's perspective. In this way one may begin to understand the meaning of being a group member. Furthermore, participant observation helps the researcher comprehend the unique meanings members place on certain actions and even words, the "meanings" of which he may have assumed to be common knowledge, shared by all. Participant observation is also the only method which allows the researcher to directly examine the behavior of people in groups. Thus it was the most appropriate method for the project at hand, which focused on the forces within the group which encourage continued group membership among individual Greeks.

Certain problems are associated with this method, however. Extensive participation introduces a new person--the observer--into the group, and his presence may influence the behavior of members. Although the extent to which situations were affected by my presence is unknown, I honestly believe that it was slight. My experience was that people felt more at ease and behaved more naturally when I participated actively than on the few occasions when I merely sat back and watched. For this reason, I played the "observer" role as seldom as possible. E.g., during Festival cooking I was not considered so much an "observer" as a willing worker who needed to be shown how to prepare the traditional dishes served in the Festival. A second limitation imposed by observation is the fact that it is much more difficult to quantify and verify observational data. Quantification is not a serious problem in this case since the project in general deals with factors which are not really quantifiable. Verification does present difficulties, however. For example, observation may lead the researcher to believe that the majority of the community members are of the second generation, or that most of them come from a certain area of Greece, or that most Greek parents want their children to date only other Greeks, but is this really so? To offset these problems of verification I conducted the telephone survey to obtain basic demographic information, as well as the semistructured interviews described above.

2. Interviewing

The semi-structured interviews were based on fixed questions, but the order and wording differed slightly according to the situation and individual respondent at hand. This flexibility allowed the interviews to be more spontaneous and personal, which was important in maintaining the interest and good will of the respondents. A common problem with such interviews is that the researcher must rely on the individual's report of attitudes and behavior. However, continued observation helped determine the veracity of comments made in interviews, and showed that informants and interview subjects generally told the truth. This is not surprising in view of the fact that I participated quite extensively in community affairs, and respondents had seen me before and knew they would see me again. This encouraged truthfulness for two reasons: first, many respondents had come to know me personally, and realized that I would not betray their confidence; and, perhaps more importantly, it was obvious that I could rather easily check up on any claim they made by asking others, or by my own observation.

A second, more serious difficulty with interviewing is the fact that the interviewer, however inadvertantly, influences the responses of the person being interviewed (on this point, see Hyman 1954). The respondent may wish to please, therefore saying what he thinks the researcher wants to hear. Moreover, by coming to the interview situation with a set of even vague questions, the interviewer determines to a large extent what will be discussed and therefore, what is "important". This problem is inherent in the nature of interviewing, and its effects are virtually inevitable. Nevertheless, it is possible for the researcher to lessen these effects by listening to group discussions, only occasionally inter-jecting a question or comment; 21 of the 72 interviews I conducted were of this type. The interpretation of data was greatly aided by these interviews, for the spontaneous discussion of relevant, shared dilemmas found in such group situations balanced the one-on-one interviews, in which responses may have been more forced, and the questions less relevant.

C. Responses to the researcher

The only topic remaining to be discussed is the effect of the researcher on the project. How did I present myself and explain my purposes? How did members of the community react to me?

It has frequently been noted that the researcher's personal attributes have a significant impact on the course of the research. The factor which most seriously affected the outcome of this research project was my being a woman. Although I have always been equally comfortable in the presence of either men or women, during the research I usually found myself in the company of women, and found it much easier to establish relationships with them. Men were not unfriendly or unhelpful, but mostly just distant. This may be attributed to the "double-standard" atmosphere which still remains a viable part of Greek American culture; only certain roles are appropriate for women, and that of "career woman" implied by graduate work is not yet one of them. Thus many men did not really know what to make of me, and may have seen me as something of a threat to their superior position as males. Furthermore, there also remains a vestige of the suspicion that sexual improprieties may result if a man and woman are alone together, which made it somewhat more difficult to interview men. One incident demonstrates this difficulty particularly well. When I arrived at the home of a man I had arranged to interview, he met me outside and we stood talking there for about two hours. I was surprised that he had not invited me in, but later found

out that his wife had been at work, and so it would not have been appropriate for me to have been in the house. Despite these problems, I
managed to talk with many men by arranging for the interviews to be
conducted in situations in which others would be present. For example,
I would interview a man while his wife (or mother, in the case of younger
men) was in the house.

Most people with whom I came into contact were cooperative, although
there were of course certain individuals who remained suspicious of me
as ἡ ξένη (i xeni), a "stranger". The Houston community is rather
close-knit, and the presence of a stranger is cause for questions. When
people asked me about my presence, I responded by telling them as much
as they wanted to hear about my project.[7] However, the more common
pattern than direct confrontation about my purposes was for one person
to ask another about me in Greek. I soon became familiar with the Greek
expressions for "Who is this girl? What is she doing here?" After
learning of my purpose, most were convinced of my legitimacy and good
will, but many remained rather guarded around me. I eventually became
almost a "permanent fixture", however, and when I occasionally missed an
activity, people would ask, "Where were you?"

Despite my acceptance at public gatherings that anyone could attend,
I was very seldom invited to private gatherings or into people's homes.
I attribute this to the fact that Houston's Greeks have very close relationships with each other, and in general there is little room for
outsiders, or thought of including them. There may be another factor
at work in this behavior, however. Much of this dissertation is devoted
to an analysis of the ways in which members of the Greek community keep

their community insulated as a means of maintaining the group. One way
to maintain the in-group is to make sure that outsiders are always aware
of their status and do not come too close, and I felt this force at work
many times in my own case. There seemed to be invisible barriers between
myself and many of the community's members, and these people always
seemed to keep me at arm's length--friendly, but superficial and distant.[8]
People's responses to me will be further discussed in later chapters.

Despite this sometimes acute sense of being an outsider, I feel that
I formed several deep and lasting friendships. The most friendly and
helpful group of people were young adults who readily took me into their
confidence. There were also several other individuals with whom I became
very close. I soon began to sense the significance of participating in a
closeknit ethnic group--the warm feeling of intimacy and closeness, and
yet the suspicion of outsiders. After I had been involved in this project for about four months, I was amused to note my reaction to an
incident. Two strangers came to the community center one day, and--being
accustomed to seeing the same familiar faces--I found myself asking a
Greek friend, "Who are those people? What are they doing here?"

D. A note on methodology

Throughout the research project I was stumbling around methods which
are described in Glaser and Strauss's The Discovery of Grounded Theory,
which I unfortunately did not read until the second draft of this dissertation was in progress. A great deal of time would have been saved had I
been familiar with their suggestions for developing theory which is
grounded in research data.

Glaser and Strauss's main point is that the researcher generates theory through the comparative analysis of data, which is coded into various conceptual categories arising during the course of research. Such analysis generates not only categories, but hypotheses about relations between them. These become the core of the emerging theory. The properties of categories, as well as the relations between them, are verified as much as possible in the course of research. The researcher simultaneously collects, codes, and analyzes his data, and the emerging theory guides the further collection and analysis of information: the researcher seeks data which will fill in gaps in the developing theory. Thus groups to observe or interview are chosen according to their theoretical relevance; this is called theoretical sampling. When no new information about a category comes to light from the examination of relevant groups, the researcher can move on to others with confidence, realizing that the category is saturated.

In general, this project was conducted along the lines suggested by Glaser and Strauss, with a couple of important exceptions. One source of headaches was the fact that too much time was spent in developing categories which were already saturated. My main problem, however, was expecting that theory would spring full-grown from my head upon completion of the project. The graduate-student practice of "one year of field-work/one year of analysis and writing" was so firmly entrenched that it was difficult to realize the possibility of developing and testing theory on the spot. Of course, some theories emerged during the fieldwork which guided further interviews and periods of observation, but the theories were not developed in the systematic way described by Glaser and Strauss. Nevertheless, one of Glaser and Strauss's comments gives me confidence to report my findings.

> When generation of theory is the aim, one is constantly alert
> to emergent perspectives that will change and help develop his
> theory. These perspectives can easily occur even on the final
> day of study or when the manuscript is reviewed in page proof:
> so the published word is not the final one, but only a pause in
> the never-ending process of generating theory (1967:40).

It is in this spirit that I offer this study.

V. Organization

This work is divided into two parts. Part I provides an ethnographic description of several major aspects of Greek American society and
culture. The Greek Orthodox church is of great importance in the maintenance of the Greek community, for it serves as the center of community
organization and affairs, and provides strong religious convictions which
reinforce ethnicity as a source of group solidarity. Chapter 2 considers
the Orthodox Church in general, and Houston's Annunciation in particular,
and concentrates on several sources of tension within the Orthodox Church
which may cause individuals to leave the church and, ultimately, the
community. Chapter 3 discusses the individual's relationships with his
family and community; both family and community act as significant forces
to keep the individual in the group, and thus his relationships with them
are important in his decision to remain within the community or to leave.
The themes of "closeness" and "respect" which are found in these relationships are used as a basis for the analyses that follow.

Part II assesses the meanings of "Greek" identification in both
senses—identification of oneself as a community member, and as a person
whose Greekness is central to his self-conception. It also examines the
ways in which identification is fostered in the Houston Greek community.

The analysis in Part II is based on the theoretical orientation developed throughout this chapter. This is the idea that the ethnic group is defined by social boundaries which determine membership in the group. Chapter 4 discusses the central social meanings of Greekness--the "boundaries" of the community--and outlines those elements which are necessary for group membership. Another section of this chapter demonstrates how these membership qualifications are applied to Greek Americans, recent immigrants from Greece, and non-Greeks. In other words, the main question considered in this section is how members of each of these three categories cross the social boundaries of Greekness, thereby entering or leaving the community. Chapter 5 considers the role of Greekness in the individual's self-conception, and focuses on the several aspects of a "Greek" self-conception. The centrality of Greekness in the individual's self-conception no doubt has a significant effect on his choices to either remain in the ethnic group or to leave it, and for this reason it is important for the future of the ethnic group that such a self-conception be developed. The role of the family and the church in fostering a "Greek" self-conception will be examined. Membership in the Greek community is the topic of Chapter 6, which focuses on the group's maintenance of those boundaries which separate Greek Americans from the larger society, by excluding non-Greeks and by keeping Greeks within the community. The ways in which family and community members act to maintain the ethnic group by encouraging the individual to remain associated with the local Greek community are therefore of particular interest. Chapter 7 considers the implications of membership in the Greek community--how membership influences one's social actions by obliging him to alter his behavior to conform to Greek standards.   Chapter 8 provides a few concluding comments.

Annunciation church

Interior of Annunciation

Polemanakos Educational Building

Greek Orthodox Community Center, entrance

GREEK ORTHODOX COMMUNITY CENTER

Pool and tennis courts

Snack bar and dressing room

ANNUNCIATION AND COMMUNITY FACILITIES

CHAPTER 2

THE ORTHODOX CHURCH

This chapter will examine one of the most important elements of
Greek American life--the Greek Orthodox Church. Life in each Greek
community is organized around the church, which serves as a nucleus for
most Greek activities, even those of a secular nature. The Greek Orthodox Church is such an integral part of Greek life in America that there
can be no understanding of the Greek American community without a basic
familiarity with its history and traditions. Thus a brief overview of
Orthodoxy, its history and religious practices, will be considered first.
This section will be followed by a discussion of the Orthodox church in
contemporary America, which will focus on its problems as they are
reflected in the Houston Greek community. Finally, the chapter will
conclude with a section which considers the history and programs of
Annunciation, Houston's Greek Orthodox church.

I. A Brief Overview of Orthodoxy

A. History

1. Early Church

The first period of Christianity was important for the formation of
several of the basic elements of Orthodoxy. Since cities were a major
part of the Roman Empire at this time, they formed a unit of administra-
tion within the early Church: a bishop, assisted by priests and deacons,
was responsible for the faithful in each city. This arrangement provided
the basis for the Orthodox idea that the local community in which the

53

sacraments are celebrated is "the Church"; the necessary formal organization, with archbishops and patriarchs, is secondary in importance to the local church.[1] The Emperor Constantine's conversion to Christianity in 312 resulted in great changes in the emerging Church. Persecution and martyrdom came to an end as Constantine made Christianity the official religion of the Roman Empire through the Edict of Milan. To form the center of his new Christian Empire, Constantine moved its capital in 324 from Rome to the site of the Greek city Byzantium, and named the new city Constantinople; there he built a beautiful church, Agia Sophia. He also called the first Ecumenical Council at Nicaea in 325, to clarify the content of the Christian faith.

2. Councils

This was the first of seven ecumenical councils which were instrumental in the definition of the Church's teachings of the doctrines of the Christian faith, and the formulation of the Church's organization into five Patriarchates--Rome, Constantinople, Jerusalem, Antioch, and Alexandria. The importance of these councils to the Orthodox Church should not be underestimated since next to the Bible, it is the councils to which the Church looks for guidance. It is through the bishops' reaching a "common mind" at such councils that God guides the Church.[2]

3. Byzantium

Byzantium has been called the "icon of the heavenly Jerusalem", for religion entered into every aspect of Byzantine life. Unfortunately the Byzantines often made the error of identifying the Byzantine Empire with the Kingdom of God, the Greek people with God's people.[3] One of the major accomplishments of the Byzantine Church was its missionary activity among

the pagan Slavs. The brothers Cyril and Methodius were chosen for this
job because of their knowledge of Slavonic. They invented a suitable
alphabet and then translated service books and the Bible into Slavonic.
Thus the Slavs enjoyed a privilege shared by no other Europeans--they
heard services and the Gospels in a language they could understand.
This incident demonstrated the flexibility of the Orthodox Church in
the realm of language. Orthodoxy's policy is to hold services in the
language of the people.[4]

4. Schism[5]

The Roman Empire from the end of the third century was divided into
two parts, the "Greek" East and the "Latin" West; Constantine's founding
of a second capital in the East furthered this tendency. Barbarian
invasions and the Arab control of the Mediterranean further contributed
to the separation of the two halves. As a result of this separation,
the Greeks and Latins became strangers to each other; they shared the
same Church tradition but began to interpret it differently. A problem
arose because in the East there were many churches founded by the
Apostles, and the emphasis was on the equality of all bishops and the
conciliar nature of the Church. In the West, Rome was the only Apostolic
see, and the Church was seen as more a monarchy than a college. Gradually the Papacy came to view infallability as its prerogative and even
to interfere in the affairs of the Eastern Patriarchates. This was a
major point of contention.

The incident which has traditionally been taken to mark the beginning
of the schism occurred in 1054, when three legates from Pope Leo IX laid
on the altar of Agia Sophia a Bull of Excommunication against Cerularius,

the Patriarch of Constantinople. Friendly relations between the East and West continued after 1054, however, and it was actually the Crusades which completed the schism by bringing the issue down to the people. The Crusaders recaptured Antioch and Jerusalem from the Turks, but then set up Latin Patriarchs. What was worse, in 1204 the armies of the Fourth Crusade were persuaded by the son of the dispossessed Byzantine Emperor to go to Constantinople to restore him to the throne, and the Crusaders sacked the city. In Agia Sophia

> a Parisian prostitute seated herself on the patriarch's throne while the knights drank from the altar vessels, trampled icons underfoot, and ripped down the silken wall hangings to make wrappings for their loot. The rape and pillage went on for three days. During that time a large part of the creative work of a millenium was undone... (Eliot 1972:180).

And so the doctrinal differences that separated the western and eastern Empires were now reinforced among the Greeks by an intense hatred and indignation for Western sacrilege and aggression. The Christian Church was finally divided.

5. Turkish domination

The Byzantine Empire had been under attack by the Moslems since the seventh century, and the Patriarchates of Alexandria, Antioch, and Jerusalem one by one came under their control. Finally in 1453 the Turks seized Constantinople; on May 29, the last Christian service was held in Agia Sophia, and then "the most glorious church in Christendom became a mosque."[6]

According to the laws of Islam, Jews and Christians were "People of the Book" (Ahl-al-Kitāb) and thus once they had submitted to Moslem rule and agreed to pay taxes to the Moslem state, they were technically free

to practice their traditional religion.[7] The Ottoman Empire's non-
believers were governed in three main religious communities (millets),
through their separate hierarchies. In this way the Patriarch of
Constantinople became responsible for governing all of his Orthodox
subjects, regardless of their language or geographical location.[8]
Thus the Patriarch, according to Orthodox tradition merely the bishop
of a local center, became the temporal head of the Orthodox Christians
(millet-bashi). He added the eagle of the βασιλεύς (basileus, ruler)
to the cross he wore on his cassock, and was invested with superiority
to the other bishops.[9]

Although the Christians technically were not persecuted, their
"rights" merely represented the mercy of the sultan, for they were
rayah (cattle) and had no real rights.[10] They could not build or repair
churches without permission, and they were required to wear distinctive
dress. Their youngest sons were taken from them and converted to Islam,
to be enrolled in the Janissary corps. A Christian who converted to
Islam was liable to a death penalty if he reverted to Christianity,
and those who met this fate became the "new martyrs" of the church.
The rights of the Patriarch were eventually reduced to nothing as well;
he was chosen by a Synod, but the Turks could easily control the election.
A complex simoniacal system arose, in which the Patriarch bought his
election from the Turkish authorities--the election usually went to the
highest bidder. This system quickly spread throughout the clergy.

Two lasting problems developed within Orthodoxy during this period
of Turkish domination. First, the conditions under which Christianity
existed under the Turks led to an appalling lack of education among the

Christian populace. Many children remained illiterate. At local monas-
teries the boy who wished to become a priest learned to read and write,
and memorized religious works; once he learned the Liturgy, his education
was through. As a result, education was so poor that the metropolitan
of Thessalonica said in the 16th century that "not one monk in the
diocese knows ancient Greek or understands Church prayers," and early
in the 19th century, Constantine Oikonomos declared that "simple reading
of the service books, and often very badly at that, as long as it was
done in a melodious voice, was the sole qualification for a priest or
deacon."[11] Furthermore, the Orthodox church under Ottoman rule had
survival as its aim; the Greeks were content to repeat accepted formulae,
and to entrench themselves in positions inherited from the past. However,
this conservatism had the advantage of maintaining the Orthodox faith
through a very difficult period.[12]

The second major difficulty of Orthodoxy arising during this period
was nationalism. The millet system may have made possible the survival
of the Greek nation through four centuries of Turkish rule, but it also
led to a confusion of Orthodoxy and nationalism. Since both their civil
and religious lives were administered through the church, the Greeks
eventually became almost unable to distinguish between Church and nation.[13]
Moreover, the Patriarchate attempted to impose Greek bishops on the other
groups--Serbs, Bulgarians, and so on--under its rule. This attempt to
turn the Orthodox church into an exclusively Greek church caused a great
deal of resentment among the other Orthodox groups.[14] Thereafter, nationalism was tainted with hostility toward other Orthodox people; this is a
problem which still plagues the church today.

With the beginnings of the Greek war for independence in 1821, the Patriarchate's situation changed greatly. Patriarch Gregory V was hanged in his vestments after the Liturgy on Easter day, 1821, and Metropolitans, bishops, and laymen followed him. The few remaining powers of the Patriarchate were severely curtailed.[15]

6. Organization of Orthodoxy today

As the power of the Turks declined, the Patriachate of Constantinople lost control of many areas; nations which had finally freed themselves from the Turks found it impracticable to remain subject to a Patriarch resident in the Turkish capital and involved in the Turkish political system. Thus a group of national churches emerged from the Patriarchate. The Orthodox church is currently organized in this manner:[16]

four ancient Patriarchates:	Constantinople Alexandria Antioch Jerusalem;
eleven autocephalous churches:	Russia Roumania Serbia Greece Bulgaria Georgia Cyprus Czechoslovakia Poland Albania Sinai;
three autonomous churches:	Finland China Japan

and three administrations among the Russians outside of Russia; and ecclesiastical provinces in western Europe, North and South America, and Australia, which are dependent on the other churches.

In North America, there are 2-3,000,000 Orthodox, divided into at least eighteen jurisdictional groups. The Greek Orthodox in the United States, headed by Archbishop Iakovos, are under the jurisdiction of the Ecumenical Patriarch of Constantinople.

B. Orthodox worship

It is beyond the scope of this paper to go into a lengthy discussion of Orthodox theology; instead, a few basic elements will be presented to help the reader to get a general "feel" for the Orthodox religion. I will first examine the source of Orthodox faith, the Sacred Tradition; and then discuss what one encounters in an Orthodox Church--the icons, the Divine Liturgy, and the church calendar.

1. Sacred Tradition

One of the most distinctive characteristics of the Orthodox Church is its sense of "living continuity" with the ancient church; this idea is summed up in the word "Tradition". Tradition to the Orthodox means the Bible, the Creed, the decrees of the Ecumenical Councils, the writings of the Fathers, the Canons, the services, the icons, "the whole system of doctrine, church government, worship, and art which Orthodoxy has articulated over the ages."[17] Thus Tradition is the source of the Orthodox faith, and the Orthodox Christian is guardian to this important inheritance which must be maintained if continuity with the ancient church is to prevail.

2. Orthodox worship

It is said that the pagan Prince of Kiev wanted to know which was the true religion, and sent his emissaries to every country in turn to find out. They finally arrived at Constantinople and attended Divine Liturgy at Agia Sophia.

We knew not whether we were in heaven or on earth, for surely

> there is no such spendour or beauty anywhere upon earth.
> We cannot describe it to you: only this we know, that God
> dwells there among men, and that their service surpasses
> the worship of all other places. For we cannot forget that
> beauty (Ware 1963:269).

What is "that beauty" which the Prince's men could not forget? The physical aspects of an Orthodox church, as well as the Divine Liturgy itself, will now be discussed in an attempt to relate the things which moved these pagan Russians to declare that "God dwells there among men."

"'If a non Orthodox makes an inquiry of you about your Christian faith,' said St. John Damascene, 'take him into the church and place him before the icons.'"[18] A distinctive feature of Orthodoxy is the place it assigns to icons, paintings of saints and events in the life of Christ. One of the major controversies of the early church concerned icons. The arguments presented in the Iconoclast controversy of 726-843 indicate the theological significance of iconography. This was not merely a conflict over religious art; it involved Christ's human nature and the meaning of Christian redemption. The Iconodules held that icons safeguard a proper doctrine of the Incarnation: God took flesh and became man, and thus matter can be redeemed.[19] The prayers and hymns used in the consecration of icons demonstrate this concept: God performed self-protraiture by the incarnation of his Son, who is "the image of the invisible God." Thus God shaped his perfect icon. The victory over the Iconoclasts, "the Triumph of Orthodoxy" is celebrated each year in the Orthodox Church.

An icon is not a piece of a religious art in the sense that one might say the "Last Supper" is. Rather, icons are considered manifestations of heavenly archetypes. Icons are a kind of window between the earthly and celestial worlds, through which inhabitants of the celestial world look down into ours, and on which the features of the heavenly

archetypes are imprinted. Many icons are supposed to be self-made, "not

made by hands"; the likeness is said to have appeared by some miracle.[20]

An icon conveys a picture of the divine world order, of how things really

are in the eyes of God, rather than of how they appear to man, from his

limited point of view. In Orthodox art, the beautiful is determined not

by the natural formation of an object, but from its sublime content, its

power of serving the ideals of the Faith.[21] A basic presupposition of

iconography is the idea of a "new" man and world through Christ. Thus,

icons of the saints must not represent their appearance before grace,

but their holiness, their forms clothed in heavenly glory. The Orthodox

iconographer attempts to express the nature of these divine persons

through exaggeration, excess, and deformation of natural reality.[22]

Thus eyes are painted large because they have been opened to the sublime;

ears have been widened to hear the commandments of the Lord; the mouth is

small, since the body has no need of material things, and so on. In

short, an icon is a picture not of a body, but of a soul.[23] The signifi-

cance of icons for the Orthodox worshipper has been stated by Calian:

> The worshiper contemplating the icon becomes the point of
> reference. He is conscious that the icon is addressing him
> in his Christian pilgrimage toward theosis. The skillfully
> distorted shapes of the icon express the metamorphosis and
> transfiguration at present taking place in the very life of
> the believer...The dynamics of deification or theosis are
> at the very heart of Orthodox spirituality, and the icons
> serve a key role as symbolic prototypes of those who have
> undergone transfiguration and address themselves to the
> worshiper in his earthly pilgrimage (Calian 1968:138).

One can begin to sense from this discussion the importance of

symbolism in Orthodoxy. Indeed, a church's entire physical structure is

comprised of symbols too numerous to discuss. The church's physical
appearance is designed to elevate the worshiper to God through contempla-
tion of the symbolism which surrounds him, as well as through the liturgy.
For example, the church edifice represents the universe: the ceiling is
heaven, and the all-ruling Christ Pantocrator is painted there, looking
down through heaven on the faithful; the floor represents earth; and the
altar is lifted from the floor by a series of steps, suspended between
heaven and earth, since its purpose is to lift the believer to heaven
through the Gospel teaching and sacraments which come from the altar.
The icons are also arranged in a similar manner. The ceiling is reserved
for Christ, and on the front wall is the figure of Mary, Θεοτόκος
(Theotokos, Mother of God), who serves as the link between God and man.
On the iconostasis (icon screen) are icons of the angels and saints, and
the floor level is left for the church members, who themselves have an
image of God within them. In worship services the priest censes the icons
and then the congregation, honoring the living icon of God within each
Christian, as well as the saints.[24] Thus through these symbols, the
entire church--on earth and in heaven--is gathered around Christ in the
Orthodox church.

Symbolism is an implement in Orthodox worship services, as well as
in the church's actual physical structure. As an example, I will cite a
passage from Holy (Easter) Week services to explain a single, but very
important symbol in Orthodox worship. This symbol is Christ as the bridegroom, who weds his pure bride, the Church, at a wedding supper in the
kingdom of God. A foretaste of this feast is found in Holy Communion,
which anticipates the heavenly kingdom. This analogy forms the basis of

the three "Bridegroom" services, on Palm Sunday and Holy Monday and
Tuesday evenings.

> Thou, O bridegroom, dost exceed in beauty all the sons of
> men, and Thou hast called us to the spiritual festival of
> Thy bridal chamber. Through participation in Thy sufferings,
> do Thou remove the mean rainment of my sins, and adorn me
> with a robe of glory, which will proclaim me a radiant guest
> of the glorious beauty of Thy Kingdom; for Thou, O Lord, art
> merciful (Papadeas 1973:69).

Orthodox hymns, as one can see, often involve complex imagery. They
frequently use contrasts and comparisons to illuminate--sometimes quite
beautifully--the deep implications of many Biblical events. Again,
passages from Holy Week will be used as examples. On Tuesday evening the
service utilizes a striking contrast between the promiscuous woman who
washed Jesus's feet with her tears and dried them with her hair, and
Judas, who betrayed him.

> When the woman who was a sinner was offering the myrrh, then
> the disciple was making terms with the lawless men; she rejoiced
> in emptying out that which was all-precious; he hastened to sell
> Him, Who was above all price; she recognized the Master, he
> severed himself from the Master; she was set free, and Judas
> became a slave of the enemy. Fearful is the rashness! Great
> is the penitence! (Papadeas 1973:99)

The contrasts on Thursday evening stress the divinity of Christ, by contrasting his treatment by men with his glory and power.

> Today is hung upon the Tree, He Who suspended the land in the
> midst of the waters. A crown of thorns crowns Him, Who is the
> King of Angels. He is wrapped about with the purple of mockery,
> Who wrapped the Heavens with clouds. He received buffetings,
> Who freed Adam in the Jordan. He was transfixed with nails,
> Who is the Son of the Virgin (Papadeas 1973:238).

The importance of symbolism, analogy, comparison, and contrast as manners
of expression in Orthodox worship should not be overlooked; whole volumes
could be devoted to this topic, but perhaps this brief discussion has made

the reader aware of the richness of religious expression in Orthodoxy.

The Prince's emmisaries "knew not whether we were in heaven or on earth." This is not a surprising reaction, for Orthodox worship represents "heaven on earth", and its outward splendor and beauty are an attempt to create an icon of the great Liturgy in heaven. The Orthodox service assaults all the senses and invites total participation of the individual--through the icons, incense, music, and other elements in the heavenly drama which unfolds before him. It is the Divine Liturgy (the Orthodox equivalent of Catholic Mass) which provides a means for man to reach upwards to heaven, as Christ reaches toward the faithful on earth through Holy Communion. The Orthodox Church

> has attempted by every element of material splendor and beauty to form the earthly Liturgy as an icon of the celestial Liturgy. Whether in great cathedral or in peasant church the prayerful attitude, the clouds of incense, the mystery and awe, have all lent an overwhelming impression of the supernatural. This experience so often remarked upon by Westerners attending the Eastern Liturgy has formed the Christians of the East much more than consideration of doctrine and discipline. These good people have been so formed in the Divine Liturgy that in the darkest periods of history whether under Muslim, Tartar, or Commissar it has been the Divine Liturgy that inspired and gave them hope--it is the most constant expression of Orthodox belief (Jacopin 1967:19).

The Orthodox approach religion in a fundamentally liturgical way; as Ware has noted, "Orthodoxy" signifies both "right belief" and "right worship", and the two are inseparable.[25] Thus the Liturgy is a central element of Orthodoxy. What is it like to attend a Liturgy?

The non-Orthodox visitor to the Divine Liturgy would immediately notice that most of the service is in Greek, with the Epistle, Gospel, and sermon usually being delivered in both Greek and English. He would also notice the presence and the participation of very small children, and even infants, who take the same part in the service as do adults. Small steps are placed before the icon of the church, so that they may climb up and kiss it, and parents hold them up to kiss the others. They learn through the services how and when to cross themselves, and even participate in Holy Communion. In short, they are full-fledged members of the Church after their baptism, which usually occurs within the first few months of their lives.

The Divine Liturgy is reminiscent of the ancient church in that it has two parts, one for the catechumens and one for the believers. This has survived from the times when the church was composed of adult converts: the catechumens were those undergoing Christian instruction who had not yet been baptized. Thus the first part of the service, hymns and readings, were open to them, but they had to leave before the second part of the service, the Eucharistic mystery. In fact, the narthax was originally the only part of the church the catechumens could enter. Although such distinctions are not made today, the liturgy still has portions which refer to this arrangement. Benz has summed up the significance of the Divine Liturgy in this way:

> The transformation of the elements themselves is not the central
> issue for the Orthodox believer. For him the central event of
> the Eucharist is the descent, the appearance, the divine
> presence of the resurrected Christ. And the full import of
> this event colors every moment of the liturgy. The believer's
> partaking of Communion, and his attitude toward the mystery
> of the Communion, are governed by the thought that he is
> actually encountering the living person of the Lord who enters
> the congregation as "King of the universe borne invisibly over
> their spears by the angelic hosts" (1963:36-7).

The annual sequence of feasts and fasts within the Orthodox Church commemorates the Incarnation and its fulfillment in the Church. The year

begins on 1 September. Of course, Easter is preeminent among all feasts,
and next in importance come the 12 Great Feasts:

> The Nativity of the Mother of God (8 September)
>
> The Exaltation of the Life-giving Cross (14 September)
>
> The Presentation of the Mother of God (21 November)
>
> The Nativity of Christ (Christmas) (25 December)
>
> The Baptism of Christ (Epiphany) (6 January)
>
> The Presentation of Our Lord (2 February)
>
> The Annunciation (25 March)
>
> The Entry of Our Lord into Jerusalem (Palm Sunday) (one week
> before Easter)
>
> The Ascension of Our Lord Jesus Christ (40 days after Easter)
>
> Pentecost (50 days after Easter)
>
> The Transfiguration (6 August)
>
> The Falling Asleep of the Mother of God (15 August)

In addition to these feasts, there are many smaller festivals. There are
also many fasting periods within the calendar, for the Orthodox Church
stresses that through fasting the body as well as the soul must be disci-
plined. The four major fasts are:

> The Great Fast (Lent) (begins seven weeks before Easter)
>
> The Fast of the Apostles (starts on the Monday eight days after
> Pentecost, and ends on 28 June, the eve of the Feast of Saints
> Peter and Paul)
>
> The Assumption Fast (from 1 to 14 August)
>
> The Christmas Fast (from 15 November to 24 December)

Wednesdays and Fridays are also fast days, with a few exceptions during
feasts. The rules of fasting are very rigorous. The individual is
generally forbidden meat, fish, all animal products, wine, and oil. Many
Orthodox find it difficult to follow such strict fasting in America,
however, and modify the rules to some extent. For example, school and
work cafeterias do not offer fasting foods, since only a small minority

of the American population is Orthodox; this is the opposite of the case in Greece, where it may be difficult to find meat during a fast. Nevertheless, many Orthodox go through periods of great austerity and physical hardship during the fasts, particularly during the first week in Lent and during Holy Week. The sequence of feasts and fasts which make up the Church calendar is very important to the religious experience of the Orthodox Christian. Hammond very accurately describes the feelings engendered by following through the church's year:

> Nobody who has lived and worshipped amongst Greek Christians for any length of time but has sensed in some measure the extraordinary hold which the recurring cycle of the Church's liturgy has upon the piety of the common people. Nobody who has kept the Great Lent with the Greek Church, who has shared in the fast which lies heavy upon the whole nation for forty days; who has stood for long hours, one of an innumerable multitude who crowd the tiny Byzantine churches of Athens and overflow into the streets, while the familiar pattern of God's saving economy towards man is represented in psalm and prophecy, in lections from the Gospel, and the matchless poetry of the canons; who has known the desolation of the holy and great Friday, when every bell in Greece tolls its lament and the body of the Saviour lies shrouded in flowers in all the village churches throughout the land; who has been present at the kindling of the new fire and tasted of the joy of a world released from the bondage of sin and death - none can have lived through all this and not have realized that for the Greek Christian the Gospel is inseparably linked with the liturgy that is unfolded week by week in his parish church. Not among the Greeks only but throughout Orthodox Christendom the liturgy has remained at the very heart of the Church's life (1956:51-2).

Thus ends the discussion of the history and practices of the Orthodox Church. This background provides a context for a closer examination of the Greek Orthodox Church in America today.

II. American Greek Orthodoxy

A. Organization

In the last section it was noted that the spheres of authority of the four ancient patriarchates of the Orthodox Church were altered by the Turkish conquest of the Middle East; the organization of the Church was totally modified when those areas which were finally freed from Turkish control formed autonomous national churches, such as the Church of Greece and the Church of Russia. These historic events were to have an important impact on the ecclesiastical organization of Orthodoxy in America.

The great influx of Orthodox immigrants to America began in the early 20th century. The immigrant Greeks had in most cases come from the jurisdiction of the Church of Greece; in the United States, however, they were included in "the diaspora", which was under the control of the Ecumenical Patriarch of Constantinople. Russian Orthodoxy had come to North America through Alaska in the 18th century, and the Russians pressed the Greek-oriented Ecumenical Patriarchate to transfer its jurisdiction over the Orthodox in America to the Church of Russia, which had a ready-made organization in the New World. Instead, its authority over American Greek churches in 1908 was transferred to the Church of Greece.[26] Because of political problems in Greece, the Church of Greece failed to appoint a bishop to the United States. This lack of centralized authority contributed to the intercommunity and intracommunity quarrels which plagued the Greek Church's early years in the United States. The royalist-liberalist quarrels which flared up in 1916 in Greece had tragic repercussions in America, by beginning a "civil war" within the Greek Orthodox Church. E.g., liberal factions supporting Venizelos split away from royalist churches, and refused to mention the king's name in the Liturgy. The "civil war" was much too complex to discuss here. Its

result was that jurisdiction over Greek churches in America was returned
to the Ecumenical Patriachate in 1922. After eight more years of chaos
and dispute, Athanagoras was appointed Archbishop of the American Archdiocese, and began the gargantuan task of reuniting the many alienated
factions and reorganizing the Greek churches in America.[27]

Incredibly enough, the "civil war" within the Greek Church was not
unique. Almost every Orthodox group has fought out similar battles over
political and international conflicts involving its mother country, and
it is unfortunate that many of these churches were eventually fragmented
into several jurisdictions each. Consequently, there are at least eighteen
national Orthodox jurisdictions in the United States, although each is
supposedly identical theologically. Schmemann has summed up the American
"situation" in this way:

> Not many words are needed to describe the American "situation";
> by 1970, Orthodoxy in America existed in the form of: one Greek
> jurisdiction, three Russian, two Serbian, two Antiochian, two
> Romanian, two Bulgarian, two Albanian, three Ukrainian, one
> Carpatho-Russian and some smaller groups which we omit here for
> the sake of simplicity. Within every national subdivision each
> group claimed to be the only "canonical" one and denied recogni-
> tion to others (1971:3).

B. Problems of American Orthodox churches

The Greek Orthodox Church is probably the central feature of Greek
American life, and yet the historical forces outlined in the previous
section point to significant questions about its future. There are a
number of problem areas within the church which cause many individuals to
critically examine their membership in the Greek Orthodox Church; some
eventually draw away from the church and, ultimately, the community.
The first dilemma to be considered is nationalism vs. "American Orthodoxy";

I will then discuss the language problem, difficulties between the several generations in the Church, and the uncertainty some younger people feel about the Orthodox religion.

1. Nationalism and "American Orthodoxy"

One of the questions which puzzles many Annunciation parishioners is why the Orthodox churches which represent different nationalities cannot unite into a single "American Orthodox" Church which uses English in its services. The Orthodox Church is one theologically, regardless of the ethnic groups represented in the various national churches. This idea was stated in an interesting way by a 3rd generation boy:

> The churches themselves--they have separate dioceses, they have separate patriarchs, and it's like really, you would think of it as a separate denomination, Greek Orthodox and Syrian Orthodox--well, politically, they are, but theologically, they are the same, one and the same. It's really... it's like buying gas from the different gas companies, they're different, and yet they're all the same. Here was my question, my big question that I thought over--I can't understand why in America they don't have it in English, and call it American Orthodox. And I asked that, and my parents said, "But we're not, we're Greek Orthodox! We're Greek!" you know. But this is America!

His parents' response indicates the very force which keeps the several American "demoninations" of Orthodoxy from forming a common, American Church: intense nationalistic pride.

At this point, I would like to give a brief summary of an excellent article by Schmemann (1971), which analyzes Greek Orthodox nationalism and its role in the "storm" over "American Orthodoxy". The Byzantine Empire was ideologically "universal", but historical events (primarily the Turkish domination) eventually dissolved this universalism into a "nationalism" and exclusiveness, as Byzantium became a small and weak

"Greek" state. The groups--such as Russians, Bulgars, and Serbs--who finally loosed themselves from Byzantine power applied this nationalistic thinking to themselves, and the concept of a Christian nation (with a corporate "identity" before God) developed. This national principle which in a different ecclesiological context had been a unifying principle (one church in one place) became, as a result of immigration to America, the opposite - a principle of division. Each national church now claimed universal jurisdiction based on national "belonging"; in other words, each Greek, Russian, or Serb belongs to his national church, wherever he may live. Schmemann suggests that the roots of Greek nationalism are not found in the "Church-nation" experience (as for other Orthodox groups), but in the experience of the Byzantine ecumene: to the Greek, the national Churches--and even the other Patriarchates--are still a part of the greater whole, the Byzantine world with Constantinople as its sacred center. Byzantium is both the foundation and the justification of Greek religious nationalism. Historical events in the Empire transformed the "imperial tradition": universalism was replaced with nationalism, "Christian Hellenism" (the Orthodox embodiment of Christian tradition) with "Hellenism", Byzantium with Greece.

> ...this "Hellenism" is the Greek expression of the secular
> nationalism common to all modern nations and whose roots are
> in the French Revolution of 1789 and in European Romanticism.
> As every nationalism of that type it is built upon a mythology
> partly "secular" and partly "religious". On the secular level
> the myth is that of a unique relationship between the Greeks
> and that "Hellenism" which constitutes the common source and
> foundation of the entire Western civilization. On the religious
> level the myth is that of a unique relationship to Byzantium,
> the Christian "ecumene", which is the common foundation of all
> Orthodox Churches (1971:21).

During the centuries of Turkish domination, the Patriarch was the symbol of the survival and identity of the Greek nation, and the Greeks came to identify "Christian Hellenism" with Greek national and ethnic identity. Schmemann suggests that the Greeks fought against autocephalies in the past because they thought "Christian Hellenism", the essence of Orthodoxy, could have no other basis than in the Byzantine Church, which was Greek; today they fight them because, having replaced "Christian Hellenism" with "Hellenism", they feel the other "Orthodoxies" must be expressions of other "essenses"--just as the Greek Orthodox must preserve Hellenism, the other Churches must protect their own national essenses. Schmemann comments:

> What makes, however, this new (not Byzantine but modern) Greek
> nationalism distinct from other Orthodox "nationalisms" is the
> certitude, surviving in it from its "imperial" antecedents,
> that within all these Orthodox "essences" the Greek "essence"
> has a primacy, occupies, jure divino, the first place (1971:25).

He concludes that the American dilemma will hopefully make it clear that it is not "Hellenism" or "Serbianism" which must be preserved, but the essentials of Orthodoxy.

There are quite a few members of the Houston community who advocate "American Orthodoxy", and their reasoning is similar to that of the young man quoted at the beginning of this section. Others, however, feel that too much would be lost if the "ethnicity" were dropped from their Orthodox church. Furthermore, the two camps are not formed along generational lines--there are people in the 2nd generation who advocate "American Orthodoxy", and 3rd generation individuals who oppose it. E.g., a 3rd generation boy made this comment:

> I don't think we're ready for that as of yet...because my
> common ties are with the Greeks, and the Syrians are two
> different things. I mean, they have their own family, they

> have their own ways, and again the Greeks have their own ways.
> ... Our Church is--you could probably consider it a way of
> life as well as a place of worship.

Perhaps this comment gets to the very heart of many Greeks' fear of
"American Orthodoxy": Greek Orthodoxy is not just Orthodoxy which Greeks
practice, but it represents a uniquely Greek way of life which is intimately tied to Greek Orthodoxy. Although Greek and Syrian Orthodoxy,
e.g., are theologically the same, they have varying religious customs,
and their church services are conducted in different languages. These
differences in themselves make the Syrian Church a "different" church to
many Greek Orthodox. A 3rd generation boy's encounter with the Houston
Syrian Church, and particularly his parents' reaction, illustrates this
point.

> One time when I was visiting the Syrian Orthodox Church, I
> said, "Well, can I take communion over there?" And Mom said,
> "Well, sure--it's the same faith". But my father said, "No,
> because you're not Syrian, you're Greek." ... He says, "Well,
> you should be going to learn all you can about the Greek
> Church, before you go to the Syrian Church. There's hardly
> any icons, it's a plain white church, and everything, and
> here you have--we're paying our membership dues, and what's
> wrong?" And then it gets--a panic in his mind, "He's con-
> verting or something, he's leaving us, what did we do wrong?"

There is another side to this nationalism, however. Besides its
impact on Orthodoxy, one must consider its importance for maintaining the
Greek group. Whereas the existence of strong nationalistic sentiments
may hinder the universalist ideals of Orthodoxy, it greatly contributes
toward maintaining the boundaries between Greeks and other ethnic groups.
The fact that Greeks have a church which is theirs alone is a powerful
factor in the continuation of the group; the refusal of many to consider
merging with other ethnic churches to form an "American" church is no

doubt partially based on knowledge of this fact.

The nationalistic feelings of many Greek Orthodox create a difficult situation for the individual who becomes a member of the church through conversion, for there seems to be a feeling that ὁ ξένος (o xenos, a stranger) cannot be a full-fledged member of "their" church. Those individuals who have married Greeks and become members of the church must struggle for acceptance into the Greek community, and many seem to feel that, after years of trying, they have still not succeeded. There is always the chance that they will be rejected as "Americans". The individual who of his own free will--not because of marriage--converts to Greek Orthodoxy is considered an oddity which few can understand. A 3rd generation boy expressed a typical reaction to such converts:

> In fact, it was very surprising for a lot of people, like my grandmother and my parents, when T came into the church. ...
> She said, "Oh, who is that American? Is he a convert?"
> Immediately, "Well, is he Greek?" or something, "Did he convert?"
> My parents always refer to him as "the American". And I say,
> "His name is T, and he's Greek Orthodox." "No, he's an American."
> Well, so am I!

It is understandable that some church leaders and laymen feel that the younger generations would be impoverished if the inheritance of Greek Christian civilization were lost to "American Orthodoxy", but others wonder whether these national traditions can be preserved without obscuring the universality of the Orthodox Church. Ware has stated the present problem of the Orthodox Church in the New World:

> Orthodox--without sacrificing anything good in their national traditions--need to break away from a narrow and exclusive nationalism: they must...not behave as if it were something restricted to Greeks or Russians, and of no relevance to anybody else. They must rediscover the universality of Orthodoxy (1963:191).

2. Language

Closely related to the question of "American Orthodoxy" is the problem of the language which is to be used in the church; the latter is the more explosive problem in the Houston Greek community, and indeed, in the whole American Greek Orthodox Church. If services were currently being conducted in English, the question of "American Orthodoxy" would naturally be much more relevant and pressing, but the big debate within the Greek Orthodox Church, and in the minds of Greek Orthodox individuals as well, is over language. Like the problem of "American Orthodoxy", the language question is a real dilemma.

Those who favor the use of English cite several reasons for this stance. One of the major points in the arguments against the exclusive use of Greek is that the language used in the Liturgy is an ancient form of Greek which bears only little relationship to the contemporary spoken language. Thus to a certain extent, no one understands what is being said when Greek is being used in the services, except through having heard the Liturgy thousands of times over the years. Many people can follow the Divine Liturgy only because they can read along in bilingual service books. In fact, a surprising number of Greek-speaking, church-going people do not even attempt to follow the service closely, but just read along in English from beginning to end paying no attention to which part of the service is being chanted at any one time. Even those who speak Greek and are very familiar with the services are sometimes surprised when--in attending a service in which the priest uses a lot of English--they realize how much they have missed by hearing services in Greek. E.g., a 2nd generation girl made this observation about a wedding she attended.

> This wedding--the thing that touched me was that it was in
> English, and I understood what was going on for the first
> time, for a change, and I got a lot more out of it in English.
> ... The only thing said in Greek was the most important stuff,
> the ritual. And I personally got a lot more out of it--it got
> to me more being in English.

Perhaps the most convincing argument for using English instead of

Greek in the services, however, is that most of the younger generation

do not know Greek well enough to get anything out of Greek church ser-

vices, and there is a very real danger that many of them will be lost

to Orthodoxy altogether if more English is not used in the Liturgy.

Here are representative comments from a young woman of the 3rd generation:

> A lot of kids are complaining now because there's so much
> Greek in the church service, and they want to change it all
> to English, you know and I tend to agree, because I mean the
> only reason I understand it is because I've listened to it
> every Sunday, and I follow along in the little book and every-
> thing. But I agree it should be changed to English, because
> we're losing the kids. I don't know of anybody who's left,
> but there's a lot of complaining among the kids, and I can
> see the reasoning behind it, because the kids now that are
> 15 or 16 I don't think are being taught as much Greek as say
> our age group was. So if they don't understand it, and if
> they don't know what's going on up there when they go to
> church, they don't know what Father's saying or anything
> else, what do they get out of it?

Another argument for the use of English in church services is that

Orthodoxy has traditionally used languages appropriate to the countries

in which it has been established. The reasoning behind this argument is

explained by a 2nd generation man:

> When I was in the GOYA I was one of the stout fighters about
> changing. I was against changing from the Greek to the English.
> 'Cause I don't know, I felt that too much would be lost in
> translation. And then one time I was teaching in Sunday school
> class about these two saints...who went into the Slavic nations
> to introduce Orthodoxy to them. And before they would go there
> they got together with their Archbishop and told him "You can

> send us up there, but before we go up there we're going to
> translate everything into the Slavic language because we
> just don't see any sense in going up there and try to teach
> these people Orthodoxy with the Greek language they don't
> understand." ...And you know I got to thinking, ya know
> this is more or less what we're faced with here. My kids
> --O.K., I send them to Greek school after school once a
> week. But what Greek they're going to learn is not going
> to be enough for them to understand the Liturgy. See we're
> faced with the same problem now, so I say "What's wrong with
> translating this into the English language so people like my
> kids can understand it?" It's the same thing they did at
> that time.

This appeal to Tradition to shed light on a current dilemma is a good

"Orthodox" way of solving problems, but in this case the situation is

not as simple as it may seem. Cyril and Methodius brought Orthodoxy to

the Slavs in their own language, true, but the Greek immigrants to Ameri-

ca brought a church with them which was already in their language:

Greek. The problem now is that the language of the immigrant generation

is not that of their grandchildren. The struggle which is necessary

for many people to understand the Liturgy is summed up by a 3rd genera-

tion boy:

> That's probably why I was turned off so much--I have to make
> myself understand, and I don't think that's what should--
> that's what people should do. I don't think they should
> try and try and try and try to understand, it should come to
> them easier.

On the other hand, there are also serious objections to changing the

Liturgy into English. The major objection is summed up by saying "some-

thing is lost in the translation," and the "something" is not just the

meaning of words, but also the beauty, mystery, and tradition of Greek

Orthodoxy; it is this loss which most people fear, since the "true

meaning" is to an extent lost to many even before translation. Beauty

and mystery are a crucial part of an Orthodox worship service, which is based more on an emotional response within the participant than an intellectual one. Thus to remove this traditional beauty and mystery is to threaten the essense of the Orthodox service. A young 3rd generation man responded to this attachment to "beauty" in this way:

> The people who are pro-Greek say, "Well, yes, but you lose the beauty of the language, especially if the hymns are translated, they would have to be altered, and you would lose the beauty of that", and I came back with "Well, what are you after? Are you after the beauty? Are you after euphonia, or the actual, if you want to be saved? - the gospel that's going to be preached."

However, many members of the younger generation do not see it this way. For them the "mystery" of the Liturgy is based to a large extent in the fact that it does represent "the unknown", and an attraction of the Greek Orthodox religion is this mystical quality, which partly results from their own lack of knowledge about what is occurring during the Liturgy. Here are the comments of a 3rd generation college student.

> I know Greek, and I've heard our service in English and Greek, and I tend to prefer the Greek. Let's say it moved me more--maybe I didn't understand completely what was going on, even though I caught every other word, let's say, it would still tend to move me more than English. I don't know, it just seems that the American--it seems that going to church and witnessing the Liturgy in completely English--it seems to tend to draw away from the--I guess religion has to be mystical up to a certain point. And it seems to draw away from that.

Perhaps one of the main reasons that people want to continue the use of Greek, however, is that it is "traditional". Even some young people feel that having an English Liturgy is "just not right". It is not at all surprising that the older generation would feel that the Greek language, traditionally an element of the Greek Orthodox Church for hundreds of years, is an essential part of their religion, as a 3rd generation girl realized.

> A lot of the oldtimers especially, there are so many still
> in the Greek Church, that don't even speak English or know
> so little of it that it would be like destroying their
> religion.
> [Except the language isn't the same as the language in the
> church.]
> It's not the same but it's just something they've always known
> and it makes it so hard for them to change.
> [I guess like King James Bible and Revised Bible.]
> It's--logically they may tell themselves--there's no difference.
> They just feel more right like you know, King James, they felt
> like it was the authentic Bible when it's King James. That's
> similar to the religion with the Greeks.

Furthermore, the mere fact that the Greek language is "traditional"

carries a lot of weight in a group which is so oriented toward maintain-

ing traditions.

Behind all these reasons for keeping Greek in the church however,

is probably a fear that "Greekness" would be somehow lost if English

were used. The church is the formal repository of the Greek language,

and if it turned to English, what would there be to keep future genera-

tions Greek?

> I think if you took away the Greek language, you'd have to
> take away the Greek everything. Because without the language,
> I don't think you'd have too much of anything really left.
> You'd still have the Orthodox Church, but it wouldn't be
> Greek Orthodox anymore.

> As they take out the language a lot of people won't be
> like their parents. It's something that draws them all
> together and if you take out the language, that's part of
> the religion. It's like taking away a part of the religion
> that they've grown up with.

The two "camps", those favoring English and those favoring Greek,

are not divided along generational lines. The two groups are mixed,

by both age and generation. Some members of the older generation may

themselves prefer Greek, but feel that the use of English would insure

that their children or grandchildren will remain Orthodox. On the other hand, many younger people support the use of Greek, even (or especially)

if they cannot speak Greek, because it makes church services more beauti-

ful and mystical. Furthermore, one should not get the idea that this

issue has all the members of the Greek Orthodox Church divided into

two warring camps; this is far from true. Although there are certainly

some individuals who take a firm stance on one side or the other of this

issue, it is probably more accurate to say that most people are undecided,

and still fighting the battle within themselves. A young 3rd generation

woman mirrored the feelings of many around her.

> I'd be sad to hear everything done in English, and I'd be sad
> to hear our hymns translated into English, but if that's the
> only way the young people are going to stay in the church,
> what are you going to do? It would hurt me, I wouldn't feel
> like it was really--well, I guess I would always feel like it
> was my church, but still...

Other Orthodox Churches apparently allow English, and use it to a

larger extent than the Greek Orthodox Church does. It seems that the

Greek Church is more anxious to maintain its language, culture, and

society in the United States than are the other Orthodox Churches. The

Archdiocese has made a large effort to teach its children the Greek

language--both Liturgical and modern. Certain portions of the Liturgy

must be in Greek, and the relative amounts of Greek and English in the

rest of the service is at the priest's discretion. At Annunciation, the

percentage of English is related to the age, generational, and ethnic

composition of the congregation attending the particular service in

question. (In my experience, however, Greek always predominates.) This

bilingual policy enables the church to please as many people as possible,

and it also has another advantage. Since sermons, letters to parishoners

from the diocese and archdiocese, etc., are bilingual, they can in effect
be two different sermons, letters, or whatever; they usually contain the
same information, but stated in ways that will appeal to the individuals
who will receive each version. Thus the Greek presentations may be
slanted toward "old country" traditions and favorite saints, whereas the
English ones may present a more scholarly approach.

3. Greek Orthodoxy in American society

A third source of problems in Greek Orthodoxy is the fact that it
has been transplanted to American society. This has had important
effects on its development here. These effects are found in the impact
of other Christian churches on Orthodox individuals and in the influence
of America's secular society on the practicing of Orthodoxy. Each of
these effects will be considered briefly.

The Greek immigrant came to America from the only country in the
world which has remained officially Orthodox. Hammond has commented,
"Hellas, when all is said as to the spread of secularism and indifference,
remains a Christian nation in a sense of which we in the West can have
but little conception."[28] In this atmosphere, the Orthodox Chruch was
the Church, rather than one of many Christian denominations, and a very
small one, as it is in the United States. This close contact with other
forms of Christianity has led to certain problems in the United States
which the Church in Greece did not have to face. E.g., strict fasting
is more difficult in the United States than in Greece; moreover, some
Orthodox have begun to question the practice itself, after having come
into contact with other Christians who do not fast. A young 3rd generation woman's comment shows the influence of contact with other chruches

on Orthodox youth:

> I don't think the church is backward like some of the kids
> do... A lot of the kids think, "Well, the Catholics don't
> have to fast any more before they take communion, why do we?
> Why do we fast on Fridays and Wednesdays? The Catholics
> don't anymore."

Although I have only given fasting as an example, there are many
other ways in which Orthodoxy has been affected by its members' contact
with other Christians. The Greek Orthodox are such a small group that
they cannot be self-sufficient (at least in Houston), and cannot avoid
social contact with non-Orthodox. Through these contacts they realize
that there are other forms of Christianity, and that these may be as
valid as Orthodoxy. One incident stands out in my mind particularly
well. During a Lenten retreat the Syrian Orthodox priest spoke on
Orthodoxy as the one true religion, and commented that Orthodox people
in America are forgetting this. Many in the audience questioned his
attitude, and afterwards, a 2nd generation friend commented that she
just couldn't see it that way, because "A lot of my friends are Americans,
and they are good people." She could not believe that these other forms
of Christianity were not valid, that her church had the only answer.

The fact that American urban industrial society is so secularized
in comparison to Greece has also presented problems for Orthodoxy, for
religious traditions which were "national" in Greece become more difficult to fulfill in America. Again I will cite fasting as an example,
since it plays such a major role in the Orthodox Church. A 3rd generation boy mentioned to me problems he had recognized in Greek Americans'
practicing of the Orthodox faith.

I don't know how many parties I've been to, where it would be

a Friday or a Saturday, and everybody'd be serving steak or
something, and I'd say, "How can these people call themselves
Orothodox if they can't sacrifice?" — I told somebody one
time, "Two days out of the week, if you can't do that, leave.
If you can't discipline yourself, you're in bad shape." ...
The thing I hear is "The world has changed! This is the 20th
century, we don't do all that!" The world has changed, but
God hasn't--he's still the same as he was a million years ago.
I said, "Yeah, it's really weird, the world's changed, but he
could flood the world now as easily as he could back in Noah's
time. It's funny, with all this technology we have, we could
still be treading water!"

This young man sensed the very real problem which faces traditional

Orthodoxy in the secularized social atmosphere of America. Furthermore,

the true meaning of a tradition such as fasting is often lost in our

technological society; people may obey "the letter of the law" but not

its spirit by making choices which were not available in the more tradi-

tional surroundings of Greece.

When Mom would fast before they had the non-dairy cream,
she would always have to drink her coffee black, she wasn't
allowed to put milk in it, but now we can use Coffee-mate.
But somehow that just takes away the original meaning.

4. Generations

A fourth problem of the Orthodox religion in America is that members

of the several generations approach their faith differently, which causes

tensions within families as well as in the church. The main reason for

these differences is probably that members of the 1st generation never

attained the level of education of their children and grandchildren.

Thus their religious practices are based on faith and tradition, whereas

their children approach Orthodoxy more intellectually, and their grand-

children even more so. The comments of a 3rd generation boy, which

explain his grandmother's conception of Orthodoxy, reflect this difference

in approach.

85

My father found a better job--and my grandmother said, "Oh, praise God!" And everything. And "Quick! Go to the room with the icons and pray!" And my Mom said, "Well, I can pray right here, you know, it's no difference, just a few feet." "No! go over here where the icons are--you see them..." And that brings in the tradition part we were talking about. ... She would say prayers and walk around the house with the incense thing, and of course her idea of the incense--I asked her, "Why do you do the incense?" And she said, "Because it's done." Yet the Orthodox standpoint, I think the smoke is supposed to be prayers or thoughts, going up to heaven or something.

One aspect of Orthodoxy in which one can see differences between the generations is in their behavior and attitudes toward saints. Most of the 1st generation and some of the more traditional 2nd generation Greeks have close relationships with the saints. They believe that there are saints who are more helpful than others in curing certain ills. E.g., one saint may be known for curing eyes and another for feet. One may sometimes make "deals" with saints: he promises to do certain things-- like fast faithfully every Wednesday and Friday if the saint will cure his illness, or go to church every Sunday for a year if his child recovers from an accident. Two saints, Cosmas and Damian--legendary Christian physicians who healed without accepting payment--are particular objects of such petitions. In conjunction with their prayers, people place on the icon of Cosmas and Damian small silver and gold medals portraying the parts of the body in need of healing. A young 3rd generation woman described this practice:

When you pray to them to intercede for you, or if someone is very ill--you know, they were doctors, physicians--you promise them, say please make that person well for you, and if they do and the person's well, you send off to the monastery--that's the only place I know where you can get them--and get those little hands and stuff like that, and then you go up and put them on the είκόνα [ikona, icon].

Many people of the 3rd generation find these practices incomprehensible,
and it is doubtful whether they will continue. The comments of a young
3rd generation man:

> [Are you supposed to have a relationship with your name-
> saint?] I believe you are. Do I? No. I don't know--well,
> you're usually supposed to ask your saint to talk to God,
> but I don't know... I usually just eliminate the middle man
> and go right to the head.

The priest at Annunciation also feels that the 1st generation's
ideas are largely a result of the inadequacy of Greek religious training
which has its roots in the Turkish occupation. There are many "pietisms"
(such as making "deals" with saints) which have no theological basis,
but which are practiced by the older generation nevertheless. A 2nd
generation man explained how many of these pietisms entered Orthodoxy:

> The thing about the old Greek immigrants I think, and you
> probably noticed this, a lot has creeped into their culture
> that they base on religious beliefs but actually have no
> religious backing. ... My mother used to say "you mustn't
> do this because of such and such," and later I found out it
> had no real religious basis at all. This is a lot of--I
> think of what--well, for instance, they're very superstitious
> people. Most of the Greek immigrants weren't well educated--
> there's a lot of custom in our religion. Customs build up
> through generations and pretty soon they become gospel.

These traditions are confusing to the younger people, who have had more
education, both secular and religious. The priest feels that he must
have respect for each group, allowing the older generation to continue
its traditional religious practices while teaching the younger generation much that their grandparents never learned about Orthodoxy.

That each younger generation is rejecting some of the religious
traditions practiced by its parents seems to support the unilinear view
of assimilation. However, I do not believe that this is the best

explanation for what is happening. Rather than a process of Americanization, this trend could be viewed as indicative of secularization, as the
Greek community gradually comes to grips with a modern world. Furthermore, by rejecting pietisms, these generations are becoming not more
American, but better and more informed Greek Orthodox. The current
changes, as well as areas of controversy, in the Greek Orthodox Church
indicate that something more complex than straight-line assimilation is
occurring. E.g., in discussions of American Orthodoxy or an English
Liturgy, one finds advocates from all generations on either side of the
arguments. Therefore, it appears that the Greek church is attempting
to respond to the needs of Greek Americans, and to become a Greek American rather than an exclusively "old-country" Greek church. This does not
mean that either the church or its members are in any sense assimilating,
because a strong sense of their own differentness from the surrounding
society remains intact.

5. Uncertainty about Orthodoxy

Uncertainties about their church plague many Orthodox individuals,
and these represent a fifth problem of Orthodoxy in America. A general
idea of the problem is found in the comments of a young 2-3* generation
man.

> I wish I knew more about it. I can't say what I don't like
> about it, because I don't know that much about it. It's a
> shame, here I am 19, I've been going that long. ... In Greece

---

*This form will be used to denote an individual of "mixed parentage",
i.e., who has one 1st generation and one 2nd generation parent. This
notation may appear rather confusing, but it is important to distinguish
these individuals from 2nd and 3rd generation people, since they form a
category with its own special characteristics and problems.

they hardly ever go to church--mostly here, because it also
has a social function. In Greece they go twice a year.
People go because that's where other Greeks are--you meet
at Athens Bar, Dionysos, Bachanale, or church. That's it.
The old people have the service memorized, they can recite
the words and know what some of the words mean, but if you
ask them some "why?" about the religion, and they can't
answer. Who should I ask? I'd have to depend on the priest.
That's the only person. Mother doesn't know, I've asked her
a lot of things.
[Well, if they know nothing about the church they're in...]
It must not be because of the religion that people are there.

This young man is really reaching out, trying to answer his questions,

and hoping that the Orthodox Church can satisfy his needs, but still

uncertain. Nor is he alone in his search for answers, for many Orthodox

individuals, even in the 2nd generation, are also uncertain about their

faith.

One of the main complaints is that the Greek Church is "too social".

One 2nd generation man who left the church was not exaggerating when he

commented that the Greek Church is as much a social as a religious thing;

one could spend his life there without ever going to a service. In his

view, the purpose of GOYA and the other church activities is not reli-

gious, but social: to get Greeks together with other Greeks, and to keep

them together. Many agree with this idea, and feel that the church is

too much like a "social club" in which Greekness is the foremost "restric-

tion". Ironically, the church has utilized "social club" terms in its

requirements for membership: every family has been required to pay $125

"dues" annually to belong to the church. The dues will be discussed in

the next section, which considers the local church, Annunciation. On the

other hand, it is understandable that the Greek church is a very "social"

institution, for it serves as the center of Greek activities. Moreover, its members form a close-knit group, because many of them have grown up together. This in itself may be a force which has kept many people in the church, as a 2nd generation man implied in his comments:

> Let's say I moved to another town away from the people I grew up with. I'm not too sure that--I probably would join the Greek Church there but there are I am sure a lot of others would, let's say strong Greek backgrounds that probably if we moved away from our early friends, probably would just decide, "Well, to heck with it, why go to a Greek Church? Let's go to something we can understand," and have just drifted away completely.

Another source of discontent for some is the feeling that the Orthodox Church in some cases stresses Greekness and Orthodoxy rather than Christianity. Thus many of the Orthodox youth are amazed at the Biblical knowledge of their non-Orthodox friends. A 3rd generation boy complained:

> A lot of the Protestant churches really teach the Bible. A lot of them, those kids know the Bible when they come out of Sunday school. And we couldn't compare to their knowledge. Our knowledge is within the Tradition, and that's what's messing us up. We know the unimportant stuff, when do we celebrate St. George, you know, really, things like that. I'm serious, really.

In reaction to this problem, some young people have begun to turn to fundamentalism and Protestant groups such as Campus Crusade.

As a result of the several problems discussed in this section, individuals and families occasionally leave the church. Such individuals will be discussed in Chapter 4. However, many people feel that their needs are met in the church, and perhaps this section should be ended on a brighter note, by quoting a young 3rd generation man's opinion of the Greek Orthodox Church.

> I've been to other churches, talked to other people, and I still think we're the one. In high school, I didn't really

> have the opportunity to visit other churches, or anything
> like that, but I have since I've been in college. I like
> my religion, and it's my choice now, because I could have
> left, gone someplace else... Most churches don't have as
> much tradition as we do. And that's one of the prettiest
> things about it.

Thus one should not overestimate the troubles of American Greek Orthodoxy,

for it is still surviving. Nevertheless, there are many individuals

within the church, as well as those who have left it, who are dissatisfied

with certain elements of Orthodoxy in America.

III. Annunciation

> [Is the church an important influence in Greek identity?]
> The church has a lot to do with it. That's the thing, that's
> where you identify, most of your friends are there, that's
> where your religion is, you see people--I do think the church
> has a definite influence. If the church were to say close the
> doors, it would hurt the Greek community greatly. I think
> everyone's kind of spread out [geographically] because of
> that--it's kind of a binding factor.

This 3rd generation man's observation is very true; Annunciation is the

primary focal point and catalyst in the Houston Greek community, in that

it serves the religious, cultural, educational, social and recreational

needs of Houston Greeks. The several ways in which Annunciation meets

these needs will be examined in this section. I will first present some

background information on Annunciation, concentrating on its history and

present organization and facilities, and then examine the numerous pro-

grams and events it offers to the members of the Greek community. The

final section will discuss recent changes in the church.

A. Background

 1. History

    Houston's Greek Orthodox community first began to organize on

23 February 1910 when 50 people of Greek extraction met and decided to organize a Greek church. Apparently nothing came of these plans until 16 April 1916 when "the few early Greek pioneers who, with the grace of God, migrated from the far shores of their Motherland, Greece, seeking new opportunities in the land of America, which was later to become their permanent home, met and formed the Benevolent Brotherhood 'Elpis'." This organization laid the groundwork for the establishment of the church, "to worship their creator and to preserve the traditions of Greek civilization and culture and the invaluable heritage they had transmitted from their homeland."[29] The first meeting of parishioners in the new church -- "Εὐαγγελίσμος τῆς Θεοτόκου" (Annunciation of the Theotokos)-- located at 509 Walker occurred on 9 May 1918. Many people of Greek descent came to settle as Houston grew, and eventually the need arose for new facilities. A Building Fund was established, and many individuals donated $1000 each to start the drive. The new church--located at Yoakum and Kipling--was dedicated on 15 November 1959, and since that time, the S. P. Martel Auditorium and Polemanakos Educational Building have been added. In 1973 the Greek Orthodox Community Center, located off South Main, was officially opened, and in spring 1974 property near the church, at Kipling and Mt. Vernon, was acquired, perhaps for the establishment of a nursing home for aged Greek men.

2. Current organization

To receive sacraments (such as wedding and baptism), one must be a member of Annunciation, which requires annual dues of $125 per family or $75 per individual. There are about 800 adults each year who are bona fide members of the church, but a much larger number than this participate in occasional services; e.g., during Holy Week the church is filled past overflowing. Furthermore, there are also many "sacramental members" who pay dues only during the years they have children needing baptism, or if they want to be married. The lay leaders of Annunciation see these "sacramental members" as one of the church's main membership problems, since they do not contribute to the support of the church except when they need certain sacraments. On the other hand, the sacramental members generally object to the "dues" concept, since it "sounds like some kind of country club instead of a church," and do not think it is appropriate to deny sacraments to those who have not paid full membership dues. Thus the "dues" have presented a major problem for many people; currently, however, there have been efforts to replace "dues" with a program in which members pledge what they feel able to pay.

The affairs of the local church are run by the members, who meet at quarterly General Assemblies. Those who are current in their membership (i.e., whose dues are paid) are given special cards to hold up for voting. These assemblies are very democratic and run by strict parliamentary rules. Apparently all church actions except those of a strictly ecclesiastical nature are decided either by votes taken at General Assemblies, or by officers on the Board, who are elected from among the members.

Through being elected to the Board, most of the men of the church are allowed to serve in an official capacity at one time or another, and thus the prestigious positions are passed around. Furthermore, those who are not elected to the Board may serve as chairmen of the

many committees which are in charge of various important aspects of
church life, such as membership, GOCC, Festival, education, or athletics.
Thus practically anyone who is interested may serve officially in one
way or another. At most assemblies there are several presentations of
plaques and certificates to individuals for their "service to the community" in some capacity, and in this way each person receives official
recognition for his position and contributions.

B. Programs

A 2nd generation man, in discussing the early years of the Houston
Greek community, made this comment:

> You probably know that Greek immigrants back in those days
> had a very very difficult time of it. ... They were consid-
> ered second-class citizens for one thing because they all--
> and probably should have been considered second-class citizens
> --because they all wanted to come over to this country, make
> money and then go back to Greece. They didn't particularly
> care about staying here. I don't think one of them did.
> They all had the thought about going back to Greece. That
> alone tells you a little bit about the Greek. He's--you can
> take him out of Greece but you can never take the Greek out
> of him.

Although it has now been more than 60 years since these original immigrants came to Houston--their children and grandchildren have been born
in America and there is no longer much of a feeling about returning to
Greece--many Houston Greeks still live in a very Greek world here in
America. It is not an exaggeration to say that many people in the Greek
community live in their own little world of Greek organizations and
church. This is not as extensive in Houston as in cities that have
larger and more concentrated Greek populations, for in these cities
people can spend their whole lives in a Greek world. In Houston the
Greek community is not large enough to be as self-sufficient as a

community such as Astoria, New York, e.g. A 2-3 generation man discussed

changes in the Houston community since his childhood, and mentioned what

his parents would have preferred for the Houston community:

> [You know, you said things were different than how your
> parents would have wanted them--how would they have wanted
> them?]
> Very ethnic-oriented, I mean, everything should be Greek,
> marrying Greek people, having Greek friends, your American
> friends, you can have them while you're in school, that's
> fine, but don't mess around with them after school. And
> I think it's basically just sticking around...Astoria, in
> New York, it's a...it's like Chinatown or something. Instead
> of the pharmacy being called "pharmacy", it's ΦΑΡΜΑΚΙΑ and
> everything is in Greek. You don't even have to leave that
> part... And I'm sure our parents would like us to stick, you
> know, be Greek, stick around with the Greeks and all that,
> but it's impossible in Houston. Well, because Houston's
> kind of spread out, and when people first moved here, they
> --most of the old Greeks lived around the church. See, now
> all the new Greeks started making money and moving out. And
> because of that, when you're out, you start associating with
> your white friends, American friends, whatever you want to
> call them, and I don't know, you just get away from this
> Greek bit.

Despite this preference--for Houston to be more like Astoria--Houston is

a smaller, less concentrated, and thus by necessity, less Greek, communi-

ty. On the other hand, it is a much larger and more Greek community

than may be found in the rest of Texas, or even in much of the South.

This "Greekness" is expressed in Greek clubs and restaurants, fraternal

organizations, but particularly in the church and its programs.

Annunciation offers much more than just church services to its

parishoners, and this fact was brought home at a welcoming reception

for newcomers, at which the president of Annunciation's Board described

the many programs and activities available for all members of the family.

He described the school, nursery, Sunday school, choir, Greek Orthodox

Community Center (GOCC), Philoptochos, Senior Citizens, GOCC Fun Club,

AHEPA, GAPA, Greek Festival, etc., etc., and then a member of the audience stood up and said, "You forgot to mention that we also have church services here sometimes." The audience got a good laugh out of this comment. (Of course, the rest of the story is that the president replied "Funny you should mention church!" which was really humorous because the fellow was one of a group that attends activities, but very seldom goes to church.)

1. Religious

In addition to church services, the church sponsors annual Lenten retreats for men, women and young adults; and adults', young adults', and children's Bible classes. During the school year there are also Sunday school classes, which use texts from the Orthodox Christian Education Commission and the Greek Orthodox Archdiocese, and catechism classes for those who are interested in converting to Orthodoxy. GOYA (Greek Orthodox Youth of America) provides an opportunity for Greek Orthodox kids aged 13-18 to socialize with others of the same background, and its purpose is religious training and fellowship. During the summer there is a two-week Vacation Bible School in which religious education, arts, and crafts, Greek dancing and Greek language are taught.

2. Educational

Besides religious education, Annunciation also has a parochial school for children from age 3 to the 3rd grade. The school follows the basic HISD academic program, with additional courses in Greek language, Greek Orthodoxy, and Greek dancing. In the spring of 1974 (and again in 1975), the church held a Benefit Dinner for Annunciation School which was very well attended by the Greek community; about 500 people paid $5 a plate. There were exhibits of work the children had done at the school, and a display of educational equipment the school needed, which people were asked to donate. Even those who do not have children in the school support it as an important "Greek" influence on the younger generation, and a wonderful opportunity for the children to go to school together.

3. Cultural

There are also several "cultural" programs which are sponsored by Annunciation. A cultural dance class meets twice a month, and non-Greeks as well as Greeks are welcome to come and learn Greek folk dances. For school children there is an afternoon Greek language school which meets after regular school hours; there are five "grades", each meeting one afternoon a week. An adult Greek language class which meets once a week provides an opportunity for several groups of people to learn Greek: Greek Americans, Americans who are married to Greeks, and Americans. The cost is $35 for members of Annunciation and $50 for non-members.

4. Social

Several social and fraternal organizations frequently meet or have special functions at the church. These include GAPA (Greek American Progressive Association) and AHEPA (American Hellenic Educational and Progressive Association) and its auxilliaries, Daughters of Penelope, Sons of Pericles, and Maids of Athena. In addition to these functions, the church has fairly regular social functions. There are "fellowship coffees" after services, special dinners (such as the school benefit dinner mentioned above and a Palm Sunday Fish Dinner), and family communion breakfasts. There is also a monthly Men's Breakfast, and the ladies' charitable organization Philoptochos has meetings and fellow-ships there, as well as get-togethers twice a month for the Senior Citizens.

5. Recreational

Recreational activities also play a big part in Annunciation's programs. The GOCC has made available an exclusive place for Greeks to come together for baseball, basketball, volleyball, tennis, and swimming. It has been proposed that other Orthodox Christians be allowed to use the facilities for a fee. (When questioned why others should be allowed in, the president of the Board replied that 60% of the parish's marriages are to non-Orthodox, and that it would be good to get the Greek kids together with other Orthodox children.) In the summer there are two sessions of "Fun Club" for children aged 4 through 12 at the GOCC. There are also a number of Greek Orthodox men's, girls', and boys' softball, basketball, and volleyball teams which compete in church and YMCA League play; in the spring there is a sports banquet which honors the players.

6. Greek Festival

The Greek Festival, Annunciation's big annual money-making project, is enthusiastically supported by the citizens of Houston; e.g., in 1973 the Festival took in $122,524.58 and netted $61,447.65 after expenses were paid. The Festival is very important to the Greek community for more than just monetary reasons, however, for it provides an opportunity for all interested members of the community to work together on a common project.

The Greeks take a great deal of pride in their three-day Festival, which involves months of preparation by all segments of the Greek community. The women begin baking the food for the October festival in July, and soon afterwards the children and young adults who dance in the shows begin learning their routines. The men plan the business end of the Festival, go to Greece for gift shop merchandise, and so on. During the three-day Festival all age groups work very hard: adults prepare food, sell food and gifts, and serve as cashiers, while the children clean off tables. There is a great atmosphere of fellowship, a group feeling of togetherness in a common endeavor, which is in itself a reward for all those who participate. A 3rd generation girl made this reply when I asked her the times when she felt most "Greek".

> Well, like let's say, like when you're with all your friends and you're Greek dancing or something, you know, and getting ready for the Festival when everyone's down at the church, and then there's all this stuff going on, and you might talk in Greek and kidding around and stuff like that.

C. Changes

There seems to be a general feeling that Annunciation has changed quite a bit in recent years—it has become a lot less ethnic-oriented, less "Greeky". Several changes were mentioned by a group of young 2nd, 2-3, and 3rd generation men and women (aged 19-30) who discussed "the old days" with me. They commented that the previous priest was much more "old-school Greek" than Father Nick, and that the church reflected a more "Greeky" atmosphere: e.g., the Sunday school rooms had Greek flags and maps of Greece. Other comments:

> D: Like just think of the church in general, like we didn't have the Polemanakos building in the old Sunday school. That was when it was mostly the kids that were really under the influence of their parents.
> T: I don't know, maybe it was a little more ethnic then...it's

becoming looser.

D: Think about how it was when you were little, as far as the recreation for the youth, stuff like that.

T: There wasn't any.

C: Lately it seems like in the church they've got all these different things going on, it seems like we've almost become like a Protestant church, you know? A lot of things like that, would not have happened you know with these older generation Greeks. They'd come to church for church and maybe have some of their old picnics, maybe have some dances but they don't do all this extra stuff. I mean, there's a lot of things, you know?

A young 2-3 generation man of this same age group also noted that there has been a significant change in the community lately, judging by a comparison of his age group and the next older one to the next younger group (aged about 14-18).

The groups are different because of the development of the church, I guess. The upper group, the church was very small, the family was for sure totally Greek, as a whole. My group got in on it when we didn't have the Polemanakos Educational Building, there was no big production--we had classes in the house that was behind the church. There was no Sunday school director, nothing humongous like it is now. Then you've got these kids who have been raised in the atmosphere of the Polemanakos building, the Polemanakos building symbolizing the growth of the church and how they're trying to make it a production like the parochial schools the Catholics have. There's a distinction in that--we're wilder than the older kids were, but these kids that are behind us, I can see much difference in... The longer you get more Americanized, like we'd never have dreamed of doing anything, because everybody would hear about it. Now it's getting--with the size, it's getting more impersonal, and so you can get away with something like that, it's no big deal. Same as everybody else. Well, not exactly--it's just not so much like it used to be.

From this discussion one senses two basic reasons for the present, less "ethnic" orientation of the Greek community. First, the community has grown greatly in recent years, and it is thus more difficult for the older generation to keep up with every movement of the younger generation and to impose sanctions on behavior which is considered "non-Greek".

The geographical mobility of Greeks within the Houston area, and the resulting lack of a ghetto-type settlement, has also resulted in greater contact with non-Greeks, which has contributed to the "Americanization" of the Houston Greek community.

An equally important factor in this process of becoming less "Greeky" is the fact that the Greeks have been in America 20 years longer than they were 20 years ago. This is a very simplistic answer to a complex question, but valid nonetheless: the gradual erosion of traditional "Greek" attitudes and practices over the years has begun to have a more noticeable effect on life within the Greek community, as more "American" programs are adopted by the church. There are several reasons why "American" influences are being felt in the church as of late, most of which concern the fact that the older generation is no longer running the affairs of the church. Virtually all of the board members and other church leaders were born or raised in the United States, which has several implications. They are naturally less traditionally Greek than the members of the older generation, who, as the reader recalls, had no intention of staying in America. Furthermore, they have had much better educations than their parents. 1st generation individuals made their living through restaurants or "ethnic" businesses, whereas the younger, 2nd generation people who are now in charge have made their way according to the American style, and tend to be professional people or managers of one sort or another. These 2nd generation board members are more accustomed than their parents were to "American" ideas and ways of doing things, and it is quite natural that under their guidance the church has become less "Greeky".

IV. Discussion

These recent changes in the Greek church and community--in which some traditional Greek practices are being discontinued--do not indicate that Greeks are necessarily assimilating, as Gordon (1964) might suggest. Perhaps the opposite is true: by remaining flexible and making a few concessions to its contemporary American surroundings, the community is able to retain members who might otherwise be lost. The situation may be most accurately viewed as one in which some traditional Greek practices are being modified into a complex of Greek American practices and values. As Chapter 1 pointed out, such cultural innovations do not indicate that the existence of the ethnic group is threatened. The community is certainly not on the verge of collapse, nor has it become so "American-ized" as to be indistinguishable from other, "American" groups.

The central feature which characterizes the Greek community and insures that its members will not become assimilated is the Greek Ortho-dox Church. In his discussion of ethnic settlements, Price commented that:

> Group settlements based on particular religious beliefs
> survive the forces of "assimilation" much more effectively
> than group settlements which are essentially ethnic in
> character. ... A host society can, and sometimes does,
> "assimilate" ethnic groups: it can rarely do more than
> "integrate" religious groups (1959:285).

How does the Greek Orthodox Church prevent the assimilation of the Greek American group into the larger society? Several religious groups--such as the Amish and Hutterites--come to mind as separatist groups which are representative of one extreme of the cultural pluralism/assimilation continuum proposed in Chapter 1, but Greek American communities have not attempted to segregate themselves in such a manner, thereby to avoid

contact with American society. However, neither has the group dissipated

and become assimilated; the major force which acts to prevent such

assimilation is the church. The close association of the ethnic group

with a church which is uniquely its own helps forestall the disappearance

of the group as a distinguishable entity. Because of the Greek Orthodox

Church, there is a point along the path toward assimilation beyond which

the Greek group will not go, since membership in the church provides the

individual Greek American with a firm identity, a sense of who he is.

The church is thus a primary means of maintaining the boundaries between

the Greek group and non-Greeks. Because of its influence, living in an

ethnic enclave is not necessary to insure that Greek Americans will re-

main in a sense "separate" from the larger society while at the same time

living in it.

Different religions and denominations naturally mark off different

"kinds" of people in America, and many people tend to "stick to their

own kind" because it is assumed that here they can find others whose

world view, values, and background are similar precisely because they

share the same religion, and hence, similar convictions; this is also

true of members of the same ethnic group. Where religious membership

reinforces ethnic membership--and to Greeks, Greek is Greek Orthodox,

the Greek Orthodox is Greek--the forces which act to keep the individual

within his religious-ethnic group are very compelling. Not only must

he be concerned that his family may be displeased if he deserts the

ethnic group, but he must also consider the more personal implications

of leaving his church. Parental threats of heart attack, suicide, or disinheritance may be accompanied by threats of hellfire and damnation; and that is a heavy burden indeed. Without a doubt, many people remain nominal members of the ethnic group because of their having been raised in the Greek church; they would not consider joining another church, because "only the Greek church seems like church." And so they remain in the group.

A serious problem arises because of the close relationship between Greekness and Greek Orthodoxy. If Orthodoxy plays such a significant role in the maintenance of the community--if being Greek is being Greek Orthodox--what effect do the numerous problems individuals sense in the church have on the ethnic group? It is obvious that some of the problems cited in this chapter are of a rather serious nature, and some people leave the church in response to them. By doing so, their membership in the Greek community is placed in jeopardy, as the reader will see in Chapter 4. A further problem with the church playing such an important part in the maintenance of the group is the increasing secularization of American society. One resulting pattern is for the individual to maintain nominal church membership by attending only a few services a year. Community members electing this pattern thereby avoid those aspects of the church--cited in this chapter--which can create conflict and uncertainty among those who attend regularly. Other individuals realize that the Greek Orthodox church is not perfect, but they conclude that no church is, and remain affiliated to it out of loyalty to their family, community, and heritage. On the other hand, some have a very deep belief in Orthodoxy. Such individuals find relief from personal anxieties through their religious convictions, which are supported by frequent attendance at church. For all, the idea that Greek _is_ Greek

Orthodox is a hard one to shake, and thus the church provides an

essential means of boundary maintenance which acts to keep Greeks within

the ethnic group. Greek Orthodoxy's central role in defining community

membership will be discussed more fully in Chapter 4, but first the reader

must be introduced to a second significant aspect of the community--the

social networks of kin, godrelatives, and friends which bind members of

the community to one another.

Annunciation's altar   Table of _prothesis_ (preparation)

ICONS

Theotokos, the Mother of God

Icon of the church, Annunciation

ICONS

Annunciation of the Theotokos

St. Marcella, patron saint of Chios

SS. Cosmas and Damian, with medals

<u>Theotokos</u>, the link between God and man

GREEK ORTHODOXY

CHAPTER 3

FAMILY AND COMMUNITY

In this chapter I will discuss the Greek family and community and
how they are related; one finds certain themes--specifically, "closeness"
and "respect"--repeated throughout the individual's relationships with
family, kin, kumbari (godrelatives), friends, and community. In general
Houston's Greek population is composed of a series of overlapping
personal networks of kin, kumbari and friends, and each of these institutions will be discussed in turn. However, I will first examine traditional marriage customs and the dating and marriage of the 1st and 2nd
generation, who are grandparents and parents today. This will provide
a background for viewing the contemporary Greek American family.

I. Marriage--the Traditional View

A. Customs

There are several traditional customs concerning marriage, and they
vary in the extent to which they are currently practiced in the United
States. Each of these customs--dowry, arranged marriage, and returning
to Greece to find a spouse--was followed more strictly in the older
generations, but can also be found to some extent today. Although they
currently tend to represent the exception rather than the rule, these
customs provide for every Greek a very familiar context which may shape
his approach to marriage and family life.

1. Prika

The dowry (προήκα, prika) is still an inescapable fact of life in

Greece, except perhaps in the largest cities. Any girl who is to be married must have a dowry to bring to the marriage. This dowry frequently includes a house and/or a large sum of cash, as well as handmade household articles. The family with many daughters is in the unfortunate position of having to provide a dowry for each of the girls. Furthermore, the quality of the husband a girl can "buy" largely depends on the relative amount of dowry she has to offer. If the father should die, it is the responsibility of the oldest son to provide the dowries. He must see that his sisters are taken care of before he can marry. It is the urgent need for sisters' dowries which sent many young Greek men to America, where it was (and is) easier to accumulate the large sums of money necessary. A number of the 1st generation men in the Houston community had to provide dowries for their sisters. A 2nd generation girl tells about her father's experience:

> He came in the early 20's... He was trying to go to school
> for electrical engineering or something, then he got into
> --the Depression, and having responsibilities in Greece, his
> father had died, and see in Greece you have to have a dowry
> to get married, and he had five sisters, and my dad was
> responsible for his five sisters. And so that kinda put a
> financial bind on him.

Dowries were probably an important factor in marriage arrangements among the first generation in the United States, but they are much less common today. The only time a dowry may usually be required is in cases which involve marriage to a "Greek" Greek.

2. Proxenia

Related to the dowry is the phenomenon of Προξενιά (proxenia), the arranged marriage. As with the dowry, this is generally the "accepted" way to be married in most parts of Greece. The arrangement is made between the families of the couple, or between the groom and the bride's family; of course either of the two young people can stop the proceedings if he (or she) is not interested in the prospective spouse. There are many factors which enter into the negotiations, but one of the major factors is whether the girl's dowry is suitable to the groom's expectations and vice versa, whether he is worth the amount of dowry the girl's family has to offer. Arranged marriages were probably the rule in the 1st generation. Neither were they unusual among the 2nd generation of Greeks in the United States; since many of these girls were not allowed to date, they had few other chances to become engaged. A 2nd generation woman describes how she met and married her husband:

> [How were y'all married?]
> Our family knew his family in Greece, and he came to Galveston, and our mother--we knew some people there in Galveston, and they had invited us down, and he was there. And that was it, we were married in three weeks... But that was it, our families arranged it, I had never met him. I had never seen him, never knew him, and yet we have lived together 27 years, and we're happy.

The incidence of arranged marriage among the present 2nd and 3rd generations is much less, however. Proxenia is generally viewed as a last resort. If an individual cannot find a Greek to marry, he (or his family) may try to arrange a marriage with someone back in Greece. A 3rd generation girl responded in this way when I asked her about proxenia:

> I know of one girl that was in our group, and her parents were from Greece; the likeliness of it happening with someone who was born here is much less. And this is girls only, mostly--you know, icky and she can't get a husband or something, they go over and find somebody in Greece. This would be the particular circumstances, because usually if the girl is halfway good-looking, or nice-looking, or at least she's not ugly, you know, she can find somebody.

3. Marriage to Greek Greeks

The final marriage custom to be discussed is marriage to Greeks from
Greece, which can take several forms. E.g., some inadvertantly marry
Greek Greeks, but in this discussion I will concentrate on situations
in which people purposely search for a spouse from Greece. A 1st generation man frequently sent for a "mail-order" type of bride from his
hometown. A 2nd generation woman described to me how her parents
came to be married:

> And she came, and the γαμπρό (gambro, groom) was waiting on
> the dock.
> [And she hadn't ever seen him?]
> No... So there was my poor father with this big box of flowers
> for our mother and these long boxes, she said--the only kind of
> thing that came in them was girdles. And she thought, "Oh, my
> God, he thinks I'm so fat that he's bringing me this big box
> of girdles!" And there were the roses!

This sort of arrangement, in which a young man's family back home
arranged for his marriage to a local girl, was of course very common
among the 1st generation of Greeks in America, for there were many Greek
men and very few Greek women here in the early years.

Those who marry Greek Greeks today are in most cases involved in an
arranged marriage ("the old fix-up with an import"). The question arises:
why would a Greek agree to marry an American whom he (or she) hardly
knows? In general, the answer is that such a marriage provides the
chance to come to America, which--in comparison to Greece--is quite
literally "the land of opportunity." A 3rd generation boy who has
spent a lot of time in Greece described in detail what Greeks have to
gain by marrying American Greeks:

> There are some Greeks over there that do get married to come
> over here. It's a fact... There's no opportunity, for anybody

> except--well, the wealthy. It's like over here a person can
> come here from over there, and work hard, for like four or five
> years, and save up some money, and open something of his own,
> and like he'll have something of his own. But there you can't
> do that--there you work and can't save any money, because the
> salaries over there are so low, it's impossible! You work, and
> just get by from month to month. So the idea of being able to
> come here and working real hard for four or five or six years
> and then being able to own something of your own is to them
> --is a dream.

Another way in which people marry Greek Greeks does not involve going

back to Greece: a Greek sailor who finds himself in port in the United

States will frequently search for a girl to marry so that he can remain

in the country permanently. Some will desert and divorce the girl after

becoming established here; Houston Greeks are on to this game, and are

very cautious about letting their daughters get involved with sailors.

However, there are occasional cases in which Greek girls marry sailors;

this was probably more true in the 2nd generation than it is now.

Marriages to Greek Greeks who join the community have a significant

impact by providing a constant flow of "new blood" into the community.

It is these newcomers from Greece who--along with the older people--

keep alive the Greek language and many Greek customs. They also help

to strengthen the community's bonds to Greece.

B. Dating and marriage - the older generations

 1. First generation

First generation Greeks most commonly married someone from Greece;

the young man either sent for a girl and met her at the boat, or went

home to Greece to find a wife, and then brought her back to the United

States. These marriages were usually arranged back in Greece by the

families of the couple.

 2. Second generation

The children of these couples, the 2nd generation, did not have to go to such lengths to find mates since Greek communities were larger and more established than they had been in their parents' time. Greeks of their own age were available as prospective mates, so sending back to Greece was not necessary. This does not mean that the familiar American pattern of courtship resulted however, for many Greek customs were still held steadfastly by the 1st generation parents.

Two customs which greatly influenced the dating process were the sheltering of women and the double standard. Sons were allowed to date and were expected to "sow their wild oats," but daughters in many cases were not allowed to date at all. This stems from the practice in Greece of letting one's daughters date very little--if at all--because a girl who goes out very much is considered loose. There are many examples of this sheltering of daughters by not allowing them to date; I will cite only one quotation, in which a 2nd generation couple discuss what dating was like when they were growing up.

> H: See, my sister didn't have any dates--well, she had some, more or less kinda on the sly, but my mother wouldn't allow her to go out with her husband until they were engaged, and then only if my brother or I were with them, then she would let her go out of the house with her fiance. That's how strong, let's say, the 1st generation was.
> [Was that common?]
> H: Oh yeah.
> W: There are many women her age, like my sister is in her 40's, and never married, because they were never given the opportunity to go out.

As a result, many 2nd generation girls were able to attend social functions only if they were escorted by their brothers or cousins. This restriction was applied not only in high school, but also when the girls were much older. E.g., a 3rd generation boy told me that his mother was permitted to go to her college senior prom only because her brother escorted her; there was no thought that she might go with a date.

Since so many 2nd generation women were not allowed to date, arranged marriages were not unusual in this generation, and extended periods of intimate courtship were definitely not the rule.

The periodic state, district and national meetings of organizations such as AHEPA, GOYA, and GAPA provided some of the best opportunities for 2nd generation Greeks to meet each other, and perhaps a majority of marriages between 2nd generation Greeks can be attributed to the couple's having met at such conventions. One should never think that these young people of the 2nd generation were in any way getting together at conventions behind their parents' backs: far from it! Parents, fully aware of this "mating" potential of conventions, took their eligible children to them in hopes that they might find suitable Greek spouses. E.g., I asked a 2nd generation man how people met and married in his generation, and he replied:

> When we were growing up and were of marriageable age this was happening: You couldn't always find someone who--you could interest your daughter in here in town, so you would take your daughter to say one of the AHEPA conventions--and you would hope they would find somebody. The more you throw these young people together the more chances you were of hitting someone who was Greek. The parent was fearful that if he didn't do this they might meet someone they like more outside the church and a terrible thing would happen.

Since these couples did not know each other well before they were married, one might wonder how these marriages have worked out. There are very few divorces among the 1st and 2nd generation Greeks. Of course this does not indicate that their marriages are necessarily happy, since many Greeks would not divorce even if they were unhappy in their

marriages. There is some evidence that some 2nd generation Greeks--
pressured by their parents, the community, and even themselves to
"marry Greek"--married simply because their spouse happened to be a
Greek who was willing, and there seemed to be no other choice.
Some 2nd generation marriages have ended in divorce; the people involved generally seem to feel that they married because of parental
pressure, and that this is a very poor basis for a successful marriage.
A 2nd generation woman described her experience in this way.

> I wanted to marry this American boy. It was O.K. for me to
> date him, but my father said that if I married him, he would
> disown me, I'd be kicked out of the family. I was so close
> to my family, it was such an important part of my life, that
> I was really afraid of what might happen if I did this, so I
> totally dropped the idea... He just wanted so badly for me
> to marry a Greek, and if I hadn't loved him so much, and not
> wanted to hurt him, I would have gone ahead and done exactly
> what I wanted to. The idea of "Marry Greek!" was so drilled
> into me that I married the first Greek that asked me--liter-
> ally! This was really a big mistake. We had nothing but
> trouble, and I was so unhappy that we were divorced in a
> couple of years.

Her experience demonstrates one of the sanctions parents can bring to
bear upon a child who wants to marry outside the group--threats of
cutting off the family's love and affection toward him. This and other
tactics will be considered more fully in Chapter 6.

II. Family

With this information on Greek customs and marriage among the 1st
and 2nd generations serving as background for the reader, I will now
consider the contemporary Greek family. I asked a college student,
"What if you were not a Greek, but an American? What would be different?"
His response was:

> I wouldn't like to be an American, because I'm different,
> and the difference I appreciate. If my family was American,
> it would have to change so much that you can't picture it.
> Would my family be the same, would it be as close as it is,
> would I have as many relatives as I do? It's stuff like that.

The first thing that came to his mind was that his family would be

different: it would not be as close, and he would not have as many

relatives. The family is indeed a major force in the Greek community,

and it is to a large extent through the family that a "Greek" self-

conception is developed and the Greek community is preserved. In this

section I will examine the main themes presented in the Greek family,

and in the next, its structural characteristics.

A. Themes

  1. "Closeness"

    The Greek family is different in many ways from the picture of "the

average American family". Greeks usually typify their families as

"closer" than those of Americans. E.g., a 3rd generation man commented:

> The closeness is very strong, emotionally. There's more
> caring and more interest about what's going on in the family.
> There's more joy and sorrow.

This "closeness" is expressed in several ways. First, family members

are expected to do things together to a large extent, as a young 3rd

generation man explained in contrasting Greek and "American" families.

> Greeks have much more of a family than Americans, they are
> much closer. They make a big deal out of namedays and other
> things that they do together that Americans just don't have.
> A heritage to stick to--it's sorta building on that. Greek
> families make such a big deal out of everything. On Christ-
> mas, you go to midnight Liturgy then go out and have break-
> fast, and then come home and open presents--with us it's a
> big deal.

The central significance of the Orthodox Church in Greek American life

is evident in these comments, for the things that family members do together are usually based on Greek Orthodox traditions; these special

customs include cutting the βασιλόπιτα (vasilopita, St. Basil's bread)

on New Year's, feasting on a traditional meal and cracking Easter eggs

at Easter, and making κουλουράκια (koulourakia, cookies) on special

holidays. Families also "do things together" that are more directly

related to the church. The obvious example of this is going to church

together, but families also frequently fast together during the fasting

periods of the church calendar.

A second way in which families make manifest their closeness is by

having members remain in the household until they are married, as a 2nd

generation girl noted:

> I notice that a lot of friends of mine go and live in apart-
> ments, and it's not that they [their parents] don't care,
> they don't mind. Whereas in Greek families, I can think of
> a lot--where they have sons that are bachelors, like in their
> 30's or 40's, and still live at home with their parents. And
> especially for a girl. If we don't stay at home when we start
> working, it's like, "What's the matter with your home? Aren't
> you happy?"

The family which is considered "close" by Greek standards generally keeps

its members together until the children marry and establish their own

households. This is because emotional closeness is thought to be

expressed primarily in social closeness. Thus, if an unmarried girl

moves out of her parents' home, the immediate speculation is, "Aren't

you happy?", i.e., "Isn't your family close?" For this reason, people

sometimes must remain at home even against their wishes. This problem

frequently arises when young people want to go away to college. Many

parents want to keep their children in the household, and persuade them,

usually through threats or insistence, to go to local colleges. In fact,

attending school out-of-town is a fairly recent development, and those
who manage to go away to school generally attend the University of Texas
in Austin and come home on the weekends.

In truth, the "closeness" does not stop when a child is married;
although he may move out of the household, he is still considered very
much a member of the family. This sometimes causes problems in the
individual's marriage, because of the conflict of interest between the
two "families"; the problems are especially acute when a Greek marries a
non-Greek, whose expectations about family life in marriage differ from
those of the Greek in-laws. The non-Greek wife of a 2-3 generation man
volunteered this comment:

> What bugs me about his family is that his Mama still thinks
> that he's their family, and that he should jump up and help
> them all the time. I don't think she really considers that
> we're his family now, and that we're our own little group,
> and have to take care of ourselves.

2. Strictness and sheltering

Perhaps it is the emphasis on the closeness of the family which
leads parents to shelter their children. A family which is close
emotionally and physically would not allow children to be exposed to
"dangers". For this reason, parents are protective of their children
and very strict about the activities they allow them to participate in.
In what ways are Greek parents "strict", and how do they shelter their
children? In discussing their "being raised Greek", a group of 2nd,
2-3, and 3rd generation men and women described what "strictness" meant
in their homes:

> C: I couldn't do a lot of things, I mean, they just didn't
> see the need to go places and do things. Like American kids,
> They're gone all day long: they're either here or at a country

club, or playing tennis, or they're out with their friends.
You see them at meals, and then to spend the night. At
night they leave too! But we were always in the house, you
know, we always had to play around the house.
D: They had more freedom, you know. Mother drops you off
at the roller-skating rink, or at the show.
S: When we used to go roller skating, my mom would go with
us!
M: I'll never forget the first day at the University of
Houston--orientation. She wanted to come with me, she wanted
to help me register for classes.

To a large extent, parents shelter their children from American society

and American ways; when activities involve Greeks, the family is much

more liberal, as a young 2nd generation woman pointed out.

Greek children are sheltered a lot, too. They can't do a
lot of stuff because they're being "protected", you know?
All the "weird" things American kids do, the Greeks aren't
supposed to do, because "They're good kids, and we have to
take care of them." Then they go to these AHEPA conventions,
and they raise hell like anyone else. But their parents think
it's O.K., because it's Greeks, see, "My kids can't do anything
wrong there." ... The parents are very trusting when they
know they're with Greek people.

To children, their parents' behavior sometimes represents not protection

but overprotection, and as such is a source of friction. Children resent

the restrictions placed on them by their families; e.g., a 2nd generation

girl complained:

The parents, especially like my mother, my mother is just
very overprotective. A very confined social circle, everything's Greek, just bombarded by Greek things. Everything's
the group. It's good to have a close-knit family, but you
want to--extend yourself. I think our family's a very tight-
knit family. We get stifled--our social life, it really does,
you know.

Thus the sheltering and, in some cases, overprotection--particularly

where "Americans" are concerned--of children frequently results in

resentment on their part. Although children chafe under these restric-

tions, there is little open rebellion, primarily because of the importance of another "theme" in family life--respect.

3. Respect

A third important element is respect for one's elders. Respect

provides the basis for traditional family roles. The man is the head

of the household, the king. He supports the family, and is due respect.

Women are definitely secondary; the wife is in charge of the house and

the children. A 2-3 generation college boy explained to me the "Greek"

family roles and how they have affected his expectations of married

life:

> Women are subservient. Not "stay home", but--their job is
> the house. Like if I get married, I'm not going to clean the
> house, that's for sure. I'm not going to wash dishes or wash
> clothes. ... I mean, that's what I expect. That's what's
> been encouraged.

There are of course some cases in which the wife wears the pants in the

family, but they are generally sources of gossip among the Greeks. One

young 2-3 generation man who was about to be married told me in obvious

disdain how his father let his mother gain control of the household:

> I realize what happened: my dad let my mom gain control.
> Because at first, I heard, my mom was scared to do anything.
> She'd call my dad up and ask to do stuff. Now, my mom just
> does what she wants. Dad's the one that's scared to leave.
> My dad didn't care about the trivial stuff, he'd let my mom
> do it.

One must respect his parents. Such respect is instilled in children;

they "feel that they owe everything to their parents." This attitude is

the basis of many things that "children" do which might otherwise seem

incomprehensible. An example was given of one man in his 40's who had

been going with a non-Greek woman for several years. When asked, "When

are y'all getting married?", his reply was, "When my mother dies." This

respect sometimes causes tensions when a Greek marries. It is difficult
to start a new authority pattern in which a man is now the head of his
own household; his respect for his parents causes him to try to follow
their wishes, which sometimes conflict with the best interests of his
wife and children. An American woman discussed the problems she and her
2nd generation Greek husband had in their marriage:

> When you become a mature person, you don't continue doing
> things for your mother's sake. You have to live your own
> life. I guess some people never really get out of that. ...
> You can't possibly feel good about yourself. It even changed
> our relationship when he finally had the guts enough to stand
> up to her as a man and tell her, "I'm a man, and I have to do
> what I think is right." And I felt like--even though I had
> never verbally said to him, I felt subconsciously that he was
> weak in some ways because he was not able to break that last
> thing.

Another woman related her 2nd generation husband's feelings:

> The idea that's constantly stressed in Greek families is,
> "Be good to your mother--she's sacrificed her whole life for
> you." What my husband wants to know is, "What's the sacrifice?
> Which sacrifice did she make that means I have to spend my
> whole life pleasing her?"

This man's comments demonstrate the ideal of respect which had been
impressed upon him throughout his life--parents, particularly mothers,
have devoted their lives to their children, who owe them great respect,
expressed in following their wishes. For him, the demands of "respect"
are too many. Against his mother's wishes, he married an American
woman and left the church and community; he refuses her pleas to return,
to once again become involved with Greeks.

"Respect" permeates one's relationships with his elders: not just
parents, but other relatives--aunts, uncles, and grandparents--as well
as non-kin community members such as neighbors and even mere acquaintances.

The community aspect of respect will be discussed in greater detail in
Chapter 4.

B. Elderly relatives in the home

A custom which logically follows from the family themes of "closeness" and "respect" is having elderly relatives live in one's household.[1]
The relative may be one of the parents of the husband or wife, or in some
cases an aged aunt or uncle. The elderly are put into institutions only
when their health is so poor that the family can no longer give them
adequate medical attention at home. A typical case is demonstrated in
this story related by a young 3rd generation woman.

> [Did any of your relatives ever live with y'all?]
> My grandmother did. Because she lived in her own house, and
> παππού (pappou, grandfather) died, and she lived not too far
> away from us, and she became unable to live at her own house.
> Then she came and lived with us for about three years, then
> she couldn't live with us anymore, and she...my mother put
> her in a nursing home. Because of the medical facilities
> that we didn't have, you know. Not like we didn't take care
> of her, but we couldn't take care of her that way.

Since Greek women generally outlive the men in the community, it is
frequently a γιαγιά (giagia, grandmother) who lives in the household.
There is another reason for this pattern, however. The older Greek
women in general have led sheltered lives, and are therefore less able
to care for themselves than the men are. The Greek men have been out
in the world of business, and have learned English at least well enough
to get along, but many of the older Greek women have never learned
English. Thus, when their husbands die, they must look to their children for help in dealing with the outside world. Having a giagia live
with the family is also customary in Greece. This custom has been
continued in America because it is a custom, but also in response to the

exigencies of the American situation. Nevertheless, having an elderly
parent living in the home sometimes creates tensions. Furthermore, the
elderly relative still wants to have his independence, to continue his
accustomed life without his children's interference, or his interference
in their lives. For these reasons, families frequently have (or build)
a garage apartment, an addition to their house, or at least a separate
room with a private phone, for elderly relatives.

III. Kin

When asked how his life would be different if he were American, the
Greek boy wondered if he would have so many relatives. This statement
points out a very important aspect of kinship ties among Houston's Greeks:
many people are considered bona fide relatives who would probably be on
shaky ground as far as American kinship tradition goes.

A. Closeness

The most outstanding examples of this widening of kinship ties are
found in cousins and in-laws. One 3rd generation man told me that in his
family, their cousins' cousins were called "cousin"; and even though
these cousins "really" (i.e., by American standards) were not relatives,
they considered them so, even to the extent that he would not think of
marrying one of them. A young 2-3 generation man said:

> I lose track of my relatives, which is all right, because
> there are 20 million of them. They try to make everybody
> your relative. ... I guess it gives them a feeling of
> security to link everybody up. Like they go back to third
> cousins, and most people don't do that. ... They try to
> keep everything united, family-wise, church-wise.

Another way of extending the family's circle of kin is considering οἱ συμπέθεροι (symbetheri, in-laws) to be relatives. If A marries B,

each member of A's family--grandparents down to children, including

aunts and uncles and possibly their children--is ὁ συμπέθερος (symbe-

theros) or ἡ συμπέθερα (symbethera) to everyone in B's family, and

vice versa. This excludes A and B, however. They are not symbetheri to

each other's families, but daughter- and son-in-law, sister- and brother-

in-law, aunt and uncle--in other words, true family members.

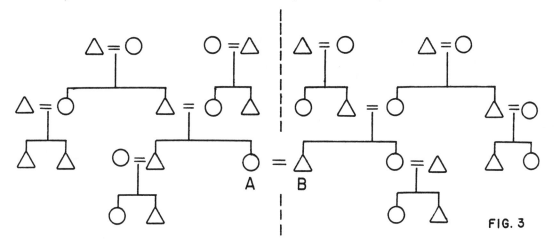

FIG. 3

Not only are the individuals on the two halves of the chart symbetheri

to each other; the in-laws of each person on the one half also have

the option of being symbetheri to those on the other half of the chart.

It is obvious that the relationship could expand indefinitely, but in

practice this does not really happen, for there is an element of choice

in the relationship along its outer edges. Those with whom one gets

along well who are marginal symbetheri can be elevated to true symbe-

theri in practice, by his inviting them over and so on. By the same

token, even though one may be fairly close symbetheri with an individual,

the relationship does not have to be practiced. Although one sometimes

should invite his symbetheri to a family gathering at his house, there is nothing other than public opinion to make him do so. People who are just not interested in each other can allow the relationship to fall into disuse. Similarly, a symbetheri relationship is more difficult to maintain if the symbetheri do not live in the same city. In some cases--siblings and parents, and perhaps also aunts, uncles and grandparents of each spouse--even though the relationship is not used, it still exists: the individuals are still symbetheri. Thus, a symbetheri relationship is not quite the same thing as a sibling relationship, for example. One cannot choose his brothers or sisters, but he can to an extent choose his symbetheri.

It is fairly easy for Houston's Greeks to maintain relationships with distant relatives because in many cases they all live in the same city. Thus the larger "family" is "close" geographically, which makes it easier to be socially and emotionally "close" as well. This "closeness" is further enhanced by the fact that one's relatives all go to the same church, and participate in the same social activities. Since the individual sees and associates with distant relatives such a large part of the time, it is easy to maintain relationships with them, and thus to consider them "relatives".

B. Respect

Respect, which was seen to be an important element of relations in the immediate family, also permeates Greek kin relationships. "Respect" is the cause of interesting variations in kinship terminology. Because of "respect" one calls cousins who are older than himself θεῖο (thio, uncle) or θεία (thia, aunt), rather than "cousin". Similarly, out of respect to an older individual, one might call him συμπέθερο (symbethero), or κουμπάρο (kumbaro, godrelative), to make him feel a part of his family group, even though the relationship is in fact a tenuous one. Furthermore, "respect" means that people who are not related, even by Greek standards, are called kinship terms and treated like relatives. Many children are taught to call all adults thio and thia out of respect. Other Greeks may not go quite that far, but still have friends of the family called thio and thia to make them feel closer. A 2-3 generation man commented:

> Like I was calling my dad's best friend and his wife aunt and uncle. ... They want the kid to feel closer to the person, but you don't want to call them a first name, so you call them Thia Soula or Thio Niko. You can associate with a person a little more. When I was younger, I always thought that these people were my aunt and uncle. I really did. I knew that so-and-so was my mother's sister, and that's why I called her aunt, but the other people--I was thinking, "Well, evidently they're related somehow." And I just never learned how. There were a lot of people like that when I was growing up.

Thus the family themes of "closeness" and "respect" are extended to include more distant relatives as well. In fact, one's family relationships are also extended to include many people who are, according to "American" standards, not relatives at all. The most obvious examples of such widening of kinship ties are found in distant cousins and symbetheri. Another example is one's godrelatives--his kumbari.

IV. Kumbari

A central institution of the Greek community is κουμπαριά (kumbariá, co-parenthood). One enters into a relationship of kumbariá with another when he serves as sponsor in either of two religious services-- baptism and marriage. A sponsor can be either male or female. A godparent, who sponsors a child at baptism, is called ὸ νουνός (o nunos, masculine) or ἡ νουνά (i nuná, feminine), and his godchild is ὸ βαπτιστικός (vaptistikos) or βαπτιστικά (vaptistika); he and the child's parents are kumbari (οἱ κουμπάροι) to one another. Similarly, the individual who sponsors a couple's wedding is their κουμπάρος/ κουμπάρα (kumbaro/kumbara), and they are his kumbari as well. The spouse of the sponsor is considered nuna to the child and kumbara to the parents in the case of baptism, as well as kumbara to the couple in marriage sponsorship.

It would be a serious mistake to assume that a kumbari relationship is only a religious one, although there are certain religious obligations involved. Rather, it is a very special social relationship. This is especially obvious when one realizes that people who seldom (if ever) go to church become very active kumbari by sponsoring a child at baptism, e.g. In fact, to many people becoming a godparent is not as important as becoming a kumbaro; the sponsoring of the child is secondary to the establishment of a kumbari relationship, as a 3rd generation girl noted with some sorrow.

> I can't help but feel that there's a closer relationship between kumbari and your parents than actually between you and your godparent. The age difference I'm sure plays a part it it, but whenever they come over to visit, it's not coming over to see you, it's to see your parents.

One of the main criteria for someone to baptize one's child is not that he be a religious person; "the important thing is to see that you can mix together." One's kumbari are closer than just good friends. In fact, they are almost like relatives. A 2nd generation girl commented:

> It's like they're special. You have your good friends, but

kumbari is kinda like between being related and being good friends. Like a lot of people that we know, when they have family events, when it's strictly family, they'll invite the kumbari. You include the kumbari.

Kumbari are considered so close that you should invite them to family affairs. Often kumbari celebrate Christmas, Thanksgiving, or Easter together. And kumbari provide the same sort of help as do relatives. They may pick one's children up from school, or keep them several days while he is out of town. If someone needs assistance, he knows he can call on his kumbari. Frequently people who are already good friends become kumbari, but ideally—and often in practice as well—the fact that they are kumbari brings them closer together, and their friendship deepens. The relationship between kumbari is a very special one, and one's kumbari are deeply respected. In fact, they are so special that one should never call them by their names, as he does his friends, for they are much closer. They should always respectfully address one another as "kumbaro" or "kumbara". Older people consider it a sin to do otherwise; the more recent generations are getting away from this tradition, but still revere their kumbari.

A. Responsibilities

I will now briefly consider the two different ways in which one becomes a kumbaro, and his responsibilities in each case.

The costs of the baptism are shared by the nuno and the parents. The nuno buys everything that is used in the service and a baptismal cross, as well as τά μαρτυρέκια (ta martirekia), ribbons with the name of the godchild and nuno which the congregation wears as witnesses to the baptism, and οἱ μπουμπουνιέρες (boubounieres), favors with candied almonds (κουφέτα, koufeta). The parents pay for the recep-

tion. One 2nd generation girl commented.

> Baptisms are expensive, they really are. You've got to buy
> the baby white clothes, you've got to buy it white socks,
> you've got to buy it white shoes--and baby clothes are
> expensive. You've got to buy the towels, the diapers, you've
> got to buy all that stuff. The whole wardrobe. And they
> (boubounieres and martirekia) are expensive too. You usually
> pay about--at E's baptism we had to get I don't know how many
> dozen, but you pay about $3 a dozen, and when you start
> inviting hundreds of people, like 200 people, it really runs
> into an expense.

It is the nuno's responsibility to see that the child leads a

Christian life. This is all that is required of him by the Orthodox

church, but there are also several social obligations. Most Greeks feel

that it is the godparent's responsibility to take care of a child if the

parents should die. Of course, this is not his legal obligation, but

they feel it is a moral one--he should want to do it, since he is the

nuno. Probably the most obvious day-to-day responsibility of a nuno

is to remember his godchild with presents on his birthdays, namedays,

and at Christmas, and also on Easter when the child is young. Usually

the child's mother will send cards and small presents to the nuno in

the child's behalf on birthdays, Mother's or Father's Day, namedays,

and perhaps Easter. It is this social obligation, rather than the

religious ones, which is that most fully observed. It is ample cause

for grumbling if a godparent forgets one's child on any of these days.

In the ideal relationship, the nuno and godchild should be almost as

close as parent and child. The nuno should love his godchild as his

own children, and the child should respect his nuno as his own parents.

Those people who are unhappy with their godparents feel that they have

not taken their duties seriously enough. In many cases this problem may have arisen because either the godparent or the child has moved

away, and their relationship had suffered, as a 3rd generation boy noted:

> Well, now, with a lot of godparents 2000 miles away, and you
> don't--sometimes you never even meet your godparent, they'll
> see you once when you are baptized, when you are very little,
> and that was it, they never see you again. It's not the--
> theological standpoint of what a godparent should be, it's
> more of a status, you know. "I'm a godparent!" And like
> that.

The marriage sponsor's main responsibility is to "crown" (στεφά-

νωση, stefanosi) the couple with wreaths of flowers (στέφανια, ste-

fania) during the wedding ceremony. He purchases the stefania but

he may or may not buy the koufeta (almond favors). He has no real

responsibilities after the wedding, except perhaps to patch up a marital

squabble; this rarely happens in practice, however.

B. Rules

There are many rules concerning kumbaria (co-parenthood), both in

the eyes of the church and in the customs of the Greek people. These

two sets of rules do not always coincide in that the people generally

accept the church's rules and add many of their own, without really

knowing which are the "official", church rules.

The only rules stated by the Orthodox church as necessary are that

the sponsor must be a member of the Orthodox church, and of good repute,

and that a parent cannot sponsor his own child. Furthermore, god-

relatives in the eyes of the church are actually relatives to the extent

that one is not allowed to marry them. The extent of the prohibition

is noted in these church rules:[2]

(1) The sponsor cannot marry his godchild.

(2) The natural child of the sponsor cannot marry the sponsor's
     godchild.

(3) Two children with the same godparent cannot marry.

(4) The sponsor can never marry the mother or father of his godchild.

(5) The sponsor cannot marry the son or daughter of his godchild.

(6) The sponsor's natural child cannot marry the child of the sponsor's godchild.

In addition to these rules, Greek tradition adds a few more. One is that all of the children an individual baptizes should be of the same sex. This is sort of an outgrowth of rule three above, which prohibits marriage between godchildren of the same sponsor. A 2nd generation girl explained the "same sex" rule:

> I can't baptize girls, because I've baptized a boy. Because you wouldn't want to have them grow up and fall in love with each other, and they can't be married. That's why, when you're baptizing, you stick to one sex only. ... One time a friend of ours wanted another friend to baptize her kid, and she said, "I only baptize boys," and that was a valid reason not to.

The most interesting traditional "rule", which has no basis in canon law, is that two individuals cannot baptize each other's children.

> [If I baptize your child, can you baptize mine?]
> No, you can't give the oil back. If I baptize your child, see, I anoint it with oil, which in our religion is the strongest point, and then you can't do mine and give me the oil back. That is not done.

Many community members flatly stated that this is "a rule", whereas others disagreed. The common response of those who were not familiar with this prohibition as a "rule" was that it just wouldn't be a good idea; one should spread kumbari ties around, since he would naturally "want to bring in more people." It is basically considered wise to increase one's ties with others outside the family.

Regardless of the original source of this rule, it is used in the Greek community to widen ties, to keep them from becoming restricted within a narrow group. This interpretation is consistent with the general feeling of most Greeks that kumbari relationships should be as extensive as possible. E.g., a woman explained to me that her family members were kumbari to another family through several sponsorships involving different family members. She was quick to add that this was not common, and not a good idea, because kumbari relationships should be spread around more. They were already close to the other family after the first kumbari relationship was established, so the other sponsorships created redundant relationships. Furthermore, for the same reasons, many people feel it is inappropriate to have relatives baptize one's children--why should a kumbari relationship be established with those to whom one is already related?

C. Comparison of the two types of sponsorship

The kumbaro who baptizes one's children is in a way more "special" than one's marriage sponsor; he has more honor. This is for two reasons. (1) He put the oil on the child, and the oil in a baptism "makes him just much closer." By putting oil on someone, the individual is bound in a close relationship with him and with his family, for the oil is a bond, and the person who puts it on is part of that bond. When a kumbara offends someone, he would likely say, "If she doesn't watch out, I'll give her the oil back," i.e., "I'll take away the thing that makes us have a relationship." (2) The nuno takes on the responsibility of the child, whereas the kumbaro actually has no responsibilities, since the people he is sponsoring are grown adults.

In accordance with his "special" place, the nuno should be treated with great respect, at least according to the more traditional Greeks.

One should really go out of his way if a nuno comes to his house. He should also do anything to avoid a falling-out with a godparent, for an argument with a nuno is a terrible thing, some say because it is very bad luck. A 1st generation woman explained why one is careful about his treatment of nuni.

> Like my daughter now put oil into the family, they have to
> respect. If something happens, they say, "We don't care,
> she put oil," you have to watch it. You say, "Oh, λάδι,
> λάδι [ladi, oil], πώ, πώ, πώ [popopo - equivalent to clicking
> the tongue]. They scared. If something happens, forget about
> it, because they put your oil. They say forgive them, because
> it's very sin to have trouble.

Traditionally the two types of sponsorship, of baptism and marriage, do not really represent discrete categories in that by custom one should ask his godparent to be his wedding sponsor, and one's wedding sponsor should baptize his first child. Problems arise when the groom (or bride) does not feel close enough to his nuni to ask one of them to sponsor the wedding, or does not want his sponsor to baptize their child. A 2nd generation woman discussed this problem:

> I don't feel close enough to her to have her be my sponsor
> when I get married, or baptize my first child. I'd rather
> have somebody else, and it's the same thing with my friend.
> We were talking about it one day, about how godparents aren't
> really as close as they're supposed to be, and she said, "I
> just hope my godmother doesn't want to be the one that
> stefanosies [crowns] me." Because you just don't feel close
> to them.

Thus the question of the difference between a kumbaro who sponsored a baptism and one who crowned a couple may seem purely academic in that they are often actually the same person, but this chain of sponsorship cannot continue indefinitely. Furthermore, even when one's nuna stefanosies him, and baptizes his first child, she does not become a kumbara, because she is already "closer" by virtue of being his godparent.

> [If he was your nuno before, does he now become kumbaro?]
> No, he's still nuno; that's about as original a name as you
> can get. You keep that name, that's a closer name. Like my
> godson will always call me nuna no matter what happens. Like
> even if I do his that [meaning stefanosi], or even if I baptize
> his kid, I'm still his nuna.

This comparison of the relative "importance" of the two types of kumbari

should not be misunderstood to indicate that the marriage sponsor does

not "count". All kumbari are considered very special to a family, but

the godparent is especially revered.

D. Significance of kumbariá

A very important facet of kumbariá is the fact that the relationship

is not limited to the individual who sponsored the ceremony and the

parents of the child (or the couple he stefanosied); his whole family

enters into the relationship with the whole family of the child or

couple sponsored. This situation is very similar to that of symbetheri.

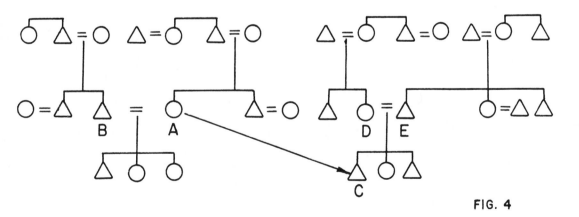

FIG. 4

For example, suppose A baptizes C. She is nuna and he is her vaptistikos.

Her husband B is nuno to C. They are kumbari to D and E, C's parents:

each calls the other "kumbaro" and "kumbara". All of the people on

either side of the chart usually consider each other kumbari as well,

and address one another as "kumbari". This is especially true when

younger people address older people (which is why the chart is so

top-heavy), for the title "kumbaro" indicates respect, which is more

important in a relationship with an older person. The same general

rules apply to marriage sponsors--the couple's family and the kumbaro's

family consider each other kumbari, as a 2nd generation man indicated:

> Oh yes, definitely, it doesn't make any difference, whether
> you christen somebody or are best man at a wedding, or some-
> thing like that. Everyone in that family are kumbari.
> [How far does it go, do you think?]
> Really as deep as you want to put it. If you want to bring
> a first cousin of C [whose child the speaker's wife baptized]
> 's into it, and I want to make him feel real close I would
> call him a kumbaro.
> [Do you consider C's brother-in-law a kumbaro?]
> Yes, I could call him a kumbaro--I could, I don't think I
> would. I don't think I'd call his sister a kumbara. But
> I'd call his mother a kumbara.
> [Because of personalities, or the closeness you feel?]
> No, I think it's sorta respect you pay an older person. I
> call the mother of the lady who baptized my daughter kumbara.
> And Mr. V, I call his grandparents kumbari. This is a personal
> thing. I'm sure there are some families who call everybody
> kumbari.

As the above example indicates, there is a large element of personal

choice along the outer edges of the kumbari relationship. This was found

to be true with symbetheri as well. Those whom one likes and sees often

may be considered and called kumbari even though the connection is distant.

As was implied earlier, there is a wide difference of opinion within

the Greek community about whether it is better to have one's friends or

relatives become his kumbari by baptismal and marriage sponsorship.

Those who favor relatives generally cite the enormous responsibilities which are a part of sponsorship, and feel that only a relative could fulfill these duties adequately. If godparents should move away, their communication and relationship with the child is often damaged, but if they are also relatives to the child, they will still fulfill their obligations should the parents die. Perhaps as important a reason for having relatives become kumbari is the expense of sponsorship, and of the receptions that follow baptisms, as a young 2-3 generation man pointed out:

> [What's the significance of kumbari?]
> Being kumbari reestablishes things [relationships] and makes them firmer. As far as relatives go you can't make that any firmer. Sometimes it's an easy way out, instead of going out and finding somebody. When you lay that deal on of being kumbari, it's also monetary too. The kumbaro has to pay for the church, he has to go out and shop for all the kiddie's clothes that they change into--he has to go out and get all that. He outlays about 100 bucks. ... It's something you would use to bond a friendship, and then you choose a relative if you didn't want to put the monetary expense on a friend.

However, a great number of Greeks cannot understand why one would have relatives become kumbari--they already have a relationship, so why waste a kumbari tie on them? The reasoning here is the same as that mentioned earlier (i.e., why one wouldn't want to "give the oil back"), that one should "spread his ties out" to include as many people as possible. In fact, it seems almost an impossibility to have relatives be kumbari as far as some people are concerned--how can someone have two relationships with the same person at once? A 2nd generation couple discussed this:

> W: You'll find that a lot of families--for instance, a friend of mine--her brother baptized her son and then her other brother baptized her daughter.
> H: Well, how can you be brothers and kumbari at the same time?
> W: Well, they do it!

One can see that ties between kumbari are quite extensive, and are an important element of the Greek community; they act to draw the community closer together by linking family groups. In fact, kumbariá may be the single most crucial of the relationships which unite the Greek community. The tendency to try to become kumbari to as many people as possible increases the number of links between individuals within the community. These forces which act to "spread out" an individual family's ties are as follows: (1) the same person does not baptize two children in a family; (2) two people do not baptize each other's children (they do not "return the oil"); and (3) the majority of people have friends rather than relatives sponsor at weddings and baptisms. The greater sense of security a man feels among his kin often results in the expansion of "kinship" networks--in some cases to include even one's enemies--through marriage (Levi-Strauss, 1949) or fictive kinship (Foster 1953, Mintz and Wolf 1950, Hammel 1968). Extending the bounds of kinship in such a manner is a significant element of many cultures.

Another series of relationships which act to unite the community is found in friendships. I will now examine friendship within the Houston Greek community.

V. Friends

A. Friendships and life cycle

For friendship in the Greek community to be fully understood, this institution must be considered in the context of each individual's stage of life, from childhood through old age. It seems that many people follow

a similar pattern in their friendships--primarily Greek through most of
their lives, with an "American" period while they are attending school.
As very young children, most people are limited in their social contacts
to their families--their siblings and cousins--but when they become more
involved in school, non-Greek friends begin to play a more important
role. Of course during this period friendships with Greeks continue
because one sees them at church functions, Sunday school, and so on,
but it seems that non-Greek friends in most cases start to take prece-
dence. Many begin to feel that they "just don't have much in common"
with the other Greek kids, as a 3rd generation boy stated:

> There's just no interest, no common interest, and my mom's
> always saying, "You should go out and meet some Greek people,"
> and well, I do, but there's no use. Because I wouldn't enjoy
> myself, and they wouldn't enjoy themselves. And they say,
> "But y'all are both Greek!" But that's to a limited thing, I
> mean--go around saying the Greek alphabet? Really, there's
> nothing.

As these kids get a little older, however, and look forward to marriage
and settling down, their Greek friends take on a new meaning. One begins
to feel that he does in fact have something in common with them--their
lives have been intertwined since they were born, and they will continue
to be as long as they live in the same city. They grew up together and
they will probably grow old together, watch their children grow up
together. A 2nd generation girl made this comment:

> I think that friends I grew up with at church, you know,
> they're people that'll always be, I know that like in the
> future we'll have a lot more contact, she'll be out of
> school and I'll be out of school, and probably married.
> These are the friends that are going to be with you all of
> your life, because most of them are going to be living in
> Houston, they're going to stay with the church, you see them
> more, that's what it is. Your kids are going to grow up
> together. ... But I do have a few non-Greek friends that

> I'm pretty close with, but it's kinda harder now; like I
> said, when the Greek friends graduate from school, you see
> them more anyway, even if you're not that good of friends,
> because they come to the same functions, and they come to
> church.

Thus once again the individual's life becomes centered around Greek

friends and activities. Although men may meet Americans at their jobs

and women may meet American housewives in their neighborhoods, a

majority of their friends, and their best friends, remain Greek. Why

is this so?

B. Why Greek friends?

 1. Parents

Parents both directly and indirectly encourage their children to

have Greek friends. An earlier section demonstrated that many parents

try to "protect" their kids from Americans. At the same time, this

encourages friendships with Greeks. E.g., allowing children to spend

the night with a Greek, but not an American, promotes the "Greek"

friendship. Sometimes the "encouragement" is not this subtle, however.

A 3rd generation high school boy told me:

> Like my sister and I wanted a party...and they [his parents]
> said, "Well, are you going to invite any Greeks over?" "No,
> this will be a school party." She said, "Well, that's fine--
> I will let you give it, only if you promise that you'll give
> a Greek party." So I said, "Well, all right." ... So I was
> real lucky. Anyway, we haven't given the Greek one yet, and
> we want to give another American one.

In this case the mother insisted that her children cultivate Greek

friends by requiring a Greek party in exchange for permission to give an

American one. The mother is actually less authoritarian than she appears,

since the young people never gave the Greek party. Nevertheless, she

used the situation to remind her children quite firmly of their Greekness

and of their obligation to Greek friends. Another more indirect way in
which parents promote friendships with other Greek kids is by forcing
"the Greek thing" so much that a feeling of "we're all in this together"
develops, as a group of 2nd, 2-3, and 3rd generation men and women pointed
out:

> S: I guess that's the only thing, permanent, that kind of
> stayed, is that our parents in all this conditioning they
> did, is that you feel closer around your Greek friends, for
> some reason, it's something that's really hard to explain,
> I think mainly becuase of the conditioning, you feel kinda
> a closeness.
> D: They had to grow up through the same stuff that you had
> to go through, you know. ... I mean, because you had to
> to up through the same Greek customs and everything, so you
> have the similar background.
> C: Yeah, you have the same problems.

2. Common background

The shared Greek background also provides a bond which unites Greek
friends. Having the same background as a whole group of people gives
the Greek a special feeling not shared with American friends. Many
Greeks experss the sense of security and belonging they feel among other
Greeks.

> It's funny, the security you can feel within a Greek group.
> There's a trust there--I can't explain it but sometimes in
> an American group at a party you have to prove yourself kinda,
> whereas in a Greek group you just feel accepted immediately
> because of the common bond between everybody and there's a
> very secure and comforting thing.

This sense of security and belonging is one of the main dividends which
comes from membership in the Greek community, and it will be discussed
more extensively in Chapter 6.

3. Interaction

Perhaps the most important factor which promotes friendships among

Greeks is that they see each other very frequently. A 3rd generation
girl commented:

> Everything we do is centered around the church--there are
> clubs, Festivals, parties, dances. ... You go to these
> functions, and so does everybody else--you see them around
> and you get to be friends. It's not that my mind's closed,
> and that I don't have any friends but Greeks--that's wrong,
> completely wrong--my best friend is an American.

Even if one has good friends who are American, he cannot see them as
often as Greek friends, because they do not participate in the multitude
of Greek activities which consume so much of his time. The fact that
one's fellow church members, club members, friends, kumbari, and relatives are all the same group of people multiplies the amount of contact
he has with them, and increases the chances that most of his friends will
be Greek.

4. "The group"

The increased possibilities for interaction with Greeks is not the
whole story, however; the fact that one's friends are also friends with
each other further enhances the feelings of togetherness and friendship.
Many of these people grew up together, and there is a real sense of
"groupness" among them. An American who had dated a 3rd generation
Greek girl had this to say:

> From year 1 till right now she's had friends at church she
> has known all her life. Not like me and not like a lot of
> people are. ... She's so close to so many people that you
> can't--all these people are sitting together, you know,
> they've known each other for 10, 15, 20 years, and here
> you've been there for nearly 30 minutes, and you never really
> feel at home. The thing that alienated me most was the fact
> that they have their culture they had for so long from kids
> right on up to where they are, and their religion--and their
> comradeship is so developed--over 18 years with GOYA and all
> of the things they've got--like an outsider coming in, there
> is no malice intended, but you have nothing in common.

This sense of "groupness" is an important aspect of the Greek community, and will be considered more fully in the next chapter.

C. Where friends get together

What areas provide places for meeting one's Greek friends? The geographic dispersion of Greeks throughout Houston is a significant factor which largely determines the answer to this question. Neighborhoods, the church, and businesses will be considered.

1. Neighborhoods

For most people the neighborhood is not an important source of Greek friends, but this has not always been true. Years ago, most of Houston's Greeks lived in one area of the city, and the neighborhood was more like a traditional ethnic ghetto. Then a second area of concentration developed around the site of the present Greek Orthodox church, the Annunciation; many of the young 2nd and 3rd generation adults grew up in this neighborhood. Increasing prosperity within the past 10-15 years has caused another move, this time to the suburbs. This process still continues today as people improve their financial position and look for housing more adequate for the needs of their growing families. Continuing geographic mobility within the Houston area has resulted in a wide dispersion of Greek families. Those who have participated in this move to the suburbs did not choose their new locations because of the number of Greeks in their new neighborhoods, but because of convenience to their jobs, and ease of getting to the Greek church. It is interesting to note that even when there are a number of Greeks in one neighborhood, they don't necessarily socialize with one another. This may be because of differences in age or generation, or perhaps just lack of interest in one another.

> There's a couple that live a couple of blocks away--they
> come over sometimes and bring us these things out of their
> yard, and they're real nice. Mother's always saying, "We're
> going to have to invite them over for coffee," you know, she's
> always said that, but we never have, never have...

2. Church

Neighborhoods then are not the important source of Greek friendships that they once were. In "the old days" people were less mobile,
and more dependent on each other in their ghetto-like area; their
neighborhoods were social areas. The recent trend has been to find
housing wherever it is available, and to keep up with one's Greek
friends by going to see them, rather than developing close friendships
in the neighborhood; and since most Greek activities take place at the
church, one sees his Greek friends there very often. Thus there is
really no geographic basis for the Houston Greek community, for its
members are scattered throughout the city. In truth, the center of
the community is the church; this is not a geographic, but a social
center for a community whose boundaries are more social than geographic.

3. Businesses

Probably the only other important place that Greek friends get
together is through "Greek" businesses, either as partners or as owners
and customers. Many Greeks are tied together because of common business
dealings, as well as (or sometimes instead of) through the church. The
pattern of the individual's running a family business, perhaps in
partnership with another Greek--a relative or close friend--is very
common in the Greek community. Many of these businesses are restaurants
or other food-industry enterprises, but in recent years service stations

have begun to play a more important role. There are also many other small businesses such as cleaners, pharmacies, and auto repair shops.

The most obvious places where Greeks interact are at the "Greek" restaurants like the Bachanale, the Dionysios and the Athens Bar and Grill. Some people go out to Greek clubs almost every weekend. But individuals patronize other Greek businesses as well; they might go to a Greek cleaners or gas station owned by a Greek rather than one owned by an American. Even professionals like doctors and lawyers have "Greek" businesses by catering to a Greek clientele. However, this system of patronage is less extensive today than it was in the past. When most of the Greeks lived and worked in one area of the city, the Greek businesses were convenient and it was easy to patronize them. Now that Greeks and their businesses are spread all over the city, it has become more and more difficult to do business with other Greeks. These days it is more likely that one patronizes a Greek business either because it is convenient, or because he has some sort of relationship with the proprietor. A 3rd generation boy noted this fact:

> [Does your family patronize businesses run by Greeks?]
> The only thing I can think of is our cleaning, we take it
> out to a cleaners in Westbury. We take all our cleaning out
> there, and Greeks own it. We could take it to Pilgrim, which
> is closer, but--but then again, those people are my brother's
> godparents.

With this important exception--taking their cleaning to a kumbaro whose business was located across town--the family patronized businesses which were convenient, rather than those run by Greeks.

Thus the geographic dispersion of the Houston Greek community makes it difficult to maintain traditional ethnic forms, such as relationships with Greek neighbors and the patronizing of Greek businesses. One might

conclude that this is one more manifestation of the difficulty of main-

taining "community" in contemporary urban society, and to an extent it

is; but the Greeks of Houston have managed rather successfully to over-

come such obstacles and to maintain a community which is centered

around the church and its programs and activities. Of course if an

energy shortage cut the supply of gasoline, the community would be in

rather serious trouble.

D. Friendship groups

Although friendship generally seems to organize the members of the

Greek community into a series of overlapping networks, there are also

two types of aggregates which are more formalized "groups". These are

the patrioti and cliques. A 2nd generation man discussed these groups:

> There's nothing about these groups that means one group is
> unfriendly with another group. It's just that whenever
> close social affairs are given, they're given in groups.
> For instance, we don't get invited to many parties with the
> Westbury bunch--and when the D's have a party they invite us
> because I grew up with them. I have almost nothing to do with
> Patmians.

"Patmians" are a group of οἱ πατριῶτοι (i patrioti) i.e., people

from the same area of Greece, in this case the island of Patmos, and

"the Westbury bunch" is perhaps the most noticeable of the cliques

within the Greek community. Each of these types of "group" will be

discussed in turn.

1. Patrioti

The term patrioti has the general meaning of "people from your area".

In its most general sense, any Greeks are patrioti, but those who are

from the same island or region or the same town are much closer patrioti, and this is the sense in which I will use this term. One's patrioti

are an important group for the immigrant. He feels more comfortable

with them, and feels that they understand him. Greece is characterized

by extreme cultural diversity, and each area, island, or even town

has its own culture and loyalties which are brought to the United States

and continued here. Many customs vary from one area to another, particu-

larly those concerning rites of passage such as weddings and funerals.

These variations may cause some tensions here in the United States,

where Greeks from many areas make up a local Greek community. Comments

from a 3rd generation woman, and from a 1st generation husband and his

2nd generation wife demonstrate this tension:

> There have been different customs in different parts of
> Greece--I know that when we got married, one of the girls
> said, "Well, where I come from, the groom buys the wedding
> dress." Where I'd come from, I never heard of such a thing.
>
> H: If somebody dies where I was born, after the funeral, in
> the church yard, they offer ouzo, or some kind of cookies
> with black coffee, and I notice here that they sit down and
> eat.
> W: Where we come from, we don't eat food--we drink the black
> coffee or the ouzo. But see, in Kefallinia or Korintho, in
> all those places, they sit down and eat a full meal.
> H: In other words, when something happens like that, they
> start the cooking, for people to eat. And I never want to
> sit down and eat then.

Thus one's patrioti are familiar with the same customs and traditions

that he grew up with, and he feels a special sense of identity and

affinity with them.

To what extent are these groups continued in the 2nd and 3rd genera-

tions? Usually the patrioti groups are not continued so strictly in

these later generations, but this depends on the sort of relationship

one's parents had with their patrioti. In those cases in which the patrioti were very close-knit and even baptized one another's children, the 2nd generation children have grown up together, and thus their friendships come very naturally. By the 3rd generation, however, the ties are very limited. Nevertheless, some groups, such as the Patmians (from the island of Patmos), traditionally seem to stick together more than the other groups of patrioti.

The Patmians are probably the largest patrioti group, and many within the group are related to one another as well. People frequently comment on their "clannishness". A 3rd generation woman commented on a Patmian family:

> I think they are very clannish. Take for instance the X family. They don't let their kids do anything with kids that aren't Greeks. Their social life centers around the church. ... She doesn't socialize with her neighbors; she couldn't tell you who her neighbors are. Her son has very few friends in the neighborhood. ... She's very strict about them even going out in the yard, outside of the yard to play. Every weekend she's got a lot of her brothers over for dinner or they go over there for dinner or the kumbari come over for dinner. ... And the kids are always either the cousins or the kumbari's kids, that group playing together.

The Patmians are such a noticeable group for two reasons: (1) several years ago, before the Greek population grew (because of an influx from other parts of America), there was a large number of Patmians within the Houston community, and (2) they have organized themselves into a Patmian Brotherhood, which is even subdivided into men's and women's groups. This society has occasional social functions and does charitable work by sending money to needy causes on Patmos.

The Χιότες (Chiotes, people from the island Chios) also have a society, the Ἅγια Μαρκέλλα (Agia Markella) which is named for the patron saint of Chois, St. Marcella. There are fewer Chiotes than

Patmians in Houston, but they are also able to participate in a society

because theirs is a branch of the national Chios Society. A 2nd genera-

tion Χιότισα (Chiotisa, woman whose family came from Chios) discussed

the activities of the national Chios society and the advantages of

belonging to it:

> It's a very strong society. And say you're a heart patient,
> and you belong. Well, if they come here, they'll call the
> president and they'll tell her, "This man is from Chios."
> "Well, we'll all pitch in and take care of him." They can
> take him to our homes, and we'll keep him the length of time
> until he recuperates.

The people from Patmos and Chios form the only patrioti groups which

are widely-recognized by the members of the Greek community. Neverthe-

less, there are groups of families from many other areas of Greece, and

even 3rd generation people generally know whether someone is a Chiotis,

Samoiotis, Kefallinitis, and so on. Young people also usually know

which individuals in town are their patrioti.

One facet of the patrioti phenomenon is particularly interesting.

To some extent, there is a spirit of competition between people from

various areas of Greece, at least among the older generation. Obviously,

the way things are done on one's own island is the best way, and those

who are from another area where things are done differently are slightly

inferior. E.g., the Greeks from Turkey may consider themselves better

than the island or mainland Greeks, because they are much more dignified

and cosmopolitan, and less "common". Other Greeks may feel that those

from Turkey and areas close to Asia Minor are "not quite as good"

because they were "too close" to the Turks; they are not true Greeks for

their blood may be mixed. There are also stereotyped comments about the people from the different areas of Greece. One concerns Cephalonia:

> That island is known for stubborn people. I'm not kidding.
> Like my aunt married a--my uncle--they're nice people, but
> they're just stubborn. "If he's stubborn, he's a Κεφαλλινίτη
> [Kefalliniti]," If he's a Kefalliniti, automatically you'll
> assume that he's stubborn.

Another is:

> F: There's one I found that was kinda funny. Καλαματιανοί
> [Kalamatiani, people from Kalamata] are--
> E: They run around on their wives--
> F: No, they're--what do you call it? σωματέμπορος--
> that's not very nice, I wouldn't go quoting that, that more
> pimps come from there, Kalamata. But I wouldn't go around
> saying that. A lot of people here are from Kalamata, and
> they're nice people.

2. Cliques

In addition to the patrioti groups, there are also a few noted "cliques" within the Greek community. The clique which is by far the most frequently mentioned is the "Westbury group", made up of about 8-10 families. This is the "elite" group that many people feel on the outside of, looking in. A 3rd generation woman explained the emergence of this clique:

> The Westbury group is a composite of people from San Antonio,
> Dallas. They're basically outsiders to Houston. They're not
> outsiders to the area. Some of it is the Galveston bunch.
> That whole bunch has made their own group because they too
> are outsiders. They probably were not really accepted by
> the old Houston clan, and basically old families.

Other cliques involve very wealthy people, and professionals, whereas some are based upon the patrioti phenomenon just discussed.

E. Greek and American friends

Those Greeks who have both Greek and American friends--which is almost all Greeks, but especially people who are in school--have interesting friendship networks. Their networks can easily be divided into two separate groups, Greeks and Americans, between which there is little

contact. A 2nd generation woman commented:

> When I was growing up, you always had your American friends and
> your Greek friends, very rarely did you ever mix them because
> --all your Greek friends know each other, and if you invite
> Americans to a party, they know each other so well that they
> kinda tend to neglect the ones that they don't know that well.

Numerous people have mentioned to me the fact that they do not "mix"

their Greek and American friends, because "it just doesn't work". The

Greeks all know each other very well because they are tied through life-

long relationships as friends, kumbari, and relatives, and see each

other very frequently at Greek social affairs, church, and the community

center, as well as informally. Because they have such "close" relation-

ships with other Greeks, they "tend to neglect the ones they don't know

that well"--non-Greeks. For this reason one usually will not bring

American friends into a situation in which they would meet his Greek

friends.

VI Discussion

After examining kinship, kumbaria, and friendship within the Greek

community, several trends appear. First it should be noted that Houston's

Greek population is most accurately described as a web of overlapping

personal networks of kinsmen, kumbari, and friends. The community may

be visualized in this way: each individual is at the center of his own

personal network, with ties to his family, more distant kin, kumbari,

and friends progressing outward in importance.

How do the many personal networks of individual Greeks fit together

to form such a web? I would suggest that of the three patterns of relationship that have been discussed, kumbaria is the most important

for uniting the community in that it creates a web of relationships

which extend throughout the community. Kumbaria is more influential

than the kinship ties between symbetheri because one's relationships

with kumbari are a more important part of his life; his kumbari are

generally closer than his symbetheri. It was mentioned previously that

friendship ties are very strong and widely extended within the Greek

community, and I would certainly not want to belittle their role in

uniting the community. Nevertheless, I feel that kumbaria as an insti-

tution is even more comprehensive and far-reaching in its effects than

is friendship. In the first place, one's close friends usually become

his kumbari. Secondly, kumbari are considered next to one's family,

or even part of the family, and as such are usually invited to all one's

parties and family affairs. This practice has a significant impact on

uniting the community into a more-or-less integrated whole.

For example, to see how kumbaria acts to unite the many personal

networks within the Greek community, consider a hypothetical family with

two children. Chances are that this family has close ties to at least

four or five other families, those of the nuni of each parent, of their

kumbaro who stefanosied them, and of their children's nuni. And of

course they would most likely have sponsored at least one or two

weddings and/or baptisms themselves, which would increase the number

of families they were close to by two or three. This is not to mention the

possibilities of close friendships with the kumbari of their kumbari,

whom they would probably see often socially, since as kumbari they would

be invited to parties along with the same group of people for every set of kumbari. In other words, the hypothetical family A is kumbari to family B (the husband's nuni), C (the wife's nuni), D (kumbaro), E (their 2nd child's nuni, assuming the first child was baptized by the best man), F, and G (their godchildren's parents). (See Figure 5.)

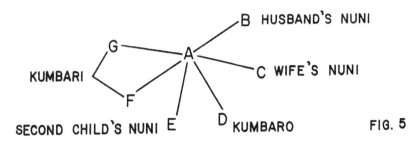

FIG. 5

Now suppose E gives a party. He would naturally invite A, who are his kumbari because he baptized one of their children. He would also invite his other kumbari H, I, J, K, and L. Since A is usually invited when H, I, J, K and L are, the chances are that they will be acquaintances, and perhaps friends.

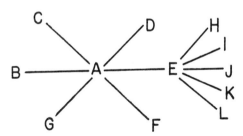

FIG. 6

The same situation also happens with his other kumbari, families B, C, D and F. It is obvious that with such things occurring, almost everyone within the Greek community has potential links to everyone else. This is particularly true because of the tendencies of "spreading out" one's kumbari ties to include many people.

Although kumbaria is probably the single most important of the institutions which unite the many networks of the Greek community, kinship and friendship are also very important factors in this unification. These three of course are not totally independent of each other; e.g., one's friends or relatives may become kumbari. Furthermore, the unifying effect of each is multiplied by their working in concert throughout the community by virtue of the fact that each individual fulfills each of these three roles for many people. An individual's best friend may be his cousin's kumbaro, his kumbaro may be his brother's friend and his friend's cousin, his kumbara's friend may be his symbethera, and so on ad infinitum. Thus each individual is tied to many others through one or more links, and their bonds with the community which their ties sustain--as well as with each other--are much stronger than they would have been otherwise.

There is an interesting term widely used within the Greek community which should be mentioned at this point. This is παρέα (parea), which does not translate well into English, but could be roughly translated as "fellowship", "company", "the group". Generally this term means "your group", i.e., one's family, kumbari, and close friends. For example, invitations to parties and dances frequently include at the bottom, "Bring your parea". In the context of our discussion, "parea" is equivalent to the closest members of one's personal network, probably those with whom he socializes the most. Almost all social life revolves around parea: most Greek social functions like dinners and dances have reserved tables, where members of a parea sit together. In such a situation, the person with no parea is in an awkward social position.

But parea also has a larger meaning of "fellowship" within the community. E.g., someone commented that the important part of everyone's working on the Festival was the parea, the fellowship with other members of the Greek community. One of the main factors which unites the community is this feeling of parea members share with each other; thus each individual's sense of parea is extended through his network to include virtually the entire community. This idea will be discussed in greater detail in the following chapter.

The themes of "respect" and, particularly, "closeness" are repeated throughout one's relationships with family, kumbari, and friends. These themes present very important forces in the Greek community, and their significance will be discussed further in the next chapter, which examines the "social meanings" of Greekness--what being Greek means to Greeks themselves.

SUMMER "FUN CLUB"--GREEK ORTHODOX COMMUNITY CENTER

Adult Greek language class

Greek dancing class

VACATION BIBLE SCHOOL

Religious education class

Greek language class

VACATION BIBLE SCHOOL
Learning Greek dancing

Play: "Soul of the Guerrilla"

Poetry recitation: "The Fustanella"

Independence Day celebration participants

PART II

ANALYSIS

COMMUNITY ACTIVITIES

CHAPTER 4

SOCIAL MEANINGS OF GREEKNESS AND MEMBERSHIP IN THE COMMUNITY

The questions to be considered in this chapter are very important,
for they involve the basic meanings of Greekness and the rules of membership in the Greek ethnic group as it is represented by the local Greek
community. When is someone no longer "Greek"? The definition of which
individuals are "in" the community and which are "out" is the fundamental
meaning of assimilation in America. The nature of "Greekness" is the
problem which will be addressed in this chapter. I will first note
several problems associated with the analysis of Greekness, and then
discuss the social meanings of Greekness, i.e., what being Greek means
to Greek Americans themselves. Based on this discussion those elements
of Greekness will be examined which Greeks consider necessary prerequisites if one is to be identified as a member of the Greek community.
The final section will then demonstrate how these requirements apply to
Greek Americans, new arrivals from Greece, and non-Greeks, as each
crosses the social boundaries of Greekness and becomes a member of, or
loses membership in, the community.

I. The Nature of "Greekness"

The first question to be examined is "What is 'Greekness'?" This
concept is actually more nebulous than one might think and it should be
considered closely. The American wife of a 2nd generation man made
these observations on "Greekness":

What is Greekness though? You say, "I'm Greek." What does

152

> that mean? My parents came from Greece, or my ancestors
> came from Greece, that's all, isn't it really? That's all
> it is to me, really. You're living in America, you're going
> by American standards and way of living, this is not the
> Greek way. We're not doing anything "the Greek way" here.
> I think that sometimes when you are of Greek descent, you
> have this little holdover--"That's the Greek way of thinking!"
> I've heard that said, or "Isn't that just like a Greek?"
> Just blanket things. You hear them, but they don't fit.
> When someone's Greek, they may be a 2nd or 3rd generation,
> they still might say, "I'm Greek." They're not Greek. My
> husband's not Greek. He's of Greek ancestry, but he was
> born in America, so he's just as much an American as I am.

She may have overstated the case somewhat, but in her comments one finds

a note of truth. Greek Americans are living in America, to a large

extent living an "American" way of life. This is not to say that the

Greek American way of life has no distinguishing features, for it is

definitely characterized by some distinctive cultural patterns. Never-

theless, the ways of "the old country" have been greatly modified through

contact with American culture.

Despite the efforts of many Greeks, the traditions of "the old

country", as the older generation remembers it, have not been maintained

intact in American society. It is interesting to note, however, that

these ways to a large extent have not been maintained in Greece either;

one may thus observe a situation in which American Greeks are in many

instances more traditionally "Greek" than their contemporary counter-

parts in Greece. A young 3rd generation man made this observation when

he said:

> Greece is not the old country like it used to be. And it's
> changed too. I mean like when my cousin moved there she
> said, "It's not like I thought it was going to be," the
> woman with the washtub at the rock and all.

A 2-3 generation boy and 3rd generation girl discussed this phenomenon in the context of their having been "raised Greek" in America, and noted

the shock they felt on seeing that Greeks are more "modern" than many

Greek Americans.

> S: What used to kill me was that before I went to Greece, or
> was really old enough to understand, Greek parents here had
> so much control over their kids, it was unbelievable! They
> were telling us, "Well, this isn't how they do it in Greece,
> you're not going to do it like this." So I went to Greece
> and found out that that's a lot of bull because there they're
> a lot looser with their kids.
> D: The [Greek American] kids--they wouldn't let anybody out
> of town to go to school, and over there the people go out of
> the country to go to school.
> S: To me, it's like the parents here had a built-in advantage,
> they could say, "Well, this isn't how it is over there, so
> you're not going to do it, we're going to do it the Greek way."
> So you go over there and find out it's not the Greek way!
> D: And you know what, S, they're not that religious in Greece!
> Remember when we were younger, it was--
> S: No, no, I was shocked. No one goes to church over there--
> hardly anybody.

This shock of realization that "Greece isn't the old country anymore"

has no doubt had an effect on the strict maintenance of Greek patterns in

America; seeing that many of the traditional Greek values they have

struggled so hard to maintain have fallen by the way in Greece itself

has made people question their conceptions of what it means to be Greek.

In his discussion of recent changes in Houston's Greek community, a 2-3

generation man implied this result of changes in Greece:

> They're becoming more American, even though they don't realize
> it. America is finally beginning to catch on to them. I think
> they're realizing that they're actually more American than
> they'd like to consider themselves. ... A lot of them left
> Greece with an impression of what it was like 20 or 30 years
> ago, and now they can afford to go back, and they've seen that
> it's just like it is here. 'Cause like I was going to go to
> Greece last summer, and I was making deliveries to these Greek
> restaurants. ... I told them I was going to quit in a couple
> of weeks and go to Greece--they said, "Ohhh!! Then you'd better
> get a haircut, they'll never let you in, everyone will make fun
> of you!" You go there, and the kids have hair. They're normal

kids! It's become cheaper--a lot cheaper--so it has become
easier for them to go. Greece is progressing. And that way
[when they see what Greece is today], they're not trying to
keep the old Greek ways as much as they did before.

Despite the unsettling effects of learning that traditional ideals have

not been maintained in Greece, most Greek Americans are not rejecting

their "Greek ideals" wholesale. Rather, they frequently feel a sense

of sadness that many of the values by which they were raised have been

somehow lost in the old country, and express a feeling of gratitude

for being exposed to traditional Greek values. Moreover, they feel

superior to their Greek counterparts to a certain extent, and consider

themselves fortunate to belong to such a unique group of people, the

Greek Americans.

Therefore when attempting to understand the meaning of Greekness

in America, one must realize that the culture he is considering is not

just an Americanized version of contemporary Greek culture, but a

complex hybrid which has been developing and changing over many decades

of contact with American and, more recently, with a new Greece as well.

Furthermore, Greek American culture cannot be simply represented as a

culture with both Greek and American elements; rather, it is a unique

culture which has resulted from the creation of new forms in response to

the situation Greeks have encountered in America. For example, one may

cite two innovations in Greek American culture which exist in neither

Greek nor American culture--conventions as a setting for mate-selection

(which will be discussed in Chapter 7), and the Greek Orthodox church as

the nucleus of the community. In earlier chapters the reader has seen

the central role the Greek Orthodox church plays in a Greek community;

it is the social as well as the religious center of Greek activities.

A 2nd generation man expressed this idea very succinctly:

> You can't really separate the Greek community from the church.
> It's an integral part of anything you want to do, or anything
> you want to say. If you're going to feel that what's in your
> paper is an ethnic group, then you can't separate it from the
> church. The Greek church and the Greek community is one.

The church has therefore served as a unifying institution in America to

an extent which was unnecessary in Greece.

For these reasons, an examination of American "Greek" identifica-

tion--both self-conception and group membership--must be based in the

context of Greek American society and culture. Chapter 5 will discuss

Greek American self-conceptions, and this chapter will consider the

meanings which Greeks themselves attach to "Greekness" and those

attributes which they consider necessary for group membership.

II. Social Meanings of Greekness

What does it mean to be Greek, to be a member of the Greek group?

This is the question I will seek to answer in this section.

A. Community

> [Is being Greek important to you?]
> It's very, very, very important. Because my friends, most of
> my friends, and that's 7/8ths, are Greek, and I enjoy being
> around them, doing things that're Greek and going to our
> church and everything. ... I enjoy being Greek, rather than
> being just like anybody else, and I enjoy the fact that my
> friends that are Greek, we have a more--our friendship is
> special, because it's not--it's just that we have this thing
> in common, and our families have it in common, you know, and
> we have our religion in common, you know. It's kinda like
> if you told jokes about what happened in your family life,
> you know, and an American person can't understand it, because
> they don't identify. So I mean, it's just nice.

In the remarks of this 3rd generation girl one can sense the central

meaning of being a Greek American: belonging to a group whose members "have this thing in common". This "thing", Greekness, is the basis for

a sense of "community"--of affinity, unity, intimacy, and loyalty--among

group members. Those with whom one shares "Greekness" are special, as

an American who married a Greek man explained:

> I see a feeling there, it's not anything overt, but there's
> this feeling. For example, the way that P and J, which would
> be his two closest friends here in Houston that are Greeks--
> the way they treat F [her husband], like "Hey brother!", it's
> almost that. It's a different way than say our best friends
> that are American would treat F. The Greek men, and women
> too, treat him as a different person. ... And it's a very
> warm, loving, different kinda thing, and I'm sure it's just
> because F's Greek and they are. It is a different feeling,
> it's a much warmer, kinda like "We're all in this boat together"
> feeling, than it would be with F around a non-Greek.

The roots of this special, "different" feeling lie in sharing a sense

of affinity in several ways, for the Greekness which unites group members

has many different expressions--biological, social, religious, and

cultural. Each of these aspects of Greekness provides a basis on which

Greek Americans can claim affinity and "community".

1. Biological Greekness

One of the main meanings of Greekness is biological, being "of Greek

blood". One is Greek because his mother and father were Greek, or in

some cases because one of his parents was Greek. Thus one cannot choose

to be or not to be Greek, biologically speaking. The concept of "blood"

carries a lot of weight with many Greeks, and its importance should not

be underestimated. E.g., a young 2-3 generation man in commenting on

his Greek identity indicated the role of biological Greekness, of "blood",

in clarifying and delineating his identity and membership.

> [You have something that other Americans don't have?]
> It's more of a unity, not being out there by yourself, but in
> a group. It's like people like to get themselves organized,

> get their bodies organized. You hear, "I'm one-fourth Dutch,
> Irish", and like that--you're true American then. But I'm
> Greek--my mother and father were both Greek, their mother and
> father both Greek. ... It's a unifier, you're in a certain
> group.

Part of the opposition to intermarriage is no doubt a response to this

emphasis on the "purity" of bloodlines. An American woman who married

a 2nd generation man sensed this objection from her mother-in-law:

> After I got my ring and everything, we went to San Antonio to
> meet his mother and I really went to her house--at that time
> she lived there alone--and she didn't come downstairs for a
> long time, and I was so nervous. And I think she probably was
> too. I'm sure she was. I think his mother was terribly dis-
> appointed because her daughter was never able to have children,
> they have adopted children that are not Greek. And of course,
> T married a girl that wasn't Greek, and I kinda think she thought
> --J was her last hope of having a Greek daughter-in-law with
> Greek grandchildren. And she just came downstairs and J intro-
> duced me, and she said, (very quietly and evenly) "I hope you
> will be happy." That's all she said.

But the concept of "blood" does not only represent biological fact;

it also has a cultural connotation, of being "raised Greek". This conno-

tation is obvious in the statements of a 3rd generation girl.

> [What if a friend of yours left the church--would she still
> be "Greek" to you?]
> That she's not Greek Orthodox doesn't mean to me that she's not
> Greek. I separate the two and you know she's of Greek heritage
> --she's born with it, she's going to always be part Greek. She's
> been shaped partly by that culture and so she's not going to be
> able to get away from that.

Being "of Greek blood" means that one has been raised as a member of the

Greek group, and that the Greek American culture has greatly influenced

his life; it is something he cannot "get away from". Thus "blood" means

much more to Greeks than mere parentage, for it is a symbol of Greekness

in general. An American who dated a Greek girl summed up the Greek

conception of blood when he said:

They don't want to lose their culture. If I marry M, it would
be lost in a sense, part of it would be. Our children would
have, you know, not that it makes any difference, but our blood
lines would be half and half.
[I think it does matter to them.]
I think it matters in that--well see, when you say the blood
thing you're saying three things right together. You're saying
by keeping the blood the same, you're keeping the culture,
heritage, and the religion, right there. I don't think it's
just like the white man marrying an Indian you know, or a
white man marrying a Negro, "I don't want Negro blood in my
children," you know, I don't think it's that. To me those
things are all one and the same, they want to preserve it,
they don't want to lose it because they love it so.

2. Social aspects of Greekness

In Chapter 3 it was noted that the intricate web of overlapping

networks of kin, kumbari, and friends which characterizes the Greek

community serves to unite the many individual pareas (fellowship groups)

into one large parea, comprising the entire community. This sense of

community parea is enhanced by the fact that community members share the

other factors being considered in this section--biological, religious,

and cultural Greekness. The large (and growing) size of Houston's

community of course limits the ability of each community member to have

ties to every other, but despite this limitation, a feeling of parea and

community "togetherness" remains an important ideal.

In fact, the community is generally considered an extension of the

family. The individual's feelings of closeness and respect toward his

family also include relationships with more distant relatives (symbetheri),

fictive kin (kumbari), and friends; indeed, these feelings extend outward

to encompass the entire community. The remarks of a 2nd generation couple

reflect the role of respect in the community.

W: I've heard the expression that Mr. So-and-so stefanosied
them, so that kind of puts him in a higher--he's pretty special

because that's what he did and he is respected. The Greeks
respect their elders and they drum this into their kids.
H: Because an older person is either an uncle or--
W: If he's a kumbaro with somebody he's important, and if
he's stefanosied them then he's important, everybody has got
a little niche. That's why you're supposed to treat them
with respect.

One may also recall the fact that many children are taught to call all

adults "thio" or "thia" out of respect. Two 2nd generation women

explained the way in which these "respect" terms bring individuals

closer together.

Calling them thio or kumbaro makes it more a personal--'cause
this means your aunt, it's kinda--not opening up, but it's
more informal than saying Mrs. So-and-so. I think in a way
it kinda warms up things. Well, when someone called you
"thia" in Greece, didn't it make you feel closer to them,
warmer?

I have had a child call me "thia", but I'm not really her
aunt. It's just something you would say rather than the
formal Mrs. S. Maybe this would make it a little bit more
of the family.

The second quotation in particular demonstrates exactly the nature of

relationships between community members--ideally, they are "like family"

to each other, and as such, are treated with the respect and closeness

which are due to members of one's family. The importance of respect

and closeness with members of the community were expressed by a 2nd

generation woman.

You're brought up, from a little person, to respect anyone
that's older than you are--they have had more experience, and
are more knowledgeable than you are. So any person--I can
remember my mother saying, "Any person that's older than you
are, you call 'em--you don't call them Mrs. So-and-so, you
call them Thia or Κυρία [Kyria, Mrs.]." You give them a
respect title. ... We lived across the street from another
Greek family, and there was an older--a giagia and pappou in
that family, that weren't my giagia and pappou, but I always
called them that and finally when I got to be a teenager, I
thought, "Well, I'm not going to call them that anymore,

> They're not my grandparents." But I never broke that habit,
> I never could. Because I couldn't call them "Mr. S" or "Mrs.
> S", that would be just terrible, that would be very disrespect-
> ful, really.
> [Why does respect involve a kinship term when they're not
> related to you?]
> Uhh--it's a respectful term, it's a closeness that's a relation-
> ship, and this is important to Greeks, relationships to people.
> [What does it mean to be--]
> Close? If you like somebody and want to be associated with
> them, related to them, or be friends with them, the only way
> that you can show this is by being close to them. And how
> do you be--how can you be close to them? Through association,
> and through togetherness. It's just a togetherness thing,
> that's what closeness means.

Throughout these examples one finds family feelings being extended to
community members. In fact, individuals have even directly commented on
the community as "a family".

> It's like one big family, instead of like a direct family thing.
> It's one big group. That's why a lot of people--that answers
> the question why people get so frustrated--well, shocked when
> people will intermarry. Because well, if you do that, it's
> like going away from the family. It's like taking the Greek
> colony and considering it one family--if you intermarry, you're
> leaving the family.

Considering members of the community like one's family is not unusual
among Houston's Greeks. E.g., young people frequently explain that they
do not date each other because they are "like brothers and sisters".
Choosing between marrying a non-Greek ("leaving the family") or a local
Greek (which seems incestuous, since the young people are "like" siblings) represents a serious conflict which is inherent in the situation.
Solutions to this problem will be explored in Chapter 6.

One has an especially close relationship with others who are members
of this Greek "family". Since friendships among Greeks have already been
discussed in Chapter 3, I will now only cite one example to demonstrate
these feelings in the community. An American married to a 2nd generation

man commented:

> I think that you're really privileged to have a heritage that
> you can keep that close with and keep in contact with, and
> identify with. I think it's great. I think it makes you feel
> just a little bit closer sometimes to your community, to your
> church, and family. ... I think it's more or less a sorta
> bond that you have with each other that I might not have with
> you, but that I would have with Greek women. It's just a bond
> of something special, something extra.

3. Religion

The Greek Orthodox religion is perhaps the primary element of Greek-

ness shared by community members. Part of its importance is the "family"

aspect which was just discussed; community members are also church mem-

bers, and the individual frequently considers his fellow Greek Orthodox

as "family". E.g., a 3rd generation woman who married into the Catholic

Church said:

> They're really quite the same, you know...but what I miss about
> the Greek church is the family feeling.

In this sense the significance of the church is social rather than

religious, as the American wife of a 2nd generation man discovered.

> W: We went to a large party in San Antonio. And I didn't
> know any of the people there, and he had lots of people there,
> some Greek and some not. And I met all these different people
> that I'd never met before, and about every third person would
> say to me, "Are you going to church tomorrow?" This was Sat-
> urday night. Finally I figured out that every person that
> asked me that was Greek. Because if I was going to church in
> the morning, that meant that they would see me in the morning,
> because there's one Greek church.
> H: Yeah, it was a natural extension of--well, if you're Greek,
> we'll see you in church.
> W: But nobody ever had said, "Are you going to church in the
> morning?" And it was just one after the other.
> H: It definitely is the center of everything.

There is a second sense in which the church serves to unite the

community, however, which was discussed in Chapter 2. Greekness and

Greek Orthodoxy are intimately tied in the minds of Greek Americans--if one is Greek, he is Greek Orthodox. A 2nd generation woman made this point.

> My mother and father both had the attitude that I had to marry someone Greek. I mean, to marry someone out of our--forget about the religion, that just goes along with it, you know, that's all a part of being Greek, is you're an Orthodox, you know, you're born an Orthodox and you are an Orthodox from then on. There's no such thing as religion-hopping or anything like that.

4. Cultural Greekness

In the sense of "community" and affinity which is the central meaning of Greekness in America, cultural factors probably play a lesser role than social and religious aspects. In an earlier chapter it was noted that Greece is characterized by a high degree of cultural diversity, and thus Houston's Greek immigrants from Greece's many different areas brought with them diverse social customs. As an example I will cite a rather humorous incident.

> P's mother told me that it's the tradition in Greek families that the best man gives a personal gift to the bride, and she said that she got her watch or something from the best man, or some piece of jewelry. So therefore C had to give a personal gift to A, because he was supposed to be the best man. ... P's mother went and bought a gold bracelet, and this was C's gift to A. ... She came up with the gold bracelet, and said, "Oh, A, here's the gold bracelet that C has given you to wear on your wedding day." But the girl's mother went "AAAHHHH! [screams] It's an evil eye" or whatever it is, "to wear gold on your wedding day." ... That really sticks in my mind because she went through this whole story about all this big tradition, and then "AAAHHH!"

Furthermore, many cultural elements which until recently were of great significance in the Houston community are gradually becoming less important. E.g., the Greek lnaguage is dying out despite enormous efforts to maintain it, as a 2nd generation woman observed.

> We're losing the language. I'm the world's worst. Our
> children understand very little Greek. And we're to blame
> for that. ... Although I speak fluent Greek, it's a lot
> easier, I mean, I express myself in English.
> [So you don't think the Greek language is gonna be something
> they'll carry with them?]
> No, uh-uh. No matter how hard we try, no matter how much we
> take them to Greek school, Donna, the children cannot get the
> language like we got it. That's all that was spoken in our
> house. My mother didn't know how to go and ride the bus--my
> mother didn't know how to go and do her own shopping. Why?
> Because she depended on us to do it. She spoke to us in
> Greek constantly, she did not learn the language. Had she
> learned the language, we would have started speaking to her
> in English--and we wouldn't have learned the language.

Another element of traditional Greek American culture, relationships

with one's patrioti, is also of decreasing significance for each new

generation, and many other examples could be cited as well.

Nevertheless, there are several central cultural elements which

continue to provide Greek Americans with a sense of their essential

similarity as Greeks, a feeling of "community". One of these is the

"close" family, and others are Greek customs which are carried out in

the home. These include cooking and foods, hospitality, music and

dancing, and religious customs. These customs will be discussed in

chapter 5.

Thus the essential meaning of Greekness for Greek Americans is the

sense of "community" and intimacy which results from belonging to a

group whose members share biological, religious, social and cultural

Greekness. This emphasis on feelings of unity and affinity among

Greeks should not be taken to mean that the Greek community is a

monolithic entity characterized by relationships of "closeness" and

"respect" between all community members; this is of course untrue.

There are a number of forces within the community which are contradictory to this "community" ideal.

B. Divisive forces

It would be surprising if there were no interpersonal friction
within a close-knit community whose members are very frequently in
contact with one another. In Houston's Greek community one can find
many examples of criticizing, resentment, and backbiting among members,
as well as individual feuds which can be quite violent emotionally:
the people involved may not speak to each other for years, or even for
the rest of their lives. Such fallings-out are very characteristic of
the Greek community, as an American who married a 2nd generation man
explained. But, despite these feuds, she views the community as acting
like a close-knit unit in adverse situations.

> I think that Greeks are the most stubborn group, and the
> meanest to each other. They harbor old hates and grudges
> for a lifetime. And I've known cases among the Greeks
> where brothers sued each other in court. And they can
> build up these terrible hatreds. And yet--it's like a small
> town in a way, when there's a death or tragedy, or something,
> they all really band together and stick up for each other.

In Chapter 3 the presence of recognizable groups within the Houston
community was noted; some of these are patrioti groups and others are
friendship cliques. The existence of such "groups", which are by
nature rather exclusive, combined with the fact that newcomers find it
difficult to enter the networks and groups of the older residents,
threatens the ideal of community closeness.

Originally the Greek community, like the rest of Houston, was
quite small; within the past about 25 years, as the city began to grow,
the Greek population also increased exponentially. Thus the older
families have been inundated by newcomers; this has caused a sense of

disorientation among some of the older residents. E.g., a 1st/2nd

generation couple discussed the changes in the Houston community since

their child had been born.

> H: At that time, when she baptized S, there were very few
> --I doubt if we were 100 families.
> W: That's right, we were very close families then. Now of
> course, we're over 1000 families here. Then, in 20 or 25
> years ago, since S was born, there were just a few families
> here, and we were just real close, you might say. Where now,
> you go into church, and we're almost strangers, there's so
> many new families that have come in.

The "original" families are therefore very close, because they have

been together for so long; they grew up together, and now their children

are growing up together, too. As is frequently the case in such a

situation, the "originals" feel that "newcomers" do not quite fit into

their firmly-established social structure; they do not have an inclina-

tion to bring new arrivals into their social circles. A 2nd generation

woman described the situation as she sees it:

> It is hard for newcomers to break into the community here,
> because it was once so small and well-knit. Many of these
> people literally have grown up together their whole lives,
> and so they are not too quick to welcome others--they seem
> to have all they need. Like people go to church to see their
> friends, so afterwards they all gather together to catch up
> on the latest, instead of seeking out a new person and taking
> the effort to welcome him. The other is just more easy and
> natural. ... Now there are so many people in the church
> that no one knows who's a visitor and who's been there five
> years. Also there's a feeling among the "originals" that
> anyone here less than about 30 years is a "newcomer". I'm
> afraid I've been guilty of this, labeling people as "not
> originals", or "newcomers", who have lived here 15 years.

It is very difficult for newcomers to break into the social circles of

the Houston community, for the parea of the established cliques appar-

ently is not easily shared with those who have recently arrived on the

scene. The American wife of a 2nd generation "Houston" Greek made this observation:

> There is the group that has grown up here together, like my
> husband and all his people. And this is what you really can't
> work yourself into, because you didn't grow up with these people
> and you can't share the memories and the times back, and they
> --you never will be included that much.

Several newcomers have expressed dissatisfaction and hurt at their lack

of acceptance here. One 2nd generation woman commented:

> We have been here more than a year, and not once has a Greek
> ever asked us over or anything. We go to the social hour
> after church, and you can just stand there and talk to your-
> self, because no one else is going to. Sure, they will say
> "Hi" occasionally, but I have as many total strangers say
> hi to me at the Galleria [shopping center] as the Greeks do.

This unhappy situation makes the Greek Festival a very important

element of the community, in that it helps foster parea between the

various social circles, which otherwise seldom get together socially.

Perhaps cooperation in the Festival is a beginning for a greater consoli-

cation of the Greek community.

The existence of feuding and close-knit groups to an extent negates

the actuality of intimacy and parea between all members of the community,

but the concept still remains intact; despite the community's hetero-

geneity, the dominant, ideal pattern of "closeness" between community

members remains. In other words, even though all members are not best

friends, they are closely bound by the essential unity of their "Greek-

ness" as it is expressed in group membership.

III. Necessary Elements of Greekness: The Social Boundaries of the
      Community

Members of Houston's Greek community have a very definite conception

of the attributes which differentiate them from outsiders. Those who fulfill these prerequisites are considered group members, and those who fail to do so are regarded as outsiders. What are these social boundaries of Greekness? Those elements which are considered diagnostic of group membership can be ascertained from the preceding discussion.

The social meanings of Greekness which have just been discussed define its social boundaries. Thus there are three necessary elements required of the individual who seeks membership in the Greek group-- these are being "of Greek blood", membership in the Greek Orthodox church, and participation in the Greek community. I will first discuss why cultural requirements are not diagnostic of group membership.

A. Cultural Greekness not required

Apparently the level of one's cultural "Greekness" does not significantly affect his group membership. This is a rather surprising conclusion, so the evidence for this claim should be examined. First of all, many community members do not live their lives in a "culturally Greek" way. For example, an important cultural element is the "close" family characterized by respect toward the father and other elders. Within the community there are several cases of divorce, and other families in which the wife "wears the pants". Or, considering other cultural patterns, some individuals may not especially like Greek food, and they do not serve it in their homes. There are also people who do not care for Greek music and dancing. Yet none of these people are considered "not Greek" because of their failure to follow Greek custom. Community members may comment on their performance of Greek roles--they may be judged "not very Greeky"--but they are not declared outsiders. Moreover, many individuals who are viewed as outsiders by the community

are "culturally Greek" in their personal lives. They may raise their
children in a traditionally Greek family, cook Greek food, and go Greek
dancing, but upholding Greek customs is not enough to insure their
membership in the community. For these reasons it is clear that
cultural Greekness is not a requirement for group membership, whereas
there are three other elements which are very definitely required.
These elements will now be considered.

B. Greek blood

"Blood" as a rule of Greek membership acts as both an exclusionary
and an inclusionary force. Non-Greeks cannot be true group members
because they are not "of Greek blood", and Greeks cannot escape their
Greekness, even if they leave the community and essentially become
"American". E.g., two 2nd generation girls made this comment:

> [What if a person wasn't involved in the religion, didn't
> have Greek friends, they weren't culturally Greek in their
> homes, say, they just decided to become American--would
> that person be Greek to you?]
> J: I think so because--
> S: They're from Greek blood, they're of Greek background.
> I wouldn't think of them as very Greeky, but--
> J: I'd consider them Greek.

The "Greekness" mentioned in these statements is more a biological than
a social phenomenon; one cannot be denied the heritage of his blood.
Thus the individual is always Greek in some sense through his blood, and
a non-Greek can never be Greek in quite the same way. For this reason,
non-Greeks who participate in the community are afforded the status of
"second-class citizens". Nevertheless, a non-Greek is in many cases
considered more a bona fide member of the community than a true biological Greek who has displayed his lack of identification with the community

by leaving the Greek church or ceasing to participate in Greek affairs. Therefore one should not overestimate the importance of "blood" in belonging to the community, for it is less diagnostic of membership than these other criteria.

C. Greek Orthodoxy

Of all the necessary elements of community membership, Greek Orthodoxy is the most crucial; the individual who leaves the church is no longer considered a member of the community. This is for two reasons, which reflect the dual nature of the Greek Orthodox Church as both a religious and a social organization. The individual in deciding to quit the church forsakes not only his faith and his heritage, but also his fellow Greek Orthodox, by rejecting a very important tie which binds them together and makes them "close".

The identification of Greekness and Greek Orthodoxy in the minds of community members, when carried to its logical conclusion, means that the individual who ceases to be Greek Orthodox also ceases to be Greek. Indeed, this is the conclusion which most people reach. That Orthodoxy is a prerequisite of "Greekness" is demonstrated in the following quote from a 2nd generation man and his American wife, who discussed people's responses upon learning that he was Greek.

> W: There's two kinds of people. The run-of-the-mill generally say, "Oh, do you go to the Athens Bar?" You meet a Greek person--"I've never seen you in church."
> H: Yeah, that's their first reaction. "How can you be Greek?"
> W: "How can you be Greek? I've never seen you in church."

Thus the Greekness of those who leave the church is highly questionable. Several instances in which people are no longer considered Greeks by virtue of their having left the church could be cited, but the following will provide sufficient example. The first excerpt is from a woman

whose husband's uncle had become Baptist; the second, a 3rd generation

boy whose cousin converted to Catholism.

> Technically, he's the head of the family, because his father's
> dead, and he's the oldest living male, outside of his uncle,
> but he's really sorta outside of the family, as far as being
> the head, because he doesn't go to the church and doesn't
> observe the traditions. So J's really considered the head
> of the family.

> A lot of people don't consider her Greek anymore, even though
> she is, really. It's because they associate Greek with being
> Greek Orthodox. Like let me give you an example—she had a
> small get-together one time, and she made some Greek-cuisine
> type things, and so some people were shocked that she actually
> did that, you know, and they said, "Oh, yeah, that's right,
> you did come from a Greek home!" Well, they didn't say it
> there—that's what it was.

There is a second reason why those who leave the church are no longer

considered members of the Greek group, however—this is because they

generally do not participate in community affairs. In many cases those

who leave the church do not intend to sever their ties with the community

—after all, they are still Greek "by blood", and many of their friends

are members of the community—but as they become involved in other

activities which replace the Greek church, they find it difficult to

maintain their Greek ties. This is especially true because active

participation in the Greek church is very time-consuming, and those who

work on church committees and projects have little time for other

activities outside the church. A 2nd generation man commented:

> We did go to some Greek dances, and stuff like that, and we
> did meet some Greek people that we liked, but it's hard for
> us to be good friends with any of the people that are really
> wrapped up in the Greek church because it's just too much of
> their life.

Thus for many people the break with the community comes through their leaving the church, as a 2nd generation man notes.

> [Do you know any people who may have left the church, but
> still participate in Greek affairs to any extent?]
> Umm--not really. I've known of some that have left the
> church, and I can't--I think that once they leave the church,
> they leave the community, too.
> [It seems that that's the big tie, and once that's broken--]
> Right, everything goes.

However, an individual need not be very active in the church to retain

community membership--one may attend services twice a year (or even

never) and still be considered "Greek" as long as he has not officially

left the church. A number of community members are active in the social

life of the community, but very seldom attend church. This type of

member will be discussed again in Chapter 7.

D. Social participation

Participation in the community has two facets--religious and social

--which are interrelated. It has been noted that participation in at

least one of these ways is essential for group membership, so the

significance of "participation" will be discussed only very briefly.

The individual expresses his sense of "closeness" to the community

through his participation in its activities. Thus those who take little

part are not "close" to the community, and are considered in a different

way than are bona fide members. E.g., a 2nd generation girl made this

remark:

> There's some kids who don't come around a lot. They're more
> at ease with Americans. Some people have not grown up close
> to the church and close to the community.

In her comments one senses that those who do not participate much are

distinguished from other Greeks. Indeed, one's not taking part in the

community may cause him to lose his membership--he may no longer be considered a "Greek". The same girl continued:

> There are some people who don't come to church so much. They
> have many more American friends, fewer Greek friends. Like
> the K family never had too much to do with church and other
> Greeks. The Greek thing wasn't too important to them. Irene
> K was married last week and I was at the church for something.
> I didn't know what was going on because I didn't know a lot
> of the people there. If it had been a real Greek wedding, I
> would have known almost everyone.

Social participation is therefore an important prerequisite for

community membership. However, this does not mean that the individual

must devote all his time to the community or remain unflagging in his

participation. Many individuals and families go through periods in which

their participation is very great, or quite limited, as a 2nd generation

woman pointed out.

> I think it depends a lot on what individual families are doing
> with their extra time and how involved they are in other things
> other than just the Greek church. And they all go through
> phases of this you know, they'll go for five years straight
> and everything's fine and all of a sudden you'll lose 'em.
> Well, you haven't lost 'em, they're gonna come back but they've
> gotten another added interest that's a very time consuming
> thing. ... That's something I think happens to a lot of
> people. Eventually they'll come back. They'll filter back
> into--of getting involved into the church situation a little
> more than maybe they have been in a certain period of time.

The important point is that such people have never really ceased to

identify with the community, for they are still members of the church.

The necessary elements of Greekness, then, are three--Greek blood,

Greek Orthodoxy, and participation in the community. Thus membership

is both ascribed and achieved, and neither qualification alone is

wholly sufficient. Those who are of Greek blood can lose their member-

ship in the Greek group by leaving the church and/or by failing to

participate in community affairs. Furthermore, those non-Greeks who join the church and take an active part in the community are still not considered full-fledged members because they are not of Greek blood. This is not to say that non-Greeks do not play a role in the Houston community, for there are several who are deeply involved in its concerns; in fact, they are virtually "Greek" in a social sense. However, an important distinction must be made between these non-Greeks and full-fledged members of the community who are of Greek blood. The Greeks themselves certainly make this distinction, and non-Greeks who have joined the community sense this. Rather than using the awkward term "full-fledged member of the community" constantly, I will continue to refer to "community members" to signify both Greek and non-Greek participants. But the reader should keep in mind that Americans who are "community members" do not have quite the same status as members "of Greek blood".

IV. Crossing the Social Boundaries of Greekness

How do Greek Americans (who call themselves "Greeks"), Greek immigrants (called "imports"), and non-Greeks (called "Americans") cross the social boundaries of Greekness? I.e., how do they become members of the Greek group, and how do they lose this membership?

A. Greek Americans

Greek Americans are born into the Greek community. Through their blood, they are members of the group. However, this does not mean that they cannot lose their membership by not participating in the community or by leaving the church.

Greek Americans who choose to stop participating generally do so because they find the community too limiting. In other words, the central aspect of the community which makes membership attractive to many people--its "closeness"--becomes the feature which drives them away--"clannishness" and narrowness. The same is sometimes true of those who leave the church as well; they reject the narrowness of the community, which is so intimately tied to the church that to escape the one, they must also leave the other. E.g., a woman commented on her 2nd generation sister-in-law:

> T has not been in the church for a long time. She went
> away just for the reasons that you say, that keep most of
> them there. She did not like the cliques, she did not like
> being part of a group. She well I guess--I know--you get
> to pretty well fit a mold, I think they wonder what's going
> on if you move a little bit this way or that way, too much,
> you know.

Furthermore, the several problems discussed in Chapter 2 which characterize the Greek Orthodox church--nationalism, the language problems, a serious "generation gap", and comparison with other American religions --sometimes cause individuals to leave the church. In doing so, the Greek American loses his community membership. One's membership is lost abruptly if he also ceases to participate in social affairs, more gradually if he tries to maintain his Greek ties, but it is inevitably lost nonetheless.

Those who leave the church or fail to participate in the community are no longer thought of as community members.

> [The P's--are they still Greek?]
> Well, how would we Greeks consider them? I, personally,
> because he left the church, to me--of course, he's still
> Greek, you know, you can't take that away from him--but
> I don't see him as a Greek, because he's not. He did that
> on his own, and because he left the church, I imagine this
> is the way he would want me to see him.

Despite their having left, they are still "Greek", as this 2nd generation woman pointed out. Even though such people may no longer be considered a part of the Greek "group" becuase of their failure to participate in the community, they are still considered, and still consider themselves, Greek, "of Greek blood". Thus one finds a rather confusing paradox in which an individual is in a sense always "Greek" because of his biological and cultural background, and yet may forfeit his membership in the Greek community. This paradox is expressed in the comments of a 2nd generation woman who discussed those rich Greeks who take little part in community affairs.

> [They obviously play a role in the community, but it's not
> a very participating one.]
> It's a financial one. ...   These are people that never really
> show up anyplace, but have the money. ... Maybe they don't
> have time. Who knows? They probably work late hours.
> [Are they Greek to you?]
> Oh yeah!
> [Are they part of the community to you?]
> Oh, no! [laughter] They're just very Greek. I don't consider
> them a part of the community just like I don't consider B [who
> left the church] a part of the community.

Similarly, a 2nd generation man commented on a fellow he no longer considered a member of the community.

> [What if someone were not in the church, or social circles,
> if they weren't very Greek in their home, but they still felt
> Greek--would Greeks say they were Greek?]
> I think most of them would feel they're Greek, and a good
> example I think would be E. If you ask me--I still say he's
> Greek. In another sense, I don't know if he's going to
> another church with his wife and children, but I still con-
> sider him Greek. Even though he doesn't participate. Except
> maybe he comes to the Festival, and he probably comes to church
> on Easter too. As far as I'm concerned, he is still Greek.

Those who have chosen to sever their ties with the Greek community are therefore still considered "Greek" because of their "blood". However,

their children, although of Greek descent biologically, are not truly
Greek because they have been raised away from Greek American society
and culture; the cultural aspect of "blood", being raised Greek, is
absent.

Although an individual has left the community, he may still
identify with his Greek background and his Greekness may remain a
significant part of his self-conception. One such person, a 2nd generation man who left the church, discussed the benefits of his Greek
identity.

> I guess the main thing is, it is a feeling you know about
> being Greek, which probably comes from--a lot of people don't
> know what Greeks are so you're an oddity. People are curious
> and everything so that makes you different. ... They're imme-
> diately interested in you--that's one way you like being a
> Greek because you're interesting, even if you're not an inter-
> esting person.

For this man, at least one of the benefits of a Greek heritage has been
kept after leaving the community: his self-conception as a Greek, which
gives him the status of an "interesting person", independent of group
membership.

B. Greek Greeks ("imports")

Members of the Greek community and "imports" who have recently come
from Greece generally consider each other almost as strangers. Although
there is a feeling of kinship because of their sense of shared "blood"
and common Greek Orthodoxy, each group regards the other with some degree
of suspicion and hostility. Greek Greeks are not immediately accepted
as full-fledged members of the Greek community despite their Greek "blood"
for two reasons. First, their cultural background is not really the
same as that of American Greeks, and because of this, they are actually

"strangers" to some extent. A 2nd generation man commented:

> In the last decade or so, there's a new Greek who's coming over
> now from Greece, who's quite different from us, who were here
> let's say with the concepts and thinking of the--the past couple
> of generations. ... The Greek customs that I have are usually
> the customs that my parents had in the past 30 or 40 years. So
> the Greek who comes from Greece now is really a different type
> of person. ... The earlier Greek came here, and he always
> looked for his Greek friends, to establish a Greek community,
> to identify with it. The new Greek that comes over is somewhat
> --he looks at the Greeks that are here, the second generation,
> he thinks that we're almost--<u>different</u> from him. So I think
> the reason he doesn't participate as much is maybe because he
> feels a certain amount of gulf between us. And eventually,
> after he's here a longer period of time, he does participate
> to some degree in the community affairs. But it's only after
> a certain amount of <u>wait</u>, and sometimes they don't ever come
> unless something big takes place, which is during the Greek
> Independence Day or Christmas or Easter, in church.

The major problem, however, lies in the differing views of the

Orthodox church held by Greek Americans and "imports". Early immigrants

from Greece attached themselves to the church with a fervor they never

felt in Greece, because in America the church became a reminder of home,

and, moreover, a social center for American Greek society. The immigrants

needed the church as an institution that bound them together and gave

them a sense of security in this strange land. The Greeks who are active

in the Greek Orthodox Church today are these original immigrants and

their descendants, who were raised within the Greek church and the Greek

society which revolves around it. Recent immigrants, however, come to

church for special holidays, weddings, and baptisms, but do not pay dues

or take part in other church activities; they probably comprise a

majority of the "sacramental members" discussed in Chapter 2. Most Greek

Americans view these people with disdain and dismay. A common reaction

was expressed by a 2nd generation woman:

> They're not involved in--they don't share in the expenses of
> the church, they come and go. They don't take an initiative,
> they don't take an active part in the life of the church, in
> the sharing of expenses, in sharing the workload. They don't
> --and yet, you see them out at the community center. They're
> not members of the church, and then when you stop 'em and ask
> 'em, you know, "You don't belong to the church, you don't
> belong to the GOCC, you're not a member, according to the
> laws--", "Well, we've just been over from Greece a couple
> of years, you know." Well, you have money to go and spend
> elsewhere, but you don't have $125 to become a member of your
> own church?

The response "We've just been over from Greece a couple of years"

reminds one of Nagata's findings in Toronto, that immigrants cannot

participate fully in the life of the ethnic community until they have

established themselves financially. This is surely one reason for the

Greek immigrants' apparent lack of interest in the church. Many of the

recent immigrants work at very demanding jobs--running restaurants, gas

stations, or other businesses--which leave them little time for any

outside activities, since their lives are not exactly 9:00 to 5:00. Of

course many are concerned with making a good living, and doing so

consumes most of their attention. A 3rd generation boy commented on

such people.

> They try to build themselves up, and a lot have. Usually
> you'll find them to be very industrious, and they'll kind
> of put aside their religious part of their life so that they
> could go ahead and make money and seem worldly and everything,
> and a lot have.

However, there are other factors at work as well. One of the central

reasons that Greek Greeks do not get involved in the American Greek

Church is because they actually did not attend church in Greece. A 3rd

generation girl made this observation:

> The only people that go to church in Greece are the real old
> ones, the little ladies in black, you know, a lady her husband

died at the age of 29, she wears black the rest of her life. They're the only ones that go to church.

One explanation for this lack of interest in the Church in Greece is that many people have had bad experiences with the Church. A 2nd generation man explained his understanding of this problem.

> They make poor community members as far as contribution-wise.
> ... I think they contribute very little. I think really the
> basic reason there is that the Church in Greece is not held in
> the esteem that we would hold our church--our church here. I
> think really they don't respect it because they hear stories
> about priests making money on the side, and are a bunch of
> money-grabbers and this kind of thing.

Their lack of participation in church life should not be taken as an indication that all the Greek Greeks are not religious, however, for their rejection of "the Church" does not necessarily mean that they have rejected God. The same man continued:

> Still these people still hold on to the old beliefs, where
> it's considered a sin to question anything religious. Not
> so much the priest for instance but certainly you have a fear
> of God and you don't want to do anything to make Him mad. I
> think they still want to believe. ... I think they've just
> been turned off by the church in Greece.

Several people indicated that Greek Greeks are "inherently" religious--even if they do not attend church often--and frequently cite their superstitions as proof that they are religiously oriented. This idea was expressed by a 3rd generation girl:

> People who are Greek and come over, they just have a kinda
> inherent religiousness. ... Like if something happens, they're
> very--they all wear their crosses and stuff like that. It
> doesn't seem that their morals are fantastic, but they just
> have like a--I don't know, something inside them. They just
> don't go regularly. ... Their kids are always baptized, and
> they always have godparents. Even if they don't come to
> communion and stuff like that. I mean, it's just unheard of
> not to have the kid baptized. Even though they don't go to
> church.

Nevertheless, many "imports" are not religiously inclined, as two 2nd

generation girls pointed out:

> R: They'll drop off their kids at Sunday school, and they
> have a place where they all meet--all men, play cards and
> have fun and talk, and then they pick up their kids from
> Sunday school and take them home. ... I remember C talking
> about that one time, saying "It's good for the kids while
> they're young." He thought we were kinda weird, still being
> in church and everything.
> M: You should graduate from religion, that's their point of
> view. After Sunday school, why go to church, you know? But
> for baptisms or weddings or funerals or something.

The reason that American Greeks find the behavior of the Greek

Greeks so difficult to understand is that the two groups are looking

at the church from different perspectives. The church is the Greek

Americans' primary tie to Greece, and they are vitally interested in

maintaining this bond, for they are not as certain as Greek Greeks are,

exactly what "being Greek" is all about. Thus they latch onto the

Greek Church, Greek social circles, and Greek language classes in an

effort to clarify and strengthen their identities as "Greeks". This

effort is not necessary for recent immigrants. They are better prepared

to enter an American way of life in that most are familiar with English

before they arrive, and have more education than the early immigrants;

in most cases, they come to America, not to make their fortune and

return to Greece, but to make America their home and take what it has

to offer. Furthermore, these immigrants, secure in their personal

identities as Greeks, do not need to cling to the Greek Church to prove

themselves "Greek". They view the church as a place to be married and

to have their children baptized, rather than as the center of their

social life. This casual attitude toward Greek church, customs, language, and culture is viewed with surprise and dismay by American

Greeks, who <u>need</u> these material aspects of "Greekness" to prove to

themselves and others that they are Greek.

Having such different conceptions of the Orthodox Church naturally

leads to tension between the two groups, and thus the major factor

barring Greek Greeks from full membership in the community is their

sporadic (at best) participation in--and support of--the church and its

programs. This tension is very evident in the comments of a 2nd genera-

tion couple:

> W: The Greek Greeks feel that their allegiance for the most
> part is still to Greece, they still plan eventually to go to
> Greece. Now many of them don't do that. They marry here, they
> raise children who become Greek Americans, and gradually they
> become--
> [Do you think the Greek Greeks participate much in the Greek
> American social circles?]
> W: They do to a certain extent, but not very much. Now when
> we were growing up, we were all basically Greek Greeks, and we
> were all the same. Our church was established so we could keep
> you know uhh the language, keep the religion, we all grew up,
> everybody knew everybody else. ... But gradually, as the
> community got larger, and after the war, more Greeks started
> coming over, that's when we first began to feel <u>different</u> from
> these people. ... And this was I think when we first started
> having this split, because during the war, people naturally
> weren't coming over, so we gradually became Americanized, and
> then of course when they came over, it was a different type of
> a feeling.
> H: I've noticed one thing though, that the Greek Greeks today
> don't support the church financially as the ones that are born
> over here. They'll go out of their way to support it, but the
> Greek Greeks--
> W: Many of them do not, that's true.
> H: And I don't know whether it's a training that they had in
> the old country, where all they did was just go in church and
> light a candle, do their blessings, and that was it. I don't
> know if that's their training. Here we're trying to teach our
> children to more or less--not to meet an obligation that's a
> <u>dues</u> or something, but to really contribute toward the church.

Those Greek Greeks who are willing to participate in the community are accepted into the group, however. Essentially, they become Greek

Americans, and are no longer considered imports, as a 3rd generation

girl pointed out.

> If someone participates, there's the possibility they're not
> really an import. That is what makes the distinction to me.
> [Do you think this is a common thing in a lot of people's minds?]
> Yeah. When they see that they're not just the part-time Greeks,
> I mean, church goers, and they get into things, then they seem
> to be more you know, people tend to think more of them.
> [Like E?]
> I don't know that I think that much more of him, but I just
> see him as being more stable. Therefore, he can't really be
> an import. ... And then they move from the import stage to
> being established. "Import" just means that they're real--
> they may work and stuff like that, but participation in any of
> these things is just kinda partial, they kind of just drift
> in and out. ... When they say, "He's not that Greek," I think
> the basis for that is how much they see 'em. Uhh, even though
> you may be an import and we don't see you that much at church,
> you're not that Greek. Like if you don't identify with Greeks.

In her statements one again finds the distinction between being Greek

both culturally and in personal self-conception, and yet not identifying

oneself as a member of the Greek community, measured by the extent of

one's participation. In this sense, Greek Greeks are undeniably Greek,

but not necessarily members of the Greek community.

C. Americans

Non-Greeks enter the Greek community through marriage to a Greek

and conversion to the Greek Orthodox religion. Either of these alone

is apparently not sufficient to qualify the individual for membership.

Those who are not engaged or married to a Greek, and elect to join the

church on their own initiative, are not regarded by the community as true

members; in general they are merely objects of curiosity. Similarly,

those who marry a Greek but fail to join the church are also considered

outsiders. Church membership is a very important element of acceptance into the community, as a 2nd generation man pointed out in discussing

American women who had married Greeks and joined the church.

> [It's interesting that these people amount to "Greeks",
> socially, and people don't think of them otherwise.]
> I don't think they do, I really don't. And I think this is
> true of about any non-Greek woman or--man, I was gonna say,
> there's not too many of those--I think once you join our
> church, you know, there it is, that tie. The tie, as long
> as you're a member of the church, you're three-fourths Greek,
> whether you're Greek or not.

This attitude is also reflected in the behavior described by a 2-3 genera-

tion boy whose uncle married an American.

> See, when we found out about the family, then Aunt T was
> baptized by my parents. She was Catholic until they found
> out, and then she wanted to be rebaptized in the Greek Ortho-
> dox faith.

In this case, his non-Greek aunt was Catholic "until they found out",

when it became necessary for her to join the Greek church. By becoming

a church member, one becomes "almost Greek", which is much more accept-

able to the Greek families involved than remaining an outsider.

But marriage and conversion are only the bare essentials, the sine

qua non, of membership; again a commitment to and identification with the

Greek community are required, reflected in participation which is at

least on a par with that of Greek Americans. E.g., a 3rd generation

girl made this observation about non-Greeks who marry in:

> See, like they just do it in the beginning for the parents
> and everything, they come around in the beginning, but then,
> you know, it's hard. ... If he tried or she tried, they
> could get into it, you know. I mean, if they tried long
> enough, sure, they can, but-- ... I think if you came to
> church every Sunday and you--I mean, they need people to help
> with everything, especially at Festival time, and if you get
> around, you get to know people, despite all the Greeky old
> ladies and everything.

The degree of participation required of an American for acceptance into

185

the community is generally much greater than that required of a Greek

American. One of the community's American women mentioned this:

> I've often wondered how these people felt about like N--I
> mean if anybody puts anything into the church, N puts twice
> as much. And she's not even--there's no way to get around it,
> she's just not Greek. And I wonder, I've often wondered how
> these people feel, sitting there watching her? Because she's
> really not in any way obligated to carry on the culture, it's
> because she feels she wants to do it. And the girls that are,
> they end up sitting back watching it. I think it's very tragic
> that you can't just be accepted without beating your brains
> out, you know. Maybe I'm on the lazy side, but I think I
> should--I think it would be nice if we all could just do our
> own thing and be liked. But apparently not. You have to prove
> yourself.

In other words, a non-Greek must "become Greek" religiously and

socially if he (or she) is to become a member of the community. The wife

of a 2nd generation man expressed regret over not having "become Greek":

> I haven't become Greek. I didn't learn to cook and I didn't
> learn the language, haven't been to church--didn't join the
> church. ... My brother-in-law married an American girl.
> They were married in the Greek church and everything. And
> his wife now has gone completely all the way to living the
> Greek life. She joined the Church, taught Sunday school,
> learning the language--she's doing it like it should be done.
> [It should be done that way?]
> I think it would be more complete like that. I feel that
> something was left out by me not going completely.

In the Houston community there are several people who, like her sister-

in-law, have "become Greek" by joining the church, participating in the

community, and faithfully following Greek traditions in their homes.

They do not take on a "Greek" self-conception, however; their identifi-

cation is with the community, as a participating member. A non-Greek

woman pointed this out:

> Several people, particularly lately--someone outside the
> community completely said something about, "Are you Greek?"
> ... And I said, "No, I'm Greek Orthodox." That's why I say
> basically it's a matter of religion. Certainly I'm not going

to be Greek because I married a Greek. I'll never be Greek,
of Greek descent, of Greek blood. There's no way, unless I
have a blood transfusion or something, you know! But I can
be Greek Orthodox. ... I feel a part of the Greek in quotations community here. But I can never say by any stretch
of the imagination that I'm Greek. There's no way that I
can be Greek. I say that my husband is of Greek descent.
... I guess that if I had to put myself with a particular
group, and some people never have a group to put themselves
with, then I would have to be identified with the Greek
community.

Despite active participation in the community, many non-Greeks sense

their status as second-class citizens. E.g., an American woman who is

active in the community remarked:

[I wonder if these people would ever get to the point where
they'd put it out of their minds that you were not Greek?]
No, I don't think so, because I heard somebody the other
day that made the comment that uhh "It's amazing the amount
of work that gets done by the Americans around here." But
you know I've often wondered too, if that would ever stop,
that "She's an American" first.

In her statements one hears a common complaint of non-Greeks who have

given much of their lives and themselves to the Greek community, and

have essentially "become Greek". They feel they have not been truly

accepted, and probably will never be. There is one major reason for

their being denied "full membership" in the community--they are not "of

Greek blood". A 3rd generation man engaged to an American discussed

this problem which his fiancee may face.

If people really want to get nasty about it, which a lot of
them will be, they'll never consider her Greek. I don't care
if she masters the language, masters the cooking, masters
every bit of the religion that you could think of, there's
still gonna be people who don't consider her Greek, because
she doesn't have true "Greek blood". I think they will feel
like she's infiltrating something that's theirs.

Virtually every American who participates in the Greek community expressed

feelings of being excluded because of not being Greek. Two non-Greek women:

> I've never been asked to teach Sunday school, although I'm
> always asked to teach Bible School. ... I know that one of
> the ladies was very hesitant about me even teaching--even
> my teaching Bible School. Because that--I was not Greek
> and could not pass on the customs, the Greek customs to
> them.
>
> For a long time I thought that it was me. Maybe I'm too shy.
> I really am sorta shy. I don't come on like gangbusters
> around the Greeks, especially around the women. And I think
> had it not--if it were really important for me--to me to
> really be a part of that whole scene, I'd probably really
> suffer. But it's not important to me. If they like me,
> fine. I want to do what I can in the church. ... There
> are several girls I've met up there that I've said, "Now,
> if I were a Greek girl, that would be the girl I'd pick to
> really be friends with," but since I'm not, she'll always
> be nice to me, but it will always be at arm's length. And
> I'm just not gonna worry myself with it. ... I really do
> feel that there's a big awareness that I'm not Greek among
> the women.

Because of their not being "of Greek blood", non-Greeks are always

to some extent "outsiders", and are frequently treated as such. As dis-

cussed in Chapter 1, ethnic groups may maintain the boundaries which

separate them from the outside world by keeping outsiders "in their

place", and treating them like "strangers". My experiences as an

"American" participating extensively in the community corroborate the

statements of non-Greeks who felt that real barriers were placed between

community members and themselves as "outsiders". For example, the Greek

language was often used when English easily could have been, which serves

as a constant reminder of one's status as an Αμερικανίδα (Americanida).

Many community members were definitely distant, and I soon became per-

sonally familiar with the frequently-expressed feeling of being invisible

when at a public gathering. Furthermore, many people were friendly on a

superficial "How are you?" level, but invitations to private gatherings or into homes were virtually nonexistent. When forcefully faced with the reality of one's "outsider" status day after day, those who are not deeply committed to community membership might decide to leave the group without a second thought, for the advantages offered by group membership do not seem worth the pain.

There is also a second, related reason for this sense of exclusion, however. Greeks may consciously place barriers between themselves and non-Greeks, but as discussed in an earlier section, much of their "exclusiveness" results from the strong and extensive social ties they have with each other, which are not necessarily shared with "outsiders". Again I will quote American women who have married Greeks and joined the community.

> I have a great sense of not being Greek. Some non-Greeks
> don't seem to have this, but I have a great sense of not
> being Greek.
> [Do you feel like you're accepted by the Greek people?]
> Well, I definitely don't feel like I'm just one of the girls.
> You know, I've never--and some of that could be my fault. ...
> Say I were a Greek girl and maybe my mother had been--well,
> say L's mother was my mother or something. Well, I'm sure
> I would be invited to luncheons and Greek parties, and we'd
> be invited to a lot of open houses, things that we're not
> invited to, because they don't know me, and they've got their
> own old friends. And I think a lot of the Greek girls--and
> they've always been nothing but nice to me, but uhh--I think
> they've got their own little cliques, their own little groups,
> and they're not gonna rush out and--and I'd probably be the
> same way. But I am always slightly aware of that difference
> there, for some reason.
>
> This one friend of mine--she's constantly battling the Greeks,
> she's constantly trying to say, "Why can't they like me?" and
> I told her, "I think the best way of surviving and getting
> along is taking everything at face value. When they say,
> 'Good morning, how are you?', everything's great." And I
> said, "Don't sit there and say to yourself, 'Well, why is
> she doing that? just because--'. Don't! Don't do that,
> because you can do that the rest of your days and never get
> anywhere." I mean, I'm gonna take it as I'm accepted. ...

> Sometimes you feel like, "Well, gee, why do I ever come here?"
> Because you go to some social event, and you feel very excluded,
> you feel like you're standing on the outside looking in, but
> again, I'm just gonna take it day by day, you know. I don't
> want to have to look ahead and say. "Gee, what's it gonna be
> like twenty years from now? If it's just like right now, what's
> the sense of staying, if I don't have any more friends than I
> have now?" So I just keep going on.

The basic insecurity we find in these comments was even more forcefully

expressed by another American woman:

> There's one thing--I've often wondered what would happen, like
> if something happened to K [her husband], what would happen to
> me and the children? ... A lot of his business is done with
> Greeks. He has enough faith that they would maintain that
> business with me, out of loyalty to him. Well, I really--I
> believe otherwise. ... I would be interested to know how
> other people felt on that, you know, how they really and
> truly feel about me and the children. Would they be "Americans"
> then. Because they're Greek kids now. Because just think of
> what a radical change it would be for my children. I mean,
> their whole life would dissolve if we were turned out like
> that. I guess I really don't feel that secure.

Even though these Americans are probably not fully accepted, their

children can become full-fledged members of the community; as this

American woman said, "They're Greek kids now." In fact it is sometimes

for the sake of their children that non-Greeks remain active in the

community, despite their sense of rejection. They want their children

to be able to have the very sense of community and security which is

denied to them.

> Such a tight little world they're in! ... I want to be able
> to carry the security over to another group, and not be you
> know in the shadow. I envy them having this, and I want them
> to have it. So I guess I push it even more, that may be one
> reason why I do.

Furthermore, they feel that it will be beneficial to their children to

be raised with ethnic traditions.

> I like the Greek community for another reason--is, something

> on the positive side--I mean, I find negative sides, but on the
> positive side is--there was very little tradition in our home,
> very little to look back on, that "We did this and this and
> this" as a child. I find, with the community, being very
> closely related to the church, we have more functions and
> things that the children will look back on, like Easter. I
> mean, Easter is a time in the Protestant church when you dress
> up and the Easter rabbit comes. But with our children, it's
> the meal after fasting, it's the breaking of the eggs, you
> know, see who's gonna be the winner. And there's a lot of
> things there that I think the children will carry with them
> as happy memories. ... I'll encourage them, to keep them close.
> I guess in the long run, I like that closeness feeling. And
> I would like for the children to be very close. And I think
> they'll be better off as adults--like I said, I'd like for
> the children to look back and see these traditions and things
> that we did, these customs and the fun that they had. Well,
> I'd like to see them keep that in their families, so that they
> will stay within you know the community.

Such a child may find "membership" a little more difficult than "full-

blooded" Greek children, but he can at least fulfill the qualifications

which his American parent could not, in that he is "of Greek blood", will

likely be raised in the community, and may even be "raised Greek".

In the case of children who are "half Greek", the principle of

"blood" can be helpful as well as detrimental. Although some people

may never forget that these individuals are "only half Greek", the fact

that they are partially "of Greek blood" insures their right to claim

Greek identity. While discussing feelings of racial superiority among

Greeks, a 2nd generation man implied this.

> They [Greek people] have a feeling that they're almost--
> their blood is different, their blood is Greek. For example,
> I would listen to my father talk about some people that are
> here, and they would be maybe partially Greek, and so forth,
> and he would say, "Well, there's Greek blood running in his
> veins!" So he's partially Greek, or "Part of his blood is
> Greek, so he has something of Greek in him."

Equally important for the membership status of the "half Greek" are the

more cultural and social connotations of Greek "blood"--he has been "raised Greek", for he has grown up within the community and has been introduced to Greek American customs and ideals. Those children who have been raised in the community alongside the children who are full-blooded Greeks generally do not find acceptance to be a problem. E.g., a non-Greek mother expressed her hopes in this way:

> I'm hoping that they will enmesh and become a part of this [community togetherness]--as these children grow up, together. [Do you think this will happen?]
> I think so, now that they're in--I have seen a difference since they started going to Greek school. Now when they weren't in Greek school, there was nothing. They didn't like Sunday school, or anything, because they were not included. They were kinda outsiders of the Sunday school group. And now they're the insiders. There's very few people who refer to them as "Americans" now. There's still a few that hold on to it, but then they'll hold on to it until.

On the other hand, the children who have not been encouraged to participate in the extensive round of Greek activities--church, language classes, Sunday school, GOYA, Sons and Maids, etc.--have a more diffi-cult time fitting into Greek circles. Of course this would be true of one hundred percent Greek children as well. Nevertheless, the child of an intermarriage is somewhat more likely to avoid exclusively Greek activities for two reasons. First, through his non-Greek parent he is introduced to non-Greek influences in family, friends, and values. Furthermore, his Greek parent may be less traditionally Greek than many Greek Americans, or he would not have married a non-Greek in the first place. These problems of community acceptance are well-illustrated in the comments of a non-Greek mother:

> [Well, are your children Greek?]
> They're Greek Orthodox but I don't think they're necessarily Greek. J and I both feel they should have their own person-alities--be individuals. So we haven't forced them to take part in just Greek functions. In fact, my daughter says the

Greeks are very <u>rude</u> people lots of times--I think this is
since she has dated "outsiders". Really I guess she's kinda
considered an outsider herself.

For a non-Greek spouse to be accepted into the Greek group is thus
a matter of taking part and working hard in community activities; if she
(or he) raises her children as Greek, they will be able to enjoy full
membership in the group. The importance of extensive participation in
the community was noted by a 3rd generation man engaged to a non-Greek:

> There's a relative of my mother's that married an American
> girl, and when she speaks of that lady, she always calls her
> <u>Americanida</u>.
> [Are their children accepted as Greeks?]
> I don't really think so. Now they never come to church, the
> wife and kids never do. He comes very rarely, perhaps on
> holidays. Easter, Christmas, maybe his name day. ... I think
> the big thing about it is--if you marry someone who's not
> Greek, and that person doesn't get involved, and gets to know
> everyone, you know--she'd probably have to push a little more
> to win people over. If she didn't do that, I think they might
> be cruel. She's gonna have to work that much harder because
> she's not Greek to kinda quote, win their respect.

V. Discussion

The findings reported in this chapter call into question several
basic assumptions and theories one finds in the literature on ethnic
groups. For example, it is generally assumed that assimilation of any
group begins in earnest when large-scale immigration from "the old
country" ends. This idea is based on the commonly-held assumption that
an influx of newly-arrived immigrants plays an important role in maintaining the "ethnic" quality of the community. A steady flow of immigrants from Greece supposedly should encourage the maintenance of Greek
traditions, values, and patterns in the Houston Greek community, but
this is not necessarily the case. "Imports" have limited impact on the

community, because they actually have little interaction with community members; the assumed pattern in which newcomers immediately search out members of their ethnic group and are welcomed with open arms by the ethnic community does not apply in Houston. In fact, there are actually two distinct groupings--those who are associated with the Greek American community, which is centered around the church, and those who associate primarily with "imports", whose community to a large extent revolves around Greek restaurants and night clubs. Why do the recent immigrants have so little impact on the Greekness of the community? For one thing, Greek Americans and Greeks are not really similar in cultural patterns-- with attitudes toward the Greek church providing the most obvious example --and they view each other as strangers. It is not until Greek Greeks have made a firm commitment to the community and adopted Greek American patterns of church affiliation and community participation that they are accepted as community members. Even when they have joined the community, however, they continue to socialize primarily with other recent arrivals, and thus their influence on the community--with the possible exception of encouraging the speaking of Greek--is minimal.

A second assumption is that unique cultural elements are a defining aspect of ethnic-group life in America and that their passing is a sign of imminent assimilation. Whereas I would not want to deny the signifi- cance of distinctive cultural patterns among American ethnic groups, the situation which exists in the Greek community of Houston indicates that in many cases cultural criteria are not particularly diagnostic of group membership: many people who are culturally "Greek" are not considered group members, and others who are members are not very Greek. This finding lends support to Barth's view of the ethnic group as a predominantly social rather than cultural phenomenon.

Furthermore, the Greek group as reflected in Houston's community is a more flexible and viable entity than one usually sees portrayed in the literature on ethnic groups. The common view is that groups are gradually being decimated by assimilation, the desertion of members to American society and culture. It is undeniably true that some individuals are "lost", but it is also true that non-Greeks enter the community upon marriage to Greeks. This further challenges the assumption that intermarriage invariably results in the loss of members for an ethnic group, for in many cases non-Greek spouses essentially "become Greek", and their half-Greek children are accepted as full-fledged community members. Therefore intermarriage does not necessarily destroy the ethnic group.

However, there is a basic problem here which may have a significant effect on the future of the Greek ethnic group; most Greeks in the Houston community are basically very hesitant about accepting outsiders, a fact which is quite evident to non-Greek members. One wonders how long such individuals can cope with the feeling of being second-class members of a group which they have chosen to be a part of--as one woman said, "What's it gonna be like twenty years from now?" Surely this question plagues many of the Americans who have married into the community, and makes it difficult for some to remain in the group. This may place the future of the group in jeopardy since marriage to non-Greeks is not uncommon, and thus some number of American spouses must join the community to replace those Greeks who for one reason or another sever their ties with the group.

The ways in which community members act to preserve the group--primarily through preventing intermarriage--will be considered in Chapter 6. The "Greek" element of individual self-conceptions provides the topic of the next chapter.

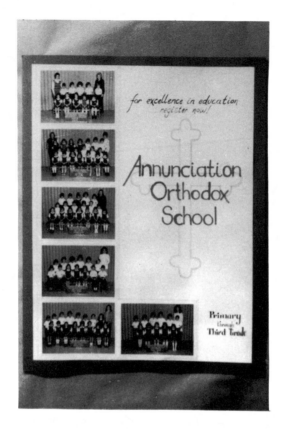

Display, Annunciation School benefit dinner

Young adults' Lenten retreat

Dancing, a wedding reception

Cyprus Day

THE 20,000 GREEK CYPRIOT REFUGEES
ARE HUNGRY, COLD AND LACK MEDICAL
ATTENTION. THEY HAVE SEEN THEIR CHILDREN
AND FAMILES MURDERED. THEY HAVE SEEN
TEIR WIVES, SISTERS AND DAUGHTERS RAPED BY
THE TURKISH BARBARIANS.
THEY TURN THEIR EYES TOWARD THAT
HOPE WHICH IS YOU. ONLY YOU CAN
RESTORE THEIR DYING BELIEF IN
JUSTICE AND FREEDOM.

Trio Bel Canto at the Dionysos

Bellydancer at the Bachanal

SPECIAL EVENTS

CHAPTER 5

GREEK SELF-CONCEPTIONS

Throughout the previous chapter on membership in the Greek community
the distinction was made between one's self-conception as a Greek and
his identifying with, and being identified as a member of, the community.
Although usually related, these identifications also exist independently
of one another; this was noted in each of the three cases discussed. It
is doubtful that the self-conceptions of Americans who identify themselves as community members have "Greek" elements. Similarly, Greek
Americans who leave the community and imports who choose to remain outside of it can still have a high level of personal identification as
Greeks, even though they do not identify themselves as members of the
community. Nevertheless, these two facets of ethnic identification
generally go hand-in-hand. Membership in the community in most cases
causes one's Greekness to be a very salient aspect of his self-conception, and the individual who has a strong conception of himself as a
"Greek" will usually remain within the Greek community. The major focus
of this work is on ethnic-group membership, and those forces which
encourage it. Previous chapters have discussed membership in the Greek
community, and Chapter 6 will examine those forces which encourage the
individual Greek to affiliate himself with the local Greek community.
One of the most precipitous of these is his personal conception of
himself as a "Greek"; thus this chapter will discuss the Greek element
of self-conceptions. I will first examine its several components and
then consider the factors which influence the individual's "Greek"

self-conception--church, family, and the larger "American" society.
The final section will discuss the flexibility of an individual's self-
conception, which at times may be more or less "Greek".

I. Components

An ethnic self-conception is a very complex thing, and sorting out
its many facets is difficult, since it is an intricate blending of many
disparate elements. Nevertheless, I shall briefly discuss some of the
more prominent elements of a "Greek" self-conception as it is found
among Houston's Greek Americans. Two historical sources of pride in
one's Greek identity--ancient and modern Greece--will be examined, as
well as the aspect of "racial superiority" which for some Greeks results
from this history. A very significant topic which must also be considered is the "American" component of a Greek American's self-conception,
as well as the role comparison of himself as a Greek to members of other
ethnic groups in America plays in his self-conception. Finally, I will
discuss the influence of the "Zorba" stereotype most Americans hold of
Greeks on the Greek American's self-conception and behavior.

A. Sources: Ancient and modern Greece

The pride which Greeks feel for their heritage from ancient Greece
is obvious; there is little point in reiterating here the accomplishments of ancient Greek civilization in philosophy, science, mathematics,
drama, poetry, and government. I will only cite the statement of a 2nd
generation man about his feelings about this heritage:

>[How do you feel about your Greek identity?]
>To me, I think it's an asset, I really do. In my work now,
>a lot of the teachers joke about Greek and everything, but

> they can't help but remember that Greece was the birthplace
> of democracy, the ancient Greek civilization and everything.
> ... I say it jokingly a lot of times, but it's one thing that
> you have to remember--the Greek civilization <u>was</u> great. Just
> like in the field of mathematics. When the students are
> reading history of math, up pops Archimedes and I tell them,
> "O.K., there's another Greek!" The class will laugh, but they
> realize that here's another famous Greek mathemetician.

A sense of pride in such brilliant and august forebears is very

understandable, but Greek Americans also find the Greek Revolution of

1821 and resistance efforts during World Wars I and II true sources of

pride in the democratic traditions of Greece.[1] They are proud of the

courage, determination, and tenacity with which Greeks resisted first

the Turks during their 400 years of oppression, and then the Germans

in World War I and the Axis powers in World War II. A 2nd generation

woman related a story which demonstrates this pride in the Greek spirit

of resistance. There is a group of Greek people from a certain area of

Asia Minor, around Pontus, who during the Turkish rule were forbidden

to speak Greek; they continued to do so, and their tongues were cut out

as a final measure to stop the Greek language. They continued to speak

as best they could, however, shouting "Ἑλλας ζεί" ("Greece lives"),

which came out "λα ζεί (<u>la zee</u>)" and so they became known as Lazi.

She commented that the people living in this area today still speak a

strange dialect of Greek, which shows how courageous and determined

Greeks can be. Furthermore, October 28 is a national festival in

Greece, Ochi Day, which commemorates the day in 1940 when the Greek

dictator Metaxas refused to allow the Italian army to enter Greece,

telling Mussolini's minister "Ὀχι! (No!)". A young 3rd generation man

explained to me how he had come to be interested in his Greekness, which had been insignificant to him until the following incident occurred.

> When I went to Greece, there was a priest there. ... I was
> really not too--not really excited about the country. I
> got the impression that the Greeks had nothing to offer in
> like two or three hundred years. I mean, I couldn't see
> what they'd done. He took me aside and told me about the
> Revolution, he told me about World War I, he told me about
> World War II--things that'd never been brought up to me
> before. All that's been brought up to me you know, on the
> home front, is ancient Greece. That's thousands of years
> ago--how long are they gonna live on that? But just that
> one talk, and it was such a change. I just walked out of
> there with a different attitude. It only lasted half an
> hour--he was really berating me because--really upset with
> me--"You have a culture that's something to be proud of, and
> you should take part in it."

B. Racial superiority

These sources of pride foster a feeling of racial superiority among

some Greeks. A 2nd generation man described this attitude: "Many

Greeks feel that they are inherently superior to any other kind of

people--the glory of the Greek civilization and all that!" A 2nd

generation woman commented:

> Growing up, in Greek school we had these old-fashioned Greek
> teachers that would tell us that--the Greek hero. In other
> words, we thought that Greeks were super-human. ... I thought
> that my father was the strongest man in the world too, because
> after all, he was my father and he was a Greek. Others were
> not as good as the Greeks. ... And we grew up thinking that
> all the other groups were just inferior to us, and as we grew
> older, we began to realize that this wasn't exactly so.

Of course, the proportion of Greek Americans which advocates this atti-

tude of racial superiority is not large and growing smaller. For many

Greeks--particularly the younger generation--the idea of inherent

superiority is a source of great embarrassment. While discussing having

to turn down dates with non-Greeks, a 2nd generation girl said:

> A boy will call you up to go out, "Why can't you go out with
> me?" "But you're not Greek." You know, that really puts you

in a tough spot. That's kinda embarrassing, to act like you
think you're superior, it's not that. No, you don't think
you're superior, but it's your parents. But if you don't say
it right, people will think, get that impression that you
think you're better--a superior race. I was taking this
psychology quiz, and it talked about ethnocentricity, it was
A-B-C-D, and one was "a minority group that thinks they are
superior to others," or something, and when I saw it I just
died laughing, because that's what people think. Well, you
really don't. It was funny at the time, if you've gone through
what we've gone through.

Many young people complain about their parents' or grandparents' narrow

view that "Greeks are the very best!", but a common reaction is probably

that expressed by a 2nd generation girl:

My father always drummed it into us, "Greeks are best" and
all this. You don't believe it when he tells you, but then
you kinda accept it deep down inside, you're kinda proud of
what they've done.

It is probably natural for any national, ethnic, or social-class

group to feel that its customs are best, that its members are actually

superior to the members of other groups, so the attitudes of superiority

among Greeks should not be overemphasized. Nevertheless, because of their

lengthy and illustrious history, Greeks may fall into a conception of

racial superiority more easily and more frequently than do the members

of other ethnic groups. This feeling of superiority is also related to

a third important aspect of a Greek self-conception, comparisons of

oneself as a "Greek" with members of other groups.

C. Comparisons with other groups

A 2nd generation man, in discussing how strict parents were when

his generation was dating, made this statement:

This is something that's strong--now, how strong it is with
the 1st generations coming over now, I don't know. I know
the 2nd generation, it's not. It's uhh, I know they're uhh--

they are dating. If not with Greeks, even with uhh--other uhh--yeah, you know.

This incident is an example of what was a common occurrence throughout the course of my research: people began sentences quite naturally, and then toward the end fumbled around for words to use instead of saying "American". They did this to avoid embarrassing me, since I am an "American" and might not understand why they did not call themselves "Americans" also. To some extent this phrase merely denotes group memberships; they as Greek Americans call themselves "Greeks", and those who are not "Greeks" are "Americans". There are other connotations to the label of "American", however, which are probably one source of the embarrassment some Greeks felt in talking about "Americans" with me.

1. American universe

Before considering the connotations of the term "American", I should perhaps first define exactly to whom it refers. Are all Americans who are not of Greek ancestry "American"? Three 2nd generation women discussed this question, and their response was typical of most Greeks' conception of how the American "universe" is divided up.

> [What groups are there besides Greeks? Are "Americans" WASPs or what?]
> G: Blacks are μαῦροι (mavri). Jewish, it doesn't apply. Jewish are different. Americans are different. Blacks are different.
> N: Do you think Catholics too?
> P: No.
> G: Catholics are American too. Maybe like someone who's Italian, whose parents are from Italy, she's born here, or someone from France, or you're from Germany, you're German, first generation like I am, you're considered German.
> P: Not to that extent though.
> G: Yeah, they're considered American. They're more American. But Jews are considered not--

```
P:   "Jewish"
N:   Not American--
G:   Hebrew, kinda, Jewish.
[Mexicans?]
G:   They're not Americans.  Well, they are Americans, but we
don't consider them--
[So Americans are Catholics and Protestants?]
P,G,N:  Wasps and Catholics, unless they're Mexican or black
or Jewish.
```

Thus "Americans" are mainly WASPs. Catholics are also included in this category, but with less certainty; those who are really "ethnic" may form intermediate groups of their own, rather than being "Americans". Jews are most definitely not "Americans", I suspect primarily because they are not Christians, and because they represent the epitome of what ethnic groups are about. The Greek language term for blacks--οἱ μαῦροι (i mavri)--is used more frequently than any English word, such as Negro, colored, or black. The term ὁ μαῦρος (o mavros) means, quite literally, "black". Blacks are not "Americans" to some extent because of their skin color, but the fact that Mexicans are not considered "American" or "ethnic" tends to imply that both blacks and Mexicans are judged as "not American" primarily because of their lower-class reputation. Greeks around the country would all surely judge mavri as "not Americans", but Mexicans outside the Southwest--in areas where they are not a highly visible, predominantly lower-class group--would perhaps be considered "ethnic" rather than a group to themselves, as blacks are judged.

How do Greeks rank these groups which together constitute the American group? Greeks are obviously on the top of the heap, and the other groups are ranked in the following manner when the issue at hand is primarily one of social status, how an individual's worth is judged by his group membership:

1. "Americans";
2. Jews;
3. ethnics;
4. Mexicans; and
5. blacks (mavri)

On the other hand, if the main concern is a more personal issue such as family structure, social behavior and so on, the ranking is rearranged somewhat, according to how similar the Greeks perceive the group to be to themselves. In this case, Americans must drop down to third, and Jews and other ethnics each move up a step. With this brief introduction to the meaning of "American" and to those groups which are seen to be in juxtaposition to "Americans", I will now turn to a consideration of how these several groups are viewed by Greeks, how the terms naming them are used, and what the connotations of these terms are.

2. "Americans"

In many cases the word "American" is used in a purely descriptive sense, as a way of denoting that the person being discussed is not of Greek descent: if a stranger shows up in church, people wonder if he is Greek or "American". Thus the term in such situations is merely a substitute for the more awkward term "non-Greek". The origin of this terminology is fairly certain; it can be traced back to the first generation of Greeks in America, who quite logically dichotomized their world into "Greeks" and "Americans", "we" and "they", the familiar patrioti who spoke their language and the strangers who spoke a foreign tongue, English. These immigrants did not really consider themselves Americans, and those who are still living today probably continue to identify themselves more with Greece than with America.

This is not necessarily the case with their children and grand-children, who were raised in the United States and have in most cases known no other home than America. Using the term "Americans" which has been inherited from the older generation comes naturally to the 2nd and 3rd generations, but they are not really comfortable with the implied dichotomy which opposes "Greek" and "American", for they identify themselves as Americans (but not "Americans", keeping in mind the distinction made earlier). Thus using the term "American" as a contrast to "Greek" causes some degree of discomfort among members of younger generations. This feeling of confusion was expressed by a 2nd generation man:

> I keep--you know, that's one thing that's always bothered me. We're always doing this, saying "Is he going out with an American girl?" And all the time I'm thinking, "I'm an American, why do I say 'that American girl'?"

The sense of discomfort is more acute when one slips up and uses the term in front of "Americans", who do not understand why 2nd and 3rd genera-tion Greeks do not call themselves "Americans", not realizing that they actually do consider themselves Americans, and are only using the term to differentiate themselves from non-Greeks. A 2nd generation girl pointed out this problem:

> It comes naturally to us. But when we're talking like to you for instance, I feel funny saying it, like when we talk to other people about Greeks and Americans, I'll call myself Greek and refer to the other person as American, without wanting it deliberately. It just comes out, and I'm worried that the other people might think that "Who does she think she is?" You know? T [a non-Greek who is dating a Greek boy] says that it makes her mad to hear people say that, and I can understand why, because we're all Americans, we've got Greek blood in us, I mean heritage in us, but we're not Greeks. I tend to use that term a lot, but I feel funny about it.

In such situations, there is also the additional problem that in many cases the expression "American" does not have a neutral connotation, but rather a derogatory one. When used derogatorily, the term alludes to all that Greeks view as inferior in American culture. E.g., a young 3rd generation man explained his understanding of the connotation of "American".

> I use it every now and then. Most of the time I'm kidding about it. But a lot of people say it, "He's an American," meaning he's a nobody.
> [What connotation does it have? Sometimes it seems to mean a creep or something.]
> I can see how it would be used in that fashion and in fact I'm sure I've used it myself. You want to say something about someone and you really can't say it--like "He's an American, doesn't that prove it?"
> [What does it mean though?]
> I think that would depend on what you were talking about when you said it. Like if you said "He didn't show much compassion for J when he fell off the bike," "Well, he's American, what do you expect?" That would be in a derogatory sense. It's kind of a general catch-all when you want to say something nasty about someone if they are not Greek. "He's an American, what do you expect?"

In the example he cites, an American is viewed as cold, not "compassionate". Indeed, coldness is one characteristic which Greeks frequently attribute to "Americans". The Greek norm is warmth, expressiveness, spontaneity, and emotionalism, and "American" reserve is seen as "cold" lack of emotion, where as "Americans" would tend to view Greeks as "unstable" people who cannot control themselves. A 2-3 generation man expressed this conception of "Americans":

> I don't know why, but maybe it's because of the way I was brought up--but I see that in a way maybe I do have a prejudice in a way, because I see that in Americans--like they'll go to parties and couples will get "Oh, honey" and they'll hug each other, but to me it looks all phoney or plastic. It seems that the people--now you're bringing out the real prejudice--you hit it!--I think Greek people are usually

warmer than Americans. I believe that, a whole lot. ...
When I see people hug each other or say goodbye, or something, to me it's kind of cold. I get this cold feeling.
Whereas Greeks to me are somewhat more emotional and
warmer.

Similarly, two 2nd generation girls noted that Greeks are much livelier

and warmer than Americans:

G: And really, a lot of the Greek kids...they're so much
livelier, so much--
D: More zing to them--
G: Yeah, really they do have more zing. Like when you're at
a party at school or something--
D: They do, really. ... They just get--like soul dancers--
they just really feel it, and they're out there Greek dancing,
and it's just like the sailors at Athens Bar. You can really
see that they are enjoying their dancing, or whatever it is.
G: Or if you go to a big Greek party, and everybody's
slightly drunk, and you compare it to a party, like I went to
at school, where everybody was still slightly drunk--but still,
there's so much more warmth at a Greek thing--people will just
go up and kiss each other and laugh. And at an American party
you just don't do that.
D: It's more formal I think.
G: You just don't go and kiss somebody. ... There's that
vitality there that's not quite fully at another kind of party.

A 2nd generation college girl commented on the connotations of the term

"Americans" and revealed another facet of the Greek conception.

[Does "American" have bad connotations?]
Maybe for Greek Greeks. No, even some first generations. Not
us, but our parents. Like "What did you expect? He's American."
For a Greek boy to marry an American girl, he's not going to be
happy with her. If he married a Greek girl, he'd be happier,
she's a better housekeeper. They tend to generalize. It's
kinda embarrassing saying this, because it's such a closed-
minded view, and you don't want people to think that Greeks
are--think that way. I don't think people our age--we are
more open-minded. When I say it, I mean non-Greek, non-Orthodox, I don't mean it as an inferior type of person or anything.
It's easier to identify, you're not Greek.

A Greek boy who marries an American is "not going to be happy", in

particular because Greeks are better housekeepers, but in general be-

cause Americans are inferior to Greeks. This feeling is apparent in the

comments of another young woman, of the 2-3 generation, who noted a
Greek language equivalent of the expression "American".

> The first thing, if you say you're engaged, they'll go,
> "Well, she married ὁ ξένος [o xenos]," that's what
> they'd call him, a stranger. I guess that's better than
> "barbarian", that's what the early Greeks used to...same
> connotation, just about, though.

In general, then, it appears that the use of the term "American" frequently carries with it an implication of American inferiority, and Greek
superiority. This is of course not to say that all Greeks use the
expression in this sense, for many use it in the merely denotative sense
of "non-Greek", with no bad connotations. Nevertheless, everyone understands the implications when the term is used in a derogatory sense.
Thus an important element of the self-conceptions of many Greeks is the
invidious comparison of themselves as Greeks with "Americans". It
appears that one's identity as "a Greek" is often based on contrast
with a fictional image of "the American", who in reality does not exist.
This process operates vis-a-vis other ethnic groups as well.

   3. Other "ethnics" and Jews

   Houston's Greeks have had little contact with other ethnics, for
the population of Houston is not characterized by large or noticeable
ethnic groupings, aside from blacks, Mexicans, and perhaps Jews. Thus,
although they would admit that "other ethnics" is probably a significant
division of American society, they themselves have not had much experience with Italians, Poles, or Germans. These groups are considered to
be basically the same sort of people as Greeks--ethnics who also have
"close" families and are loyal to their religions and old country
customs.

This also describes their evaluation of Jews, with one important

exception. Jews are considered wealthy and successful, characteristics

which Greeks also attribute to themselves. Therefore Jews, perhaps more

than any other group, are considered to be like Greeks. Of course

Greeks still express negative stereotypes of Jews, and consider their

own religion, heritage, and customs superior to Jewish ones. Neverthe-

less, of the visible groups in the Houston area--"Americans", blacks,

Mexicans, and Jews--Jews are considered the most similar to Greeks.

4. Mexicans and blacks

In general, Mexicans and blacks are looked down on and considered

inferior to Greeks. E.g., a 2nd generation woman discussed how Greeks

feel when they are mistaken for Mexicans.

> I think they feel insulted that you would think that they
> were Mexican. ... I think if someone told me that when I
> was a teenager I would have felt insulted. If somebody [a
> Mexican] at school maybe - a kid - a boy would flirt with
> me and I'd think "Well who do you think you are flirting
> with me?" This is terrible. ... Well I guess we think we're
> actually better than the Mexican people--that's what it
> boils down to.

Another 2nd generation woman commented on her mother's bahavior and

attitude toward blacks.

> We had a restaurant and my mother would never let me go to
> the back of the restaurant--the kitchen--because the black
> people were back there. Occasionally I had to go back and
> help dry silverware when they were in a rush. But she'd
> always think of them as something dirty. Not so much that
> they would really hurt me but they were people that you
> just didn't associate with.

In these two passages one senses the feelings of Greek superiority

reflected in avoiding contact with Mexicans or blacks, and even thinking

that Greeks are "actually better" than these groups. I do not want to

overemphasize prejudice toward blacks and Mexicans among Greeks, since
it is undeniably true that many other Americans also consider these
groups in some way "inferior" to themselves. Nevertheless, one senses
an attitude among many Greeks that Mexicans and particularly blacks are
not quite people in the same way that Greeks are, to a greater extent
than among Americans of their general class and educational level.

There are two reasons for this prejudice toward Mexicans and blacks.
First, the immigrant had no experience with these groups in Greece and
thus his response to them was greatly influenced, if not determined, by
the attitudes he found among Americans. This fact was pointed out by a
2nd generation woman:

> Back then you couldn't sit with them. It wasn't just the
> Greeks that were prejudiced. When they probably saw all this
> they thought there was something wrong with them.

It is important to note that Greeks did not take on American prejudices
to ingratiate themselves to Americans or to become "more American"
themselves. Rather, they naturally acquired the local practices as a
response to groups with which they were unfamiliar, toward whom they had
no "customary" attitudes. A second explanation is found in the comments
of a 2nd generation man, who expresses a common attitude:

> We still feel that we're a minority group too and that every-
> thing has gone their way lately. Though nothing was ever
> given to us--nothing was given to us and yet we worked hard.
> Our fathers got pushed around but they made it--couldn't speak
> the language, and yet they somehow managed to succeed.

Thus many Greeks feel that their group has also been subjected to discrimination, and yet they have been successful; in fact, they have accomplished
considerably more than these minorities with much less help. However,
there is a problem here in that both of these explanations of prejudice

--a reflection of attitudes Greeks found in America, and a response to their differential success in the face of similar treatment--apply primarily to the 1st generation immigrants, but less well to their children and grandchildren. Thus a third factor is at work here as well, and this may be the feeling of Greek superiority discussed in the previous section, which is engrained in Greek Americans from child-hood.

5. "Whites"

At this point, it is interesting to note that there is another Greek word for "Americans" besides i xeni and the literal οἱ Ἀμερικανοί (i Americani); this is οἱ ἄσπροι (i aspri), which literally means "whites". This term is used to contrast "Americans" not from blacks, but from Greeks. Thus in this terminology the dichotomy is "white" vs. "Greek", which is not meant to place the Greeks in the same group as blacks, but nevertheless does seem to place them in somewhat lower esteem than "Americans". This usage is rather peculiar, for many Greeks consider themselves superior to "Americans". A 3rd generation girl tried to explain the term "white":

> "She's marrying a white boy" and stuff like that. That's
> just something that's been picked up. I think it's semi-
> recent. For about five to ten years. It's not something
> that's traditional. I guess it's picked up from the fact
> that you're American, I mean, if you're a white American,
> you'd say, "She married a black," from the other group, you
> know, from the idea that there are two racial groups. But
> when you are Greek and you marry someone that's not Greek,
> they're white. I don't know how it is really. Maybe it's
> not a good analogy. ... In other words, we're separated from
> the regular whites; you're white, black, Greek, or Jewish.
> I guess.

A young 2-3 generation man gave his view of this terminology:

> [Have you heard people say "white"?]
> Yeah, "white" and "black" is Greek. I really don't know what
> started that. It's weird, isn't it? I guess they figured
> that--although there are blue-eyed blond-haired Greeks, I
> don't know what it is, I guess a majority are dark-haired
> and -skinned, and we just picked it up. I think that's a
> little more of a joke. It's not taken seriously, I think
> it's taken quite--funny, in a way.

This view--that "white" is a joking term--is probably accurate, at least
as the term was originally used. Now it has become a more normal, everyday word, although it is not nearly so common as "American". I believe
that the connotation of "white" is generally a play on words--as "whites"
are seen by blacks as a threat to their safety and "personhood", so do
many Greeks view "Americans". The term is used almost exclusively by
younger Greeks, and it appears to be a gibe at this xenophobic reaction
of more old-fashioned, older-generation Greeks to "Americans", who are
seen as a very real threat to Greek culture, society, and even identity
among their children and grandchildren.

D. American elements of a Greek self-conception

It is not without reason that members of the 1st generation are
concerned about the destructive impact of America on Greekness, for even
among people of the 2nd generation--those least likely to be influenced
--American ways have made significant inroads on Greek culture and
identity. The previous section showed that members of the 2nd and 3rd
generations are not comfortable with the distinction between themselves
and "Americans" which is natural to 1st generation Greeks. Generally
they identify themselves as Americans who are fortunate to have a Greek
background and culture to draw on for a "special" element of their
self-conceptions. The extent to which either the American or Greek

aspect of their identities is more important and the situations in which
one's self-conception is more Greek or American will be discussed later;
for the time being I will concentrate on the 2nd generation's unique
status as a marginal group whose members struggle with identification
as "Greek" and "American".

Members of the 2nd generation are of course marginal in the sense
that they live in two different cultural situations, at least while they
are still living with their parents. Their parents are much more Greek
than American culturally, socially, and in their national identities.
Thus the child is raised in a very Greek environment at home--he learns
the Greek language, eats Greek food, and goes to Greek church. But he
must also adjust to the very different American culture he meets when he
is at school and in neighborhood play groups. This sort of adjustment
frequently causes problems for 2nd generation people. E.g., a college
girl made this comment:

> It's our identity now, it really is. We talk about Greece
> being Greek, that's us right there. It's just a part of us
> now. Like with your teachers, you know, when they ask some-
> thing about it, you say, "I'm Greek!" You think, "That's it,"
> just a part of you. When you're in Greece, though, and they
> ask what you are, you say, "I'm American". You're torn between
> two cultures, you're right in between. You're not completely
> Greek, but then you're Greek enough that in a completely
> Americanized culture, you feel kinda like you're losing
> something. ... You can't stay too long in either, you've
> got to be kinda in a little bit of both to feel comfortable.
> It's a lot of confused inner feelings that you can't explain.

This emphasis on the 2nd generation's conflicts is not meant to
imply that the 1st generation is exclusively Greek and the 3rd generation
exclusively American, thus having no cultural and identificational
problems themselves. Many older 1st generation people have adapted

very well to America; they have learned English and become citizens, and even though they may feel nostalgic about Greece, most insist that they are Americans and that life is better here, in their adopted homeland. This is probably more true of men than of women, who have had less opportunity (and necessity) to leave an exclusively Greek environment. Similarly, members of the 3rd generation are not so far removed from Greek culture and society that they identify themselves as Americans exclusively. Their situation is similar to that of the 2nd generation, though not so basic and acute; the specifics may differ in each case, but the basic issues are the same. The 2nd generation lives in a primarily Greek-speaking, and the 3rd in an English-speaking home; 1st generation parents may insist more on the practicing of Greek social customs than do those of the 2nd generation; the 1st generation home may be more male-dominated than the somewhat more equalitarian 2nd generation home; but still the conflict between Greek and American culture is present in both situations. Third generation kids chafe under their parents' strictness and restrictions, protest at not being able to do things their American friends are allowed to do, fight about having to go to afternoon Greek school, are embarrassed about the older Greeks' closed-mindedness, and so on.

Thus the struggle between the two self-conceptions and cultural heritages, Greek and American, exists to some extent in each generation, but this conflict is more immediate and pressing for members of the 2nd generation, whose lives are closely involved in both Greek and American culture. The main difference is probably that 1st generation parents expect their 2nd generation children to _live_ the Greek culture, whereas 2nd generation parents expect their 3rd generation children to appreciate it. For example, a 2nd generation individual is able to speak Greek because this was the language used in his home. Perhaps his mother never learned English, and he had to use Greek to be able to communicate with her. The 3rd generation person, on the other hand, is a step removed from this process. It is his grandmother who speaks Greek, and the language predominantly used in his home is English. Nevertheless, he is sent to Greek school to "learn" the language, or rather, to learn to appreciate it. Unquestioning obedience toward parents is another aspect of Greek American culture which is modified in the 3rd generation. A 2nd generation couple commented on this:

> W: He [her father] was so strict that when I left junior high, they gave a party that afternoon in the home of one of the children, at her home, right after school for everybody in the whole class, and my parents wouldn't let me go.
> H: When we tell our kids what we went through, "Oh no, no!"
> W: "Well, why'd you stand for it?", that's their reaction. "Well, you didn't have to take it!" [laughter] Well, the way my children are brought up, they're not gonna take it. But the way we were brought up, we were submissive. I mean, we never thought to question our parents' authority or anything like that.

The conflict for the 2nd generation is therefore a real one between American and Greek ways, whereas the 3rd generation's conflict is more a sense of rebellion at having to learn "all this culture crud" and at having strict parents.

This discussion of the different problems of 2nd and 3rd generation individuals should not lead one to think that Greek culture, society, and identity are on the wane in the United States in the younger generations, for this is not the case. In general, 3rd generation Greeks are probably much more involved in their ethnicity than are many other ethnics of the

same generation. This difference may be attributed to the Greeks'
having a religion which is exclusively "theirs", which is closely tied
to their personal self-conceptions as "Greeks". In this respect, Greeks
are probably more similar to Jews than to other European ethnic groups
(except other national Orthodox groups). This is not to say that some
individuals have not chosen to disregard their ethnicity and become
"Americans of Greek descent", rather than to stay involved in the cycle
of Greek events which revolves around the Greek Orthodox church; nevertheless, Greekness is very much alive in Houston.

E. Greek elements to keep: Zorba image

As the length of time Greeks have been in the United States
increases, however, there is a natural drift toward more "American"
cultural patterns. Each succeeding generation is more comfortable with
American ways and adopts patterns which are more consistent with those
of other, non-Greek Americans. "You're lucky," a 1st generation father
told his child, "you can look at Greek and American culture and take
the best of each." And this is indeed what many Greek Americans have
done: they have adopted those elements of American culture with which
they can identify and rejected Greek elements (like superstitions and
arranged marriages) which are inconsistent with American culture, while
retaining those elements of Greek culture which they consider valuable.
E.g., one very central aspect of Greek culture which is considered by
most to be necessary is the "Greek" family--the closeness of family
members, the idea that "family comes first", and family customs. Other
Greek elements which are thought to be worth retaining are warmth and
spontaneity, close friendships, and colorful aspects like traditional

foods, dances, and customs, and so on.

The Houston Greek community is rather young, and the great majority of its Greek families are composed of 2nd generation parents and their young children. Thus Americanizing influences have not been at work within the community for an extended period of time covering several generations, but already some 2nd generation individuals are concerned that they will not be able to hold on to certain aspects of Greek culture and identity they consider valuable; all these aspects are associated with what one might call a "Zorba image". E.g., a 2nd generation woman commented on her family's inability to be Greek in certain ways:

> There are many good things in the Greek culture that should be kept, even though we reject some of the customs. One of the things that comes to mind first is the flair for life that Greeks have. They can really have a good time, they really enjoy life. Our parents had this, but I'm afraid that we've just become too American to be able to pull it off. Another part of this is hospitality and love of friends. We have these ideals, but we're too American to achieve them with the vim and vigor that the older generation has. Some of the second generation still has this trait, but we've lost it. Other things to keep are the Greek's love for family, and for food. And especially hospitality!

Another 2nd generation woman repeated this feeling when she related what happened to her husband on a trip to Greece:

> The Greek warmness with friends and relatives. If they see a friend, they hug and kiss him. This is something we should definitely keep, but such hugging and kissing is not part of the American way, and it's embarrassing even for Greeks raised in America to express themselves like that. When we went to Greece, our relatives there ran up and hugged and kissed F. When the men came at him like that, I saw him sorta stiffen up and back away because he was so unaccustomed to it, and being an American--he felt that there was just something wrong with it. But by the time we left, he was hugging everyone too, and it was a wonderful thing to see.

It is true that in general the members of the younger generations are
not as spontaneous and outgoing as those of the first generation, because
they have become more "refined" under the influence of American norms.
Nevertheless, it has been my experience that generally they are still
much more vibrant, warmer, and more expressive of their emotions than
are non-Greek Americans.

It is interesting to note that many Greeks feel that this "Zorba
image"--being warm and open, fun-loving, carefree, and emotional--is an
important part of their being Greek, and plays a significant role in their
Greek self-conception. For instance, a 2nd generation couple discussed
the special feeling one gets at Greek parties and made the following
remark:

> H: In Greek they say εἶναι ψόφιο (ine psofio), it's dead.
> It's a very typical Greek saying, that when someone doesn't
> get the feel of something--
> W: The κέφι (kefi), when you don't get the kefi. It's a
> feeling that you get, it's a feeling that you have when you're
> at a party, that you really enjoy yourself.
> H: And it's a different type meaning--you don't have to drink
> to enjoy yourself.
> W: But most of the time there is a little wine around!
> H: To dance yourself or to see someone else dance with you, all
> joining together, men and women, there's a tremendous exhilarat-
> ing feeling that's very difficult to explain, to verbalize to
> someone who doesn't experience this.
> W: This usually takes place at engagement-type parties if you
> haven't gotten too sophisticated for this. There are many
> Greek Americans who feel that they are too sophisitcated you
> know, for this type of thing. This is below them that they
> all of a sudden want to play the part of the elite, you know,
> and forget and push aside this. It's sort of I guess being
> ashamed you know--
> H: The peasant-type party.
> W: They look at it as if, yeah, as a peasant entertainment.

One cannot help but wonder to what extent Greeks are influenced in their
self-conceptions and behavior by the fact that Americans generally hold

a "Zorba" stereotype of Greeks. In the next section the way in which American attitudes toward Greeks can influence the centrality of Greekness in one's self-conception will be further discussed.

II. Forces in Ethnic Identification

There are several elements in the Houston Greek community which have an important impact on the individual's self-conception as a "Greek". These are the church, friends, and particularly the family, and each will be considered in this section. But first a force from outside the Greek community will be examined--this is the current interest in ethnicity, the fascination of many Americans with the myriad of ethnic subcultures in America.

A. "In" to be Greek

Many Greeks have mentioned the American public's current interest in ethnic groups as an important influence in their self-conceptions as "Greeks". They are now more able to be proud of their identification with Greekness, whereas before they were embarrassed because of their being so different from "Americans". To be a member of an ethnic group is no longer the great source of embarrassment which it once was. A 2nd generation girl expressed this idea in her comment:

> It seems like our whole community's come up in the world.
> I don't consider it that important, but it's become more
> social. ... It's come up in society--to be Greek, is kinda
> neat now. And so you're not embarrassed anymore. You've
> come to be proud of it and then you begin to show it off
> more, so you do Greek things and stick around with Greek
> friends and let people kid you and call you "Greek". So
> it's changed. I think it's a whole change in the whole
> community as it's grown up. And then as the individual
> grows up, he becomes prouder too.

A group of 2nd, 2-3, and 3rd generation men and women in a discussion of

the fact that it is now "in" to be Greek, tried to discover the explana-

tion for this phenomenon.

C: But weren't we just a whole lot more embarrassed of it
before? Now it's really neat--
M: Now it's O.K. to be Greek and stuff. Before, it wasn't
so hot, because like they said, when AHEPA was founded, a lot
of it was founded because there was a lot of discrimination
going on.
D: Yeah, the Ku Klux Klan.
M: It's funny how things have changed so much now, they've
just--it's almost gone the other way around.
C: Yeah, now it's neat, see. Before--
S: Maybe we've just grown up.
D: Well, Americans are different, you know, people are more
acceptant of other cultures rather than being so prejudiced
and discriminatory. ... About fifteen years ago if we'd 've
had a Greek Festival, for people to come and learn about our
culture--
C: We wouldn't have done it.
D: I know, you wouldn't have done it, and if we did, nobody
would have come.
C: What changed it? What happened? Lots of Greeks got rich,
for one thing. So once you're rich, you're not ashamed to say
what you are, you know?
D: Yeah, but people are just becoming more educated.
S: I think it's because there weren't enough of us. I mean,
that's a theory, that there weren't enough of us before.
T: It wasn't that large of a minority to be--
C: Yeah, now we can kind of depend on each other.
T: You know, like 25 percent of the city's black, that's a
large minority. It becomes noticeable. Same thing with the
Mexicans, you know.
[Well, you wouldn't be proud in Houston to be black or Mexican,
I mean you might be, but that wouldn't be because people were
interested in your culture.]
C: That's true, so why did our culture get what the others
didn't? We don't look as different for one thing as a black
or Mexican would.
T: We were darker once, I mean, we still are. But then up
North when they have the large Italian families, they get
discriminated against.
D: Yeah, Greeks are more discriminated against up North.
T: Well, they were because they were larger numbers. I think
we're just too small here to feel it.
C: I think the money also has a lot to do with it. Because a
lot of the big names are Greek, and they begin to be not ashamed
to say that they are Greek because they've got the money to back

them up, you know. And then we depend on them, you know.
D: Also the Greek restaurants opened up with the Greek music
and stuff like that, and in <u>National</u> <u>Geographic</u> Athens Bar
was considered one of the really neat places to go about
five years ago.
S: Well, it is, it's a very unique place to go because you
walk into another world when you go there.
T: Because of where it's located.
D: Well, it's also part of the--instead of being icky, now
it's being unique, it's Greek.
C: I still, you know, don't know why it changed from being
icky to being unique.
T: It could have been just a state of mind, uhh, you know,
our state of mind.
D: Well, Houston didn't have that many Greeks years ago. And
they've established themselves.
S: Well, what it is--like before us, you know, the embarrassed
part of being Greek, but like my friends, they want to learn
about Greek dancing. Maybe people are becoming more educated
in the sense like they want to learn something different that's
really not that far out of line. Like being black is really
different. It's obvious. I mean, it's just a color, it's
there. But like they can associate with us because we talk
just like em, we look just like em, you know, more or less,
and you know, we're white, and they can associate with us.
More, and they're becoming educated and wanting to learn,
you know, it's in to learn about other cultures. They make
you feel wanted or part of them. In a sense it gives you a
special feeling.

From this discussion one can find several clues about the reason for the

current "It's neat to be Greek!" attitude which prevails in the Greek

community, as well as in the general public.

One theme is expressed in the statement, "Maybe we've just grown

up." The young adults here have themselves only recently come to accept

themselves for what they are, particularly their Greekness. Just a

short while ago they were adolescents still struggling with their

individual identity crises, and being Greek just made the struggle that

much more painful. Thus there is reason to suspect that part of their

sense of Greeks being considered "icky" was related to, and perhaps only

an outgrowth of, their own sense of awkwardness at being "different".

Despite this, there is more to this phenomenon than just the interpretation of people who are leaving their identity crises behind and becoming more comfortable with themselves as Greek Americans, for discrimination against Greeks was not uncommon, as they point out in their discussion. ("There was a lot of discrimination going on. - Yeah, the Ku Klux Klan.") What is the explanation for this change from "icky" to "neat", for this new-found pride in being Greek?

As Chapter 1 pointed out, the recent movements among the blacks, Chicano and American Indian minority groups has no doubt had an effect on the "pride" of other ethnic groups. This is not to say that Greeks have not always been proud of their heritage, but this pride has until the past few years been expressed mainly within the context of the Greek community. Exposure to the recent cries of "Black is beautiful!" and so on have encouraged other ethnic groups, including Greeks, to "go public" in their expression of their cultures to a much greater extent than they ever have before. The feeling seems to be, "If blacks can be proud of their heritage, we can certainly show ours off a little bit!" This pride has also been accompanied by an increasing interest in ethnicity on the part of the American public in general. ("It's in to learn about other cultures.") The pendulum seems to have swung back in the opposite direction from the period of xenophobia and the "Americanization" movement of the early 20th century. The ideology of cultural pluralism is now accepted, and many people are genuinely interested in ethnic customs, food, dancing, and handicrafts. There also seems to be a particular interest in Greeks, perhaps because of the recent rise of people like Aristotle Onassis to the public attention. As one person said, "Lots of Greeks got rich, and once you're rich, you're not ashamed to say what you are."

The unique position of the Greek community in Houston is also a factor, however; the community is neither so small that it cannot function ("There weren't enough of us before."), nor so large that it is perceived of as threatening, thus becoming an object of discrimination. ("The Greeks are more discriminated against up North. -- We're just too small here to feel it.") Furthermore, Greeks are not physically as easily distinguishable as the city's larger minorities, blacks and Chicanos. ("We don't look as different.") For these reasons, Greeks are more objects of interest than of prejudice in Houston, and Greeks are more able to be publicly proud of their heritage than Houston's blacks and Mexican Americans are, or even than Greeks in many other cities are.

Therefore the "it's neat to be Greek!" phenomenon is a result of several different factors, working in conjunction. The young 2-3 generation man accurately assessed the situation when he said, "Maybe people are becoming more educated, in the sense that they want to learn something different that's not that far out of line." Greeks are considered different enough to be interesting, but not beyond the pale.

The attitude of "it's in to be Greek" acts as a pressure from outside the Greek community, which goads some Greeks into having Greekness play a more central role in their self-conceptions than it might otherwise. This attitude also encourages others to be more "Greek" than they would otherwise be, at least publicly. Thus people "start coming out of the woodwork" during the three days of the Greek

Festival to exercise their "Greekness" which has been dormant throughout the rest of the year. These "Festival Greeks" will be discussed in Chapter 7.

B. The Greek Orthodox Church and "Greek" identity

The next topic to be considered is a very important one: the role of the Greek Orthodox Church in the development and maintenance of an individual's self-conception as a "Greek". The significant part the church plays in this process should not be underestimated, for the local church is the center of Greek American life in the Houston community. I will first consider the way in which being a member of the Greek Orthodox Church and participating in its traditional customs makes a child realize--in some cases, for the first time--that he is "different" from other American children, and that the reason he is different is because he is Greek. The dual nature of the church--as both a religious and a social institution--provides the topic for the second part of this section, and the relationship between "Greek Orthodoxy" and "Greekness" will be examined in an attempt to separate these two closely related aspects of the individual Greek's self-conception.

1. Reactions to Orthodox Church

The important role that Greek Orthodoxy plays in the Greek community and in the individual's Greek self-conception is mirrored in the fact that one's first realization that he is Greek often comes through the reactions of non-Greeks to his Greek Orthodox religion and its customs. One of the first indications that one is "different" from others often comes from the realization that the Greek Orthodox Church is not like other churches. E.g., a 3rd generation girl commented:

[When did you first realize, how did you come to feel Greek
and know that you were?]
When we lived in B we went to the Episcopal Church there, but
whenever we came to Houston, we couldn't understand the Liturgy
--it was Greek and we knew that we had something different in
that we had to come all the way to Houston because there wasn't
this kind of church in B. There's a special big church in
Houston and also it's unique--not just because it's in Houston
it's unique but because there's a different language being
spoken. So through the church and my grandparents, I was first
aware of being Greek.

For most Greek kids, there were also uncomfortable moments associated

with their belonging to the Greek Church, particularly because many

Americans are unfamiliar with Orthodoxy.

And nobody's ever heard of Greek Orthodox. They ask, "Are you
Christian? Do you believe in God?" You feel so funny, you
feel so embarrassed.

The biggest thing in my life was "You're Greek Orthodox, is
that Christian?" And people still--you don't know how dense
people are. They ask you, "Well, what is Greek Orthodox? Is
that a Christian religion?" They think it's Orthodox Jew.

A source of embarrassment for Greek children is the fact that Orthodox

Easter is seldom on the same date as in other Christian Churches, and

is sometimes as much as a month later. Despite such feelings as

children, however, many later enjoy the uniqueness of this custom,

because it makes them stand out in a crowd, as a young 3rd generation

man explained:

[What kind of religious traditions has your family kept that
make you different from Americans?]
...Expecially Easter, because it even falls on a different day.
[Is that important?]
It seems that you get out of the Easter spirit, everybody's
celebrating Easter and then all of a sudden it sorta goes in
the bucket, and then you're celebrating Easter. The Greek
kids really like it now. You know, because it is so different,
so odd, and so hard.
[How did you feel about it? Was it embarrassing?]
It was, especially taking a hard-boiled egg to school a week
later, a dyed hard-boiled egg. You know that was embarrassing

when it was two weeks later, when it was a month, that was <u>bad</u>.
I'd say it has its hardships.
[Was it a hardship on you?]
I think so--I mean taking a hard-boiled egg a month after Easter,
it tends to make kids really wonder you know.

Along with these feelings of embarrassment, however, there is also

a sense of pride in having customs which are not shared with Americans.

As one gradually realizes that many of his religious customs are Greek,

they take on a special meaning because they are rather unique. E.g.,

when I asked a 3rd generation girl whether being Greek was important to

her, she responded:

> When people talk about what they like to be at Christmas time
> or Easter time or just family traditions. Talk about Greek
> traditions--I love that. Because there are so many that I love.
> So I'm proud to talk about things that make the Greek family
> unique. When people ask about Easter services or our Greek
> Orthodox services. ...When people get in religious groups and
> talk or just talk about what families do on certain occasions,
> then I'm very proud to be Greek. I don't know if so much of
> it stems from being Greek or if it stems from a family pride--
> this is what our family does tradition-wise at Christmas and
> Easter and whether or not it was Greek doesn't matter, is not
> important. But the fact is that that family tradition is there
> because of Greek tradition.

There are many such customs which are practiced during holy days; the

family in practicing them asserts its Greekness and shows its children

an important way of "being Greek". One can cite several examples of

these customs, for each holiday has a complex of traditional foods, and

practices associated with it. E.g., during the New Year's holidays the

priest blesses the house and a special bread, vasilopita (St. Basil's

bread) is prepared with a coin inside; whoever gets the piece with the

coin will be lucky during the coming year. After Easter services, the

family eats roast lamb and traditional soups and plays a special game,

described here by a 3rd generation man:

> You know breaking of eggs at Easter--You get all your eggs, dye
> them, fancy them up, do whatever you want with them, then on
> Easter Sunday, before dinner you grab an egg, the egg of your
> choice, and you know you have the round or the sharp end, and
> you hit the same ends with someone. The first person says,
> "Χριστός ἀνέστη (Christos anesti, Christ is risen)" and the
> other person says back, "Ἀληθῶς ἀνέστη (Alithos anesti, He
> is risen indeed)." And you bump eggs. It's kind of a game, and
> nobody else does it that I know of. It's a custom we've done
> in this house since day one. ... The last person without a
> busted egg wins. It's a lot of fun. It's kind of like good
> luck, but I don't know if there is a real meaning behind it.
> It's just something we've always done.

From these brief comments one can begin to appreciate the importance

of the Greek Orthodox Church in the individual's self-conception as a

Greek. Orthodox customs are not the only influence the church has in

developing and maintaining ethnic identity, however; several other factors

will be discussed in the next section.

2. The Church, a religious and a social institution

The central role which the Greek Orthodox Church plays in a Greek

community--such as Annunciation plays in Houston--makes it an important

influence on individuals within the community, as both a religious and

a social institution. In other words, influence on the development and

maintenance of an individual's Greek self-conception is exerted by the

church on a social as well as a purely religious level. I will first

consider the religious, and then the social influence of the church.

Some people's only tie to Greekness is through membership in the

Greek Orthodox Church; they consider themselves Orthodox first and Greek

second. Nevertheless, this religious tie does maintain many Greek re-

ligious customs, if not social ones, in their lives. A young 3rd gen-

eration man's discussion expressed this idea.

> I think if you took away the Greek Orthodox religion completely,

> I'd just have to consider myself American, really. It's strict-
> ly the Church that has brought in Greek that has--like I say,
> Greek food, Greek dancing, Greek language has all been through
> the church really. So when you say, you cut out the church, you
> cut out everything, because that is sort of like the source--of
> everything, really. Customs, food, the works.

In fact, the identification of Greekness with the Greek Orthodox Church

is so pervasive that some people might "consider" themselves Greek by

virtue of being members of the church--they identify themselves as

"Greek" because theirs is the "Greek Church". In this case ethnicity

has a religious basis. E.g., a young woman who became engaged to a

Greek boy and joined the Greek Orthodox said:

> My parents, right now they consider me a Greek. "Well, she's a
> Greek now." I'll go somewhere--"This is my daughter, the Greek,"
> that's how they introduce me.
> [Do you really feel like you've taken on a Greek identity?]
> I feel like I really belong, I really do. Sometimes I wonder if
> I shouldn't've been born a Greek. It's just something--it seems
> like it fits.

And when I asked a young girl whether a certain friend of hers were

Greek, she replied, "No, she's Presbyterian." It would probably be very

difficult to belong to the Greek Orthodox Church and not have this

membership play an important part in one's self-conception, since it is

not just the Orthodox Church, but the Greek Orthodox Church--and just

"the Greek Church" to some. A 2-3 generation girl's comments on Greek

language in the church explained this relationship of Greek Orthodoxy

and Greekness:

> A lot of people really try to keep with the Greek language. I
> think that makes it the more Greekish if they really can relate
> with the service, plus if you really enter your religion and you
> take part in religious celebrations which in turn have so many
> traditional customs and activities carried over from Greece, then
> you're more related to that world. So if you're in the church,
> you probably want to be more Greekish too.

Furthermore, the church also plays a major role in the maintenance of Greekness as the one formal repository of the Greek language, at least in Houston. Through the Greek language ties to Greece and Greek traditions are maintained which might be dropped if the church used English exclusively.

Thus the Greek Orthodox Church as a religious institution greatly influences the salience of Greekness in the self-conceptions of its members; its role as a social institution within the Greek community is of equal importance. For many people, the local church is the center of their social world: their friends, relatives, kumbari, activities, school, clubs, and interests--as well as religious services--are all found there. Just as some people are associated with "Greek" social circles primarily through their Orthodoxy, others are "Orthodox" primarily through their Greek associations. The former see Greek friends at church services, and the latter seldom attend services, but meet at social functions which take place at the church. A 3rd generation girl discussed the roots of this latter sort of association in America.

> Coming to America people kept the religion and kept the Greek families centered together because they'd all be in the same church and do all their activities there, so you would naturally assume that a person that was Greek would center his activities within his church and therefore a Greek would be Greek Orthodox.

The church, then, is a center for the Greek community and its social functions, and for many people this, rather than its role as a religious institution, is of foremost importance in their everyday lives as Greek Americans. It is this "group" (parea) aspect which makes it difficult for many people to leave the church, for in doing so they are leaving their social world as well, as a young 3rd generation woman explained.

> [If you said, "I think I'll start going to the Russian Church," how would people react?]
> Well, the fact of leaving the church, leaving them, the people you've always grown up with, it's something they'd probably have a very hard time accepting. Most people probably wouldn't look at it this way, but the more open-minded people--would think, "Great, Orthodoxy in any language is Orthodoxy."

The important role such feelings of parea play as a central meaning of "Greekness" for the members of Houston's community has already been discussed. This topic will be considered more deeply in the next chapter, which examines the forces which encourage the individual to identify himself as a community member.

3. Greek Orthodoxy and Greekness

Throughout this section the effect of Greek Orthodoxy on an individual's Greek identity has been discussed. Orthodoxy is one of the elements considered necessary for membership in the Greek group; in fact, many people identify Greekness with Greek Orthodoxy. The two are so intertwined that it is very difficult to separate them; this is particularly true in America, where the Greek Orthodox Church has served as the nucleus of Greek communities to a greater extent than in Greece. Saloutos explains the immigrant's attachment to the Greek Orthodox Church in America in this way:

> In the United States Hellenism and Greek Orthodoxy--the one intertwined with the other--served as the cord that kept the immigrant attached to the mother country, nourished his patriotic appetites, and helped him preserve the faith and language of his parents. The receptiveness of the immigrant to this spirit cannot be underestimated. Absence from his ancestral home, the fear that he might never see it again, the thought of losing his nationality and of dying in a strange land, caused him, at least for a time, to embrace his religion with a fervor that he never had in Greece. He attended church because it reminded him of home (1964:122-3).

In this section I will discuss why Greekness and Greek Orthodoxy are so

closely identified in the minds of Greeks, and attempt to separate these
two factors and determine the extent to which each is important in the
individual's personal identity.

The close relationship between Greekness and Greek Orthodoxy is
demonstrated in the observation of a young 2nd generation woman:

> They tend to think that their religion is for Greeks only.
> ... I guess since most Greeks are Greek Orthodox, and since
> not many non-Greeks are Greek Orthodox, unless you married a
> Greek or something like that, they tend to identify their
> religion with their nationality, and they're so clannish.

Many people also feel that not only is the Greek Orthodox Church for
Greeks only but Greeks should not join (or attend) any other--non-Greek
--Orthodox church. A 2nd generation woman who became disenchanted with
the Greek Church occasionally attended the local Syrian Orthodox Church,
where services are conducted in English. She found that she enjoyed
the services and got a lot more out of them than she had in Greek, and
tried to encourage her husband to begin attending the Syrian Church with
her, but he wouldn't hear of it, for it may be Orthodox, but it is not
Greek, and Greeks have no business going to a non-Greek church.

It is not difficult to understand this confusion of Greekness and
Greek Orthodoxy in people's minds, for two reasons. First, there is
historically an intimate relationship between "Greekness" and Orthodoxy,
which is still an important influence today. Second, these people's
everyday lives represent a complex blending of Greek and Orthodox
customs, and it is difficult to sort out which of these two traditions
is represented in certain customs. As an example one might cite
superstitions and miracles.

Many purely secular Greek superstitions are closely tied to religious beliefs in the minds of Orthodox people. E.g., many people believe in the evil eye, and to ward it off, wear on their crosses a <u>mati</u>, a small blue stone resembling an eye. This juxtaposition of secular superstitions and religious practices is not considered at all unusual by Greeks, although many of the younger generation are beginning to realize the incongruity of such practices. However, many Greek people, even in the 3rd generation, believe in such superstitions. A 3rd generation girl told me about some Greek superstitions:

> See, these things that are called 'eyes', 'evil eye', it's called μάτι (mati). It is light blue, and it has a blue dot in it...A lot of people wear them on their cross. That keeps off evil spirits and curses.
> [Do a lot of people believe in them?]
> Yeah. Like you know the F brothers? They came over from Greece, it was like seven brothers, my grandmother told me. And they wouldn't take their mother with them, when they were coming over. And they wouldn't bring their mother. She gave them a curse, and said that "None of you will get married, and none of you will have children!" Now all seven mind you.
> [Is that what happened?]
> Yeah. Of course, that could be a total coincidence, but out of seven guys? ... My aunt from Greece--she's not really my aunt, but married to my third cousin--he was born here of Greek born parents, and they went to Greece and got him a wife, that's exactly what happened. So she's got a daughter that's got beautiful eyes, and whenever someone says something about her eyes, that's kinda in a way giving a curse, because something might happen to them. And she always laughs and says something in Greek. I forget what it is, but there's something you say-- to counteract.

Other superstitions are tied in with miracles, which actually have a basis in Orthodoxy. Many Greek islands have special saints whose relics are preserved locally, and there are many miracles and superstitions associated with them. For example, a 2-3 generation girl reported:

> There's this one that every year on the celebration of his name-day, they have a service, and every year they change his shoes.

> Because every year the shoes are all grass-stained and worn out.
> It's in Corfu. I guess Protestants don't go for miracles--I
> still do, 'cause I've never had any personal contact with them,
> but I know relatives that have.

On Kefallinia the body of St. Gerasimos is preserved, and each year the

local priests carry his relics in a procession. Those who are mentally

ill lie down before the procession, and are supposed to be cured as the

body of the saint passes over them. These are just two examples of

scores of miracles and superstitions associated with Greek saints.

Although Greek Greeks are on the whole more superstitious than

American Greeks, one should not think that superstition and belief in

miracles is on the wane in the United States, for Greek Americans, even

young 3rd generation people, are more superstitious and certainly

believe in miracles to a much greater extent than most Americans. This

is understandable, since they have been raised in an atmosphere steeped

in superstition; furthermore, many of them have visited the areas in

Greece where miracles are said to have taken place. Furthermore, the

Orthodox Church is very much oriented toward miracles, so many of these

superstitious beliefs are not entirely incongruous with religious beliefs.

Despite the close relationship and confusion between Greekness and

Greek Orthodoxy, there are two situations in which it is possible to

observe people's reactions to determine whether the "Greek" or "Orthodox"

element of their self-conception is of greater importance. These are

their reactions to American converts to the Greek Orthodox Church, and

to their children's dating and marrying other Orthodox, such as Russians

or Syrians. Converts are not readily accepted by Greeks, as a 3rd genera-

tion boy commented.

> See, that's how come the Russian Orthodox Church has grown,
> because they accept their converts. A lot of them are converts.
> They're friendly towards them. Whereas the Greek Archdiocese
> is not that friendly towards its converts. There's still hostil-
> ity towards them. It's there. I don't think they'll get rid of
> it, they just can't.

In such reactions to converts one can discern the nationalistic element

of Greek Orthodoxy described in Chapter 2.

The question of dating and marrying a non-Greek of course strikes

closer to home than that of accepting converts. Almost every young

person I talked to was sure that his (her) parents would still object

very strongly to his marrying a non-Greek, even if she were Orthodox.

A 3rd generation boy made these observations:

> [Would a Greek not in the church be better than an American who
> converted?]
> Yeah, because of what I said about people putting more emphasis
> on Greekness than on the church.
> [What if you were dating a Russian Orthodox?]
> They'd still be hostile, even though she'd be Orthodox, she's not
> Greek. They're still going to be--What would my parents like
> best? Greek Orthodox, then Greek.

These feelings were echoed by a young 2-3 generation man:

> [What do parents object to in marriage to an American, Greekness
> or Orthodoxy?]
> Some of both--You can't divide it.
> [What would happen if someone were to marry a Syrian or Russian
> Orthodox?]
> That's what I was just about to say--I don't know. I'd love to
> see that happen. That would be beautiful, I'd love to see it
> happen but I don't know. You wouldn't know until it would happen,
> and there's not that many around. In honesty I'll tell you--
> I bet mostly it's the culture and not the religion, because you
> check, and very few of the people that are Greek know that much
> about the religion at all. Because it's so steeped in ancient
> Greek, and there's very little instruction, mostly just following
> ceremonies. Now I'm not knocking any of this, I'm just telling
> you what it is. And most of it is tradition. The religion is
> not known. ... Greekness is more important than Orthodoxy for
> many people. Even when I was talking to this priest about the
> idea of marrying a non-Greek, he said that "If you did that,
> you'd probably be giving up a lot of your Greekness, and that

234

The reactions to converts and marriage to other Orthodox cited

was one thing to consider, how important being Greek is to you"
--not necessarily Greek Orthodox, he didn't stress that--he
said "Greek".

The reactions to converts and marriage to other Orthodox cited
here certainly seem to indicate that for many people, Greekness is at
least as important as--and sometimes more important than Orthodoxy. Of
course there are also other Greek Orthodox who would disagree with this
perspective entirely; this is particularly true of those whose participation in Greek life is secondary in importance to their Orthodoxy. Nevertheless, this latter "Orthodox" group seems to be outnumbered by the
former "Greek" group.

Another way to sort out the elements of Greekness and Greek Orthodoxy is to examine the reactions of those who fulfill one of these roles,
but not the other--Greeks who are not Greek Orthodox and Greek Orthodox
who are not Greek. In the course of my research I have interviewed
several people who for one reason or another left the Orthodox Church;
they discussed their "Greek" self-conceptions, how they were maintained
outside the church, and which elements of Greekness they considered
worth saving. In general, however, for all of these people, Greekness
seems to be much less important than it is to Greeks who have remained
in the church. A friend of a 3rd generation boy whose parents left
the church made this comment:

> There is a great pride, especially with Greek to be a heritage
> that is something to be proud of. With all the Greeks who are
> in the Greek community, they identify with that, they hold on
> to that. Those people who live down the street, I don't sense
> that. I sense just common American persons going through their
> daily life, and the fact that they're Greek is just something
> that is there. It's not something that's redundant through
> their house, and redundant through their conversations, you

235

know, 'cause I don't even think of them as Greek and I don't
think they do.

In fact, the excessive Hellenism of the Greek Church was in most cases
a major factor which prompted such people to leave the church. The
"Greek" elements which were considered important to most of these
nonchurch Greeks were expressed by the American wife of a 2nd generation
man:

> The festive parts of it. The Greek dancing. We've taught a
> lot of our friends who are not Greek, Greek dancing. ... I
> don't know what else besides food. What makes up a culture?
> Besides religion? All the other things. He likes the handwork
> that they do, he appreciates the different artwork. But I don't
> think he feels like it's to the exclusion of everything else.

Many also mentioned that they are raising their children in a rather
"Greek" way by stressing the importance of the family and togetherness.
This is not so much out of intent to "keep Greek" as because it is the
way in which they themselves were raised, and so they use similar
techniques of child-raising and family life. Several of these people
felt that their main ties to Greekness were now through relatives who
themselves had remained in the church. Friends also provide a connection to Greekness in some cases, but as Chapter 4 pointed out, one
generally falls out of touch with them, for the main place he sees these
friends is at church and church functions; once the church--the social
locus--is gone, friendships begin to fade. But relatives are usually
always present to encourage at least a minimally "Greek" self-conception.

There are a few non-Greeks who are members of the church, and also
people of Greek descent to whom "Greekness" is of little or no importance
in comparison to Orthodoxy. A 2-3 generation girl who is in this latter
category expressed this idea.

> [It seems that to many people what's important about being Greek
> Orthodox is Greek more than Orthodox.]
> I see the exact opposite--as long as they're Orthodox whether
> they're Syrian or Russian or Armenian or whatever, the basic
> doctrine, Orthodox doctrine, the basic services, the basic feast
> day celebrations are all identical and the only difference is
> language. ... I think the way I've always been made to feel is
> that it's Orthodoxy that you want. It doesn't matter what you
> call a religion, Greek or English, it doesn't matter what langu-
> age it's in. It's the beliefs, especially regarding the sacra-
> ments--in that idea alone there is such a contrast between Ortho-
> dox and Protestant churches that it seems to me that it's Orthodoxy
> that they're striving for not just the Greek in it.

A 2nd generation woman who also subscribed to this idea that "it's

Orthodoxy they're striving for" described how she and her husband are

raising their child to be Greek Orthodox, but not "Greek". She said,

"Our feeling is that the Greek customs are nice, but we just don't keep

them. We don't even think of ourselves as Greeks, but as Americans of

Greek descent." They take their son to Sunday school, try to instill in

him a love for the Liturgy, and look forward to the day he will become an

altar boy. They are trying to raise him in such a way that the church,

rather than Greekness, is important to him. The people who fall into

this category generally seem to reject the purely "Greek" elements of

the church, such as the Greek pietisms which have no theological basis.

From the examination of these four indicative situations, one can

perhaps make a rough summary of the relationship between Greekness and

Greek Orthodoxy. First, the two are very closely related in the minds

and daily lives of most Greek Americans, but for many, the "Greek" aspect

is more important than the "Orthodox". A much smaller number reject

Greekness in favor of Orthodoxy. Between these two extremes is a more

moderate group for whom Greekness and Orthodoxy are of approximately

equal importance. Correspondingly, one can also find a continuum of customs, attitudes, and traditions which range from purely Greek to purely Orthodox. (See Figure 7) Those for whom Greekness is a more central part of their self-conceptions than Orthodoxy will stress the elements on the "Greek" end of the continuum, and those whose self-conceptions are more "Orthodox" will tend toward the choices on the "Orthodox" end. Thus this section is concluded with a tentative proposal for measuring the extent to which an individual considers himself as more "Greek" or more "Orthodox". The reader has seen the great extent to which Greek Orthodoxy influences an individual's self-conception as a Greek. It is through one's family that he enters the church, and the next section will examine the role of the family in establishing and maintaining one's "Greek" self-conception.

C. Role of the family

It is primarily in the context of his family--the people in his household--that the individual learns "what it is to be "Greek". This conception of being Greek as different from being American develops over a fairly extended period of time. As one young man said,

> When I'm used to all this [Greek stuff] that's around me, it's
> different for me to look at somebody else see it and say,
> "What's all this?", you know. And I can't imagine why they
> can't understand it. So I guess I'm still learning the dis-
> tinction.

Several elements within the family promote feelings of "Greekness". These include "blood", names, language, social customs, direct instruction, elderly relatives, and Greek activities.

First, if one's parents are Greek, it is easy for him to consider himself as Greek "by blood". The significance of blood for Greek identi-fication has already been discussed in Chapter 4, but there is a second

GREEK	MIXED--MORE GREEK	MIXED	MIXED--MORE ORTHODOX	ORTHODOX
naming children in certain order	nameday celebration		namedays	naming children for saints
Greek foods	holiday foods	Greek fasting tradition	fasting foods	fasting, religious food
should have Greek friends		should have Greek Orthodox friends		should have Orthodox friends
marriage to Greek preferred		marriage to Greek Orthodox preferred		marriage to any Orthodox O.K.
superstitions--mati	pietisms and deals with saints	local miracles	local saints	miracles
	should attend only Greek church			can attend other Orthodox churches
	don't accept non-Greek converts			accept converts
	only Greek in service			English in service O.K.
social obligations of kumbari		special treatment of godparents		religious obligations of sponsorship
	Easter egg game			
worry beads, etc.				
dancing and music				
hospitality				icons in home--altar

FIGURE 7

very basic way in which the family encourages a "Greek" self-conception:
through names.

1. Names

The individual's family and given names are a source of Greek
identity which is so obvious that it is easily overlooked. For many
people, having a Greek name was an important sign of their "Greekness"
while they were growing up. Some have no negative feelings toward their
names, but for others, the embarrassment that they felt as "different"
kids whose name no one could pronounce still continues into adulthood.
E.g., two 2-3 generation brothers discussed their name and how they
felt about it.

> J: The last name, mine's P-----------, like twelve letters,
> everybody else's name is like Smith and Jones. So we always
> had fun in school with the names. You grew up with that.
> Everytime it would stop, it would always stop on you, you
> know.
> N: So when they count roll the first day, when they say roll,
> there's a little laugh. P-----------. Ha ha.
> J: Well, to me, [I felt like a] minority because of the name
> and--I don't know, I associated with the group. I was differ-
> ent from most people, and that's just the way I thought of
> myself...Still, at work, when they ask me for my last name,
> I still, I just say, "John speaking" I won't do it, out of the
> time that I was a little kid, something happened that I cannot
> break.
> N: I can't either.
> J: And I notice how, when my friends introduce me, or when
> they want to talk to me, "Well, you ought to speak to John
> P-----------." They just say it, like Smith. It boggles me,
> man, really, my friends will call me by my--
> N: Yeah, that's true. My boss does that, and all the people
> that introduce me. "This is Mr. P-----------." But when I
> pick up the phone, I either say, "Hello," or whatever office
> I'm in, I'd say the office, you know, uhh, "Shipping Office,"
> or just "Hello." Because I don't know why, but I feel like if
> I say my name, "This is Mr. P----------- speaking," they'll
> go, "What??" or "What?? Who??" But it is funny, because I
> don't, I never say my name when I pick up the telephone.
> J: Some of these people that I meet, they say, "What's your
> name?" and they go, "Oh, what a beautiful name!" They go on

> about what a beautiful name it is, they wish they had a beauti-
> ful name like that, and really, as they say it, I keep thinking,
> "Are they just being nice? Are they really being sarcastic?"

One's last name is also in many cases a reminder of specific aspects of

his Greek heritage. For example, "Papa-" was added as a prefix to the

first names of individuals who were priests, and this combination became

the family name. Thus a man named Antonis became Papantonis, and the

prefix was passed on to all his descendants. Similarly, someone whose

name begins with "Hadji" had an ancestor who made the pilgrimage to be

baptized in the River Jordon.[2] Even those whose family name was

shortened or Anglicized on coming to the United States know what their

name was, and why it was changed. One young 3rd generation man told me:

> I would love to have our original name back...It's something
> that stands out, it's unique, it pulls you away from someone
> with a name like Smith or Jones. It's like part of your identi-
> ty. When my grandfather came over, he wanted to Americanize
> himself, so he changed it to H---. Whereas now I want to
> Greekanize myself, and I really would like our original name
> back.

First names are usually less likely than family names to call

attention because they are either names that make sense in English--

Mary, Katherine, George, Irene--or names which are translated into

English equivalents. There are two classes of names in this latter

category: (1) names which translate directly into English (Gianni =

John, Eleni = Helen); and (2) names which have no American equivalents

because they are based on Biblical events, Greek words, or lesser saints

which are not well-known in the United States. People in this class

have two names: thus, if one's Greek name, which is recorded on her

baptismal certificate, is Fotini (this name comes from Epiphany, when

Christ was baptized), her birth-certificate, American name may be Frances.

Similar names are Stavros (Stephen), meaning "cross", and Haralampus

(Harry). There is no true one-to-one correspondence between all Greek

and American names, since many of the American names are just approxima-

tions of their Greek equivalents. Thus if a girl's American name is

Evelyn, her Greek name might be Evangelia, Eudoxia, etc; similarly, if

her Greek name is Evangelia, her American name might be Evelyn or

Angela. Both the Greek and American names are used, as a 2nd generation

college girl noted:

> Every once in a while, they'll call you your Greek name—they
> use both. You identify with both names, because they're used.
> You've been called both all you life, so it's nothing new.

Why does it matter so much what someone's Greek name is, since his

legal name is the American one? He was not given his name because it

appealed to his parents; he was named for someone or something. Given

names are not chosen randomly, or out of a "What shall we name the

baby?" book. There are certain rules which should be followed in the

naming of children.

(1) The child should bear the name of either a saint or a holy

day; this is the only rule as far as the Orthodox Church is concerned.

Greek tradition supplements this rule with several others, however.

(2) The first two sons and daughters should be named after their

grandparents. The usual order of naming is:

1st son—father's father
1st daughter—mother's mother
2nd son—mother's father
2nd daughter—father's mother,

although there are a couple of exceptions to this rule. Sometimes the

father may demand that both the first son and daughter be named for his parents. Some people feel that if one or more of their siblings has already named children for a certain grandparent, the individual does not have to do so, but may choose another name. This general rule of naming children for one's parents sometimes causes uncomfortable situations. One American woman reported:

> My husband's sister had to name her child Harriet, and she hates the name. And she felt compelled, and I think that's very sad. This couple that we know had a child, and they didn't want to name him after the father, but they ended up doing it. So they called the child John Damian--they really wanted to name him Damian, and the father's name is John. So when they're around the parents, they call him John, and when they're around somebody else, they call him Damian. It's really bad.

(3) When the four grandparents are represented, the next child should preferably be named in honor of another relative, like a favorite uncle.

(4) The child should not be named for either of his parents. Some people say that to do so would be bad luck, a curse on the child. Others say that this is just a superstition, and that it's "just not done" or that it's "incredibly poor taste". A 2nd generation girl noted this.

> Like my cousin...they couldn't name the baby the same name as the grandmother because the daughter-in-law and the grandmother had the same name, and they don't name names after the mothers. They don't name the sons after the fathers, either, by the way; they do it here, but you're supposed to recognize the grandfather, not the father. Greeks have done it here, but I've never seen it done in Greece.

(5) In some circumstances, the naming of children does not follow the above rules. This is particularly true if unusual circumstances surrounded a child's birth. One woman lost a child and promised that if another were born to her, he would be named for the cross-Stavros. A second woman, had an underweight child born near the time of the

Annunciation (Evangelismos), and she named him Evangelos, in hopes that the name might "help in some way".

(6) There is also a custom which is becoming less widely practiced in America today. In Greece a child's "middle" name is not really a name at all, but the genitive form of his father's name: e.g., John of George, Γιάννης τοῦ Γεωργίου. This practice is particularly helpful because there are often many sets of first cousins with the same first names, since they were all named for the same grandparent. For example, if John Pappas has three sons, named Vasili, George, and Michael, their first sons would be named John Vasili, John George, and John Michael Pappas respectively: thus people could distinguish which family each John Pappas represented. This custom is generally continued among the first generation parents in the United States, and for this reason, one finds women with names like "Irene John". Second generation parents seem to continue the tradition primarily in the naming of their sons, because they feel it is inappropriate for a daughter to have a man's name. The "middle" name is still in many cases an important means of identification in the Houston Greek community. People make a point of including the middle initial when talking about men who have cousins with the same first and last names: Mike S. Poulos, Mike N. Poulos, and so on.

A second reason for the importance of an individual's Greek first name is that it determines his name-saint, with whom he is supposed to establish a special relationship. Furthermore, the individual celebrates his nameday on the day set aside in the church calendar to honor his name-saint. In Greece, the nameday is more important than the birthday, and is celebrated instead. Among Greeks in the United States, the

birthday is celebrated in the usual American way, but the nameday is

also recognized. For females, the nameday is a special day, but it is

not recognized with a party. Rather, friends call up and say " Χρόνια

πολλά (Chrónia pollá, Many happy returns)", or maybe come over for

coffee. Or one may get a card from her relatives or godparents with

a few dollars in it. Sometimes people take communion in celebration

of their nameday. It is much the same for a younger man as for women,

until he becomes the head of his own household. Then he is honored on

his nameday with an open house, at which at least sweets and a drink are

served, and to which most of the Greek community is invited. A 2nd

generation woman discussed how nameday celebrations have changed since

the early days of the Houston community:

> The whole idea originally was when it was your nameday, people
> would honor you by coming by to greet you, to see you. You'd
> offer him a drink, something sweet to eat, and that was it.
> But now people--well, naturally, let's face it, I can recall
> years ago too my mother used to keep the house clean and ready
> for company for two weeks at a time, because people who couldn't
> make it the first day would make it the next day, the next day,
> or the next day. Life now is such that you can't do that. So
> naturally they have it, "O.K., we're having open house at a
> particular time." But now instead of saying, "We're having
> open house, anybody that would like to come," they send out
> written invitations, so you're not honoring an individual
> spontaneously, coming to greet him, when you are sent an invi-
> tation to come. So it has changed, the whole thing has become
> one big cocktail party.

Since such an open house is trouble, and can run into great expense, it

is not always given by every family every year, except among the more

"Greeky" Greeks, or those who are fairly rich. Nevertheless, having a

nameday as well as a birthday is another aspect of being Greek which

sets the individual out from the crowd, makes him different from Americans, and thus plays a role in his self-conception.

What is the significance of one's name, to himself and to other members of the Greek community? Anyone's name is an important element of his personal identity (Strauss 1959), and this is especially true in the Greek community. First, just having a name like Angelo Papadopoulos is a constant reminder to the individual and to those around him that he is Greek. More importantly, his last name serves as a reminder of his family's history; his first name ties the individual closely to the rest of his family, and gives him his place in the scheme of things. Almost everyone is named "for" someone, which gives the individual and the members of the Greek community a sense of continuity with the past, and of where everyone "belongs" in relationship to the past, present, and even future. The importance of naming "for" was expressed by the American wife of a 2nd generation Greek:

> It is much more of an honor in the Greek community to have a child named after you than it is for Americans. Americans choose a name they like, but Greeks choose the name of someone else. The idea is that "Now you've got your own little Helen," since you admired Helen enough to want your daughter to be exactly like her. All Greek names mean something, and all little Greek kids know why they are named their name, and who they are named for. These customs make sense, and really, it's a much better way of doing things, because it gives a closer family tie, a very real sense of belonging. It draws people closer together.

An important aspect of naming is that "it draws people closer together"; again one sees the significance of "closeness" in the Greek community.

2. Language

One of the first "clues" a child gets that he is "different" is the presence at home of a different language than most Americans speak, as a 3rd generation girl noted:

Kids would come over to the house, and my grandmother would be there, and she couldn't say "Hi" to them. "This is my giagia, she's my grandmother. She can't speak English." Most of the kids that I hung around with, they eventually found out I'm Greek. ... And if I'd take somebody to church with me, some real close girl, it'd be all in Greek, you know, and I'd realize that my grandmother spoke Greek, and my mother would speak Greek, and we'd go to church and speak Greek.

The group of 2nd, 2-3, and 3rd generation people also noted this.

C: Also I remember that I learned, I probably learned Greek before English, because my parents always spoke Greek around the house. ... I do remember in kindergarten, like letting a word slip that was Greek, you know, and not knowing it, just letting it slip. And being embarrassed, because I'd said something that let everybody know that I wasn't like them.
D: This is my καρέκλα (karekla), uhh, chair.
M: Well, like when we say "Open the light." I still say that, and all my friends look at me, "What did you say?" "Open the light." "It's supposed to be turn on the light." Open the TV. In Greek, that's what you say.
D: Ἄνοιξε τό (Anixe to) TV.
C: I think lately I've just learned to say "Turn on the light".
M: But there's several phrases like that--my friends would die laughing.

The Greek language also differentiates those whose parents were born in Greece from other people, because their parents speak with an accent.

You notice it right off. Your mother speaks differently, at least ours did. You know they're different, and you know it from the start. Before you start school, you're really not too aware of it; everybody who talks to you is Greek, like when you go to church. One example is the room mothers-- all the other Anglo mothers speak normally. ... You love your mother and everything, but she's different. And you get the differentness. It's very obvious that you're different.

The Greek language is not so prevalent in some 2nd generation homes, but even those individuals whose parents speak English primarily have at least some relatives who speak little or no English. Some Greeks who do not know the Greek language try to learn it, and others usually try to keep up what they do know by using it when possible. Because of the problem of having to communicate with older people--one's grandparents

especially--most 3rd generation people know at least some Greek. A

3rd generation high school boy said:

> The only reason I'm taking Greek is so I can communicate with
> my grandmother, and some of the Greeks here. And probably
> because I think it's my responsibility, that I should learn
> Greek, since that's my ancestry.

The Greek language can be a rather explosive issue, for the older

generation expects parents to teach their children Greek. A 3rd genera-

tion boy reported this incident:

> During the Greek Festival last year, this old lady came up to
> me...and she started talking to me in Greek. But she was talk-
> ing to me in a very obnoxious way, and of course I wasn't about
> to get entangled in that, so I told her, "I can't speak, I don't
> understand you." And she got mad at me, and she got mad at my
> grandmother, blaming it on her that she didn't raise her daugh-
> ter properly to raise me to talk Greek. Because in her house
> Greek is spoken. Well, she thought that Greek was spoken in
> every house, and she got mad and was looking down on us. "Well,
> they know English instead of Greek! What's happening?"

Teaching the children Greek seems necessary to older Greeks because the

language is such an integral part of their being Greek. If the language

dies out, so will Greekness, they reason.

Those who are familiar with Greek seem to find it most useful for

saying things they do not want others to hear. Almost everyone mentioned

this to me as a definite advantage of knowing Greek, since it is not a

language with which most people are familiar. A 2nd generation woman:

> Like a lot of times I'll be with Greek friends, shopping or in
> class, and you want to say something about somebody--not bad,
> but just make a comment. You don't want anybody to understand.

The language is an important cement which binds the community together.

People who are in no way related to each other still share something in

common in the language, a few words at least. This common "Greek" bond

is demonstrated in a ritual which women almost invariably go through
when greeting each other. They usually clasp each other's hands and
return the greeting:"Κάλη μέρα, τί κάνεις;" "Καλά." ("Kali mera,
ti kanis?" "Kala.", "Good day, how are you?" "Fine.") After establishing their common bond to the community through this standard Greek
greeting, they usually change to English.

3. Social customs

There are many Greek customs--religious and social--which are
learned within the context of the home. Those religious customs which
are important in the individual's "Greek" identity have already been
examined and several social customs--cooking and food, hospitality, and
dancing and music will now be discussed.

One way that the individual learns "Greekness" in the home is
through the special foods and cooking that form a basic element of any
culture. A 2-3 generation boy and 3rd generation girl discussed Greek
foods in their homes:

> We eat Greek food pretty often. You're always reminded [that it's
> a Greek house] by the salad bowl and the vinegar, oregano, and
> garlic. Or the feta cheese. That's almost every night.

> My mother used to cook Greekier, but--she doesn't spend so much
> time you know, like she used to start in the afternoons or in
> the mornings, baking. But she still makes αύγολέμονο (avgo-
> lemona) soup...and when we have broiled chicken, she's kinda
> Greeky with the oregano, and with the olive oil in the salads.
> She doesn't cook as Greeky as some people cook, 'cause you have
> to take time. American stuff is quicky-fresh-frozen. Greek
> stuff takes a long time to make.

There are also special "Greek" ingredients which figure prominently
in cooking even American foods. These include olive oil, oregano, garlic,
cinnamon, and basil or βασιλικό (vasiliko). In his comments, a 3rd

generation boy implied that basil is used sometimes <u>because</u> it is "Greek".

> And sometimes, like some of the seasonings are used like sweet
> basil and mint are not exactly the same, but to me, I can't tell
> the difference. But to my grandmother, because it's called sweet
> basil, she'll use that instead of mint.

It is said that vasiliko is a very special plant which was at one time
reserved for the royalty; the name vasiliko is related to the word for
king, vasileus. When the cross on which Christ was crucified was found,
supposedly vasiliko was growing on it; during the holy day called "Adoration of the Holy Cross", vasiliko figures prominently in the service.
Many Greeks have such "Greek" plants as vasiliko and mint growing in
their yards.

Related to cooking practices is the custom of hospitality. When
there are guests in a Greek home, they must be served something.
Traditionally, this is a liqueur or coffee, and a sweet. A 3rd generation girl:

> Whenever someone comes over, you always try to give them some-
> thing to eat. I tell you, you go to a Greek house and try not
> to take something to eat, it's very hard. Even if they just
> try to give you a glass of water. [They] try to feed you and
> everything, just because they are super-hospitable.

In fact, one of the ways that Americans are spoken of disparagingly is
in the context of their lack of hospitality, and what an inadequate meal
they give their guests:

> I'll tell you one thing Greeks say about Americans. When a
> Greek has people over, she has all kinds of food. She'd be
> embarrassed to invite you into her home if she didn't have a
> big spread. ... If a couple of Greeks go to a luncheon, and
> all you get is like a salad--"Well, what would you expect,
> she's American." If you go to a Greek home and this is what
> you get, "My gosh, just like an American! What's the matter
> with her? Does she think she's American?"

Here then is another way in which Greeks compare themselves to "Americans":

they are much more hospitable. This provides another "Greek" attribute
which may play a significant role in the individual's conception of
himself as a Greek.

Another group of social customs first learned in the home revolve
around Greek music and dancing. Most community members have collections
of Greek records in their homes, and when a special Greek group is in
town, the parents might take the whole family out to a club to hear their
performance. Dancing is learned in the home, out with the family, and in
Greek organizations, as a 3rd generation girl noted:

> [How do you learn to dance?]
> Well, when you're little, you hang on the end of the lines, and
> eventually you start learning. And then when I was in GOYA, a
> couple of times we'd put on some shows, we went and danced for
> these other youth groups, so I learned it in that. And Maids,
> we used to go and dance for International Day at Sharpstown,
> and like that.

There are also several traditional practices carried out when people are
dancing. Some hiss through their teeth, while others may shout "Γειά
σου (Gia sou)!" in encouragement to the person who is leading the dancing. This phrase is generally a greeting, like "Hi!" but in this case
it means "Right on!" or "Do your thing!" The leader will often hold on
to the line by a handkerchief, instead of holding hands or clasping arms
like the others in the line, so that he may more easily do his fancy
(and sometimes gymnastic) variations on the steps of the dance.

  4. Teaching

The individual learns "how to be Greek" not only by observing his
family's behavior; he is also directly taught how Greeks should behave,
and how he should feel toward his Greekness. E.g., several people
mentioned that they were raised on stories of how the proud and

courageous Greeks danced off the cliffs rather than be ruled by the

Turks. Two college boys of the 3rd and 2-3 generations, told me about

their parents' instructions in Greekness:

> [Did your parents ever say "Greeks should do this or that"?]
> Dad used to do that a lot--if I'd be down in the dumps about
> something when I was small, he'd say, "You've got something
> special, that others don't have. You're Greek, you can do
> better." It was kind of a pounding-in like that. "You've
> got something better. Let people take note of it."
>
> "You should have common sense, you're Greek." You know, "Some
> dumb American would do that, but you're Greek, you should know
> better." It's just little bitty things, ways to get ahead. It
> might be something small like standing in line at a movie. Why
> go stand in line and freeze when you know the theater isn't
> going to fill up? Things like that. Or like blacks--they've
> all got big cars or color TVs in their houses, that sort of
> stuff. "You're Greek, you should know better than that."
> Smart Greek, in other words.

The constant "pounding-in" of the idea that one is "something special",

that he is better and smarter than others because of his being Greek, is

bound to have some effect on the individual's conception of himself, of

the kind of person he is. Precisely because Greekness makes him special,

it tends to occupy a central place in his self-conception.

5. Elderly relatives

A very important factor in a family's maintenance of Greek customs,

and consequently, in the self-conceptions of its members, is whether an

elderly relative lives in the household. The presence of a giagia,

pappou, thio, or thia usually insures that the household will be more

"Greek" than it would have been otherwise; there are several reasons

why this is so. The elderly relative (from now on I will just say

giagia, since this is the most common case) is more familiar with Greek

traditions than her children and grandchildren. This is especially

obvious in the case of the Greek language, for many of the giagias speak
only Greek, or just a few words of English. Thus, out of necessity the
family must speak a fair amount of Greek at home, as a 2-3 generation
boy pointed out.

> [Does a grandmother live with your family?]
> Yes, that has a lot to do with it, especially here. My grand-
> mother's been living with us since--about six years...My grand-
> mother doesn't speak any English, so everyone in the family
> knows Greek, some more than others, and that has a lot to do
> with keeping it all Greek.

The giagia also expects Greek customs to be carried out. Several people
felt that their household had been more "Greek" while their grandmother
was living there than before, and had become more lax since she had
died or moved away. A 3rd generation boy noted how his giagia had
affected his family's Greekness:

> [Has your grandmother had any influence on your home?]
> Yeah, I feel that she does have an influence. Maybe we picked
> up on our Greek a little bit, because--you know, that's all she
> could speak, so I'd have to speak it to her. As far as the
> language is concerned, I'd say yeah, because there's more Greek
> spoken.
> [What about customs?]
> She'd sometimes say, "Well, where is it?" It's a matter of,
> "Well, this is what you're brought up to do so you do it."

Another reason for the increased Greekness of such a household is
that a giagia not only wants to see Greek customs continued; she also
has the time to devote to carrying them out. Many traditional foods
require almost all day to prepare, and only someone with few other
responsibilities has the available time to prepare them and to teach
children and grandchildren how to do so. This is also true of special
religious "foods" like κόλυβα (koliva), the boiled wheat which is taken
to the church for memorial services, and προσφορον (prosforon), the

bread used in communion. It is generally the older women who prepare
these foods for the church services. The giagia also has time to teach
her grandchildren the Greek language, and to tell them stories about
Greece and the exploits of Greeks. One boy summed up the role of
grandparents in this way:

> [Are grandparents an important source of Greek language and
> customs?]
> Definitely, much more than parents. Because they are more
> Greek. In just mostly everything, really--small things you
> pick up from them in your childhood, the language too.
> [What will happen when the old people die?]
> It will go Americanism more and more and more and more. So
> that all will be left will be the church maybe, what they can
> pick up from the church.

6. Greek activities

One of the most important ways in which the family encourages a
Greek self-conception in its children, and at the same time helps to
maintain the Greek community, is by encouraging the participation of
its members in "Greek" activities. The comments of a 2-3 generation boy
reflect the types of activities parents push to encourage "Greek"
identity in their children.

> I don't know if this is being Greek, or if it is just strict
> parents and using that Greek power. It's just being raised
> --they try to force you to learn Greek, and they want you to
> go to Greek school, and learn poems, and force you to hang
> around Greek friends, and date Greeks. Like I couldn't date
> --I had to date Greek girls until I got out of high school,
> so I didn't even bother going out--or I lied. It was just
> mainly trying to keep you with--you know, connected with the
> church, learning Greek, being Greek socially. They didn't
> want you to socialize with Americans. ... And you know, being
> close to your parents, being close to the whole thing--in a
> sense, I kinda rebel sometimes. Like the music, it's good,
> but it always associates with your parents' trying to force
> you to learn all this culture crud.

The dating problems which he mentions will be discussed in Chapter 6 as will Greek organizations and friendships.

Many Greek children go to afternoon Greek language school, except
in extenuating circumstances, like a working mother who cannot get her
children to the classes. Second generation parents remember going to
Greek school "every afternoon of the world", and so the two-hour class
their children attend once a week does not seem like an unreasonable
requirement. But of course the kids dislike going to the class because
it cuts out an afternoon of other activities after having already been
at school all day. In retrospect, some young adults feel that they did
not really learn much in the Greek school anyway, as a 2-3 generation
boy noted.

> [Did you go to Greek school?]
> I went for about three years. I already knew how to speak it,
> and was supposed to have learned how to read and write it. But
> I never did get too far. There were no grades, and the parents
> weren't that concerned about it. They figured, "Well, we sent
> you, we've done our duty."

However, the purpose of Greek school is not only to have the children
learn Greek, but also to have them associate with other Greeks. Many
if not most Greek activities have this "socializing" purpose, which
will be considered in greater detail in Chapter 6.

Another important way in which the family encourages "Greekness"
through Greek activities is by sending its members on trips to Greece.
These trips may be sponsored by a Greek organization like AHEPA, or
by the church, or the family might go independently. Regardless of the
means of getting to Greece, having been there is a major aspect of
many people's enthusiasm for Greek culture, society, and identity. Here
are a 3rd generation boy's comments on his trip to Greece:

> In fact, anybody that goes to Greece and really sees how the
> people live will be influenced and touched by it so much that
> they will actually stress it in their later life. It happened
> to me...I don't know if it happened to anybody else, I think
> it has. Mainly it tended to strengthen my belief in my particu-
> lar religion to a great degree, which will probably make me
> much closer to my church.

In fact, it seems that some people don't care at all for "Greek" things

until they make the trip; then their attitude changes.

> [Some people have said they had no interest in their Greekness
> until they made a trip to Greece.]
> My sister's a good example of it. Here's all these customs and
> traditions and heritage that the people have been trying to...
> either forcing them down their throat, or they've been around
> them, and maybe it's never really clicked. But then you go to
> Greece and you see it, and you see all these people, and you talk
> to them in Greek, and they get excited because you're American
> but you can speak Greek, then you just come back with a different
> attitude. You get to like it. That's what happened to my sis-
> ter, she actually started liking it. Whereas before she resented
> the fact that she couldn't go out of town, and she had to go
> to the University of Houston, which she didn't like.

Apparently, for some individuals the forces described in this chapter--

which encourage one to have Greekness play a positive role in his self-

conception--are not successful. It takes a visit to "the old country"

to enable the individual to see for himself the traditions and history

which his group finds important, to sense a feeling of belonging and

identification with other Greeks. His being Greek then takes on a

positive meaning, and Greekness becomes a more salient part of his

self-conception, whereas before he could only see the disadvantages of

being brought up as a Greek, e.g., strict parents and a sheltered life.

Thus the family has an important influence on the centrality of

Greekness in an individual's self-conception; because of his Greek name,

customs and language in the home, and participation in Greek activities,

the individual comes to identify himself as "a Greek". The Greek

Orthodox church as well as the American public's interest in ethnicity is also a significant factor in the individual's "Greek" self-conception, and that encourages the individual to be more "Greek". In the next section the variability of ethnic self-conceptions in America will be discussed.

III. Flexibility of Ethnic Identity

In 1915, Woodrow Wilson commented: "A man who thinks of himself as belonging to a particular national group in America has not yet become an American." Parenti (1967) notes that Wilson made the commonly-accepted assumption that one's identity represents an either-or situation, that identity choices are mutually exclusive; one must consider himself either "Greek" or "American", and there are no choices in between. This idea has also characterized the thinking of many sociologists who have considered American ethnic groups--they have assumed that ethnics must inevitably become "Americans", that over the generations ethnic identification is transformed from "ethnic" to "American" as members are Americanized. The introductory chapter took issue with these ideas, and implied that there are in fact many levels of "Greek" identification available to the individual--measured by the centrality of ethnicity in his self-conception--and in this section I will discuss the continuum between "Greek" and "American" identifications, and the flexibility of ethnic identities.

A. Ethnic self-conceptions in America: A continuum

In discussing her self-conception, a 2-3 generation girl made this observation:

> I guess I identify myself as being an American more than Greek. It's nice to have another group that you can associate yourself with. You know--in this hodge-podge of people to have a certain little something of Greek that you can--the Greek heritage is such that I'm proud of that very much and even though if you asked me if I'm Greek or American, I'd say American, I'm proud to be Greek-American. So as far as identifying, first is American, second is Greek.

These comments, which are representative of the feelings of many Greek Americans, certainly refute Wilson's conception of American ethnicity as a yes-or-no proposition. During the course of my research, I have definitely found that a choice between identifying oneself as either a Greek or an American is not really appropriate. There are many choices available to Americans of Greek descent; they may identify themselves at any point along a continuum from "fully Greek" to "fully American". (These terms represent an easier way to denote the fact that one's Greekness may be the most central element, or may play no part, in his self-conception.[3])

By "fully Greek" I mean that the individual considers himself in no way an American, but a Greek who by some chance lives in America. Greeks have for centuries been forced by circumstance to live in areas which are not politically part of the Greek state, but have nevertheless clung tenaciously to their identities as Greeks. As an example one might consider the Dodecanese, twelve Greek islands off the coast of Turkey, in the Aegean Sea. The islands passed from independence to control by Rome (from 200 B.C.), then by the Byzantine Empire, the Venetians and Genoese (from 1204 A.D.), the Knights of the Hospital of St. John of Jerusalem (from 1310), the Turks (from 1523), and the Italians (from 1912); finally in 1947 the Dodecanese were united with

Greece.[4] Throughout these centuries of alien rule, however, the Dodecanesians remained Greek, and resisted all attempts of their foreign
rulers to strip them of their Greek culture, loyalty and identity. Nor
is the case of the Dodecanese unusual. The same has been true of Greeks
in Asia Minor, Crete, Cyprus, Samos, Chios, and so on. The tenacious
retention of Greek culture and identity among people from such areas
provided the basis for a major cause of the Greek people during the
late 19th and early 20th centuries--ἡ μεγάλη ιδέα (i megali idea),
"the great idea" that the Greek state should include all people who
spoke Greek and professed the Orthodox religion.[5] Greeks living in
such territories outside the political boundaries of Greece have generally
responded to i megali idea with demands for ἕνωσις (enosis, union)
with Greece. The Cyprus incident during the summer of 1974 demonstrates
that i megali idea is still a very vital force among many Greeks.

In addition to those who live in areas which are culturally but not
politically Greek, there are also Greeks living in non-Greek areas who
still consider themselves wholly Greek. E.g., a young 2-3 generation
man in discussing his financee, an Egyptian Greek, commented:

> The Greeks in Cairo consider themselves Greeks. This is what I
> don't understand because she was born there and her passport
> says she is Greek. There's some legal thing--some special--like
> my dad was also born in Egypt, but he's a Greek citizen. What
> you do is if your parents are Greek, you can claim that you want
> to be a Greek citizen, they allow it, so that way they don't
> lose their identity. So that's why they consider themselves
> Greek, because even on their passport it says they're Greek.
> My passport says I'm American.

This attitude--in which individuals "consider themselves Greek"--is
probably not at all unusual among Greeks who live in non-Greek areas.
The Greek custom of considering an individual born to Greek parents

as Greek, regardless of the place of birth, contributes to this
conception of one's being "a Greek who just happens to live outside of
Greece". Just as Egyptian Greeks may consider themselves true Greeks,
so many Greeks living in America may also think of themselves as "Greeks"
who happen to live in America. This is surely only among some of the
1st generation who originally immigrated to the United States, and not
among their children, who are American citizens by birth, and who have
in most cases been raised in the United States. Thus, even though their
number is probably relatively small, one must allow for the presence of
people who consider themselves 100 percent Greek, even though they may
have lived in America fifty years. Considering that the Dodecanesians
retained their Greek identities after more than 2000 years of foreign
rule, this retention of one's Greek identity in America should come as
no surprise.

On the opposite end of the continuum one finds an "American"
identity. Chapter 4 noted that there are some individuals who decide to
sever ties with the community and "become American" rather than to
continue living their lives as members of the Greek group. These people
have left behind their social Greekness, and their Greekness may or may
not continue to be a salient aspect of their self-conceptions. I can
cite the case of one 2nd generation man who left the church and considers
himself "American". His wife commented on his "American" identification:

> N would say that he's American, 100 percent. Sometimes the
> Greeks will call up and say, "We're celebrating Independence
> Day, why don't you come on over?" And he'll say, "Funny, I
> thought Independence Day was in July!" They say, "Come on,
> N, you know what we mean!" and he'll reply, "Well, I'm an
> American, and our Independence Day is July 4th." He thinks,
> "Why should I be so concerned with something that happened

between the Greeks and the Turks so long ago? This isn't Greece
we're living in, it's America!"

As long as an individual retains his membership in the Greek Orthodox
church, he will probably never identify himself as "fully American",
because of the identificational ties to Greekness which the church
encourages. Thus, although each generation may identify itself as "more
American" than that which preceded it, there will continue to be an
element of Greekness in the self-conceptions of those who belong to the
Greek Orthodox church. A split with the church, however, enables one
to take the final step of identifying himself as an "American".

Between these two relatively rare extremes of the continuum there
are many intermediate points, from "more Greek" through "equally Greek
and American", to "more American". E.g., a 3rd generation boy demonstrated his identification as "more American" when he said:

> I consider myself American. If Greece was in a war, I wouldn't
> die for--I wouldn't go over to Greece and help fight. Not that
> I don't like it, and not that I wouldn't want it, inside, "Oh,
> I hope Greece wins." ... Same way like in school, I'm not going
> to go parading around on March 25, "This is Greek Independence
> Day!" and wear blue and white or little banners and flags or
> something, because I'm not Greek, I'm American.

B.   Flexibility of ethnic self-conceptions

It is easy to sense that within the self-conceptions of Americans
of Greek ancestry many levels of "Greek" or "American" identification
are possible, but it is an oversimplification to think of one's
position on this continuum as permanent. The salience of one's ethnicity
may change from one period of his life to another, according to external
circumstances, or even by personal decision to do so. I will now discuss
the extent of this personal variability in ethnic self-conception, citing

cases in which people have become more and less "Greek", and also times at which Greek Americans are identified as more "Greek" or "American".

A 2-3 generation man, engaged to a Greek Greek, made this comment about his own Greekness:

> One thing that might tip the scales is that I am marrying a Greek girl. And I will eventually probably become more Greek.

This comment should not come as a surprise, since the reader has already noted that during different periods of his life, the individual is more and less "Greek", i.e., Greekness is not particularly central to his self-conception, and his membership and participation in the community are not of importance to him. E.g., during school years, he associates more with Americans--and is less concerned about his identity as a "Greek"--then at the time when he marries and has children, thereby re-entering Greek social circles to a greater extent (assuming he "marries Greek", of course).

One may also become less Greek, however. Some people even decide to "become American", but this is just an extreme instance of the more general tendency to become less Greek. The individual may become less Greek as a result of marriage to a non-Greek or of leaving the Greek Orthodox church, e.g., by entering non-Greek social circles, thereby reducing the importance of his Greekness. I have also seen a more interesting situation occur--in several instances, individuals have consciously decided to be less Greek. One woman commented that she was much happier since she had decided not to worry about being Greek anymore; she was now more her own person. She was _herself_, not "a Greek".

One of the situations in which it is most interesting to compare personal self-conceptions and the ways in which they change is the case in which Greek Americans travel to Greece. A 2-3 generation boy expressed a common feeling when he said:

> We are considered Americans in Greece, and we're considered Greeks here, so--we're in a vicious circle sort of like. We're our own breed. I wouldn't consider us Greek, and I wouldn't consider us American--we're Greek American.

Many Greek Americans have mentioned that while visiting in Greece they are identified--and identify themselves--as Americans, whereas in America they always identify themselves as "Greek". This does not mean that they feel no sense of identification with Greece and Greeks; as an earlier section noted, a trip to Greece often moves the individual greatly, giving him a deeper sense of the value of his cultural heritage, and often strengthening the salience of Greekness in his self-conception. Nevertheless, while in Greece the Greek American is seen, and sees himself, as an American. Perhaps this is because he realizes in the Greek surroundings that he really is much more an American than he has been led to believe by his family, his church, and himself as well. Despite his being "raised Greek", he often discovers that culturally the Greek people are rather strange to him, more so than his "American" neighbors or co-workers. I am reminded of the comments of a young 2-3 generation man about being a Greek American.

> To me, the whole Greek thing is kinda silly, it's very ethnic Sometimes it's cool to be ethnic, but then when someone asks you, "What are you?" I don't think you should say Greek. Because you're born here and raised here, and you do have all the Greek ideas, but your whole life is here. You speak in English--you may learn some Greek, and all that. To me, you're not a Greek unless you live in Greece. And if I ever moved to Greece, and tried to become part of their society and

finally did, talked with them and--became friends with them,
and just lived their life, their type of life, then I think
I would have to consider myself a Greek. I don't know if
they would accept me as that, but why not? Because I'm living
there, and doing everything they do, I mean, I was born somewhere else, yeah, but I would try to consider myself Greek.
I think it would be stupid to go over there and say, "I'm
the American, take me or leave me. I'm going to do everything
my way." You can't do that, you've got to adjust to their life.

IV. Discussion

Chapter 1 noted the fact that the centrality of ethnicity in one's

self-conception is closely realted to his identification as a participa-

ting member of the ethnic community. These two facets of ethnic identi-

fication are so closely related that they are generally assumed to be

inseparable, and measures of the salience of ethnicity in one's self-

conception frequently depend on examining the extent of his community

participation. I have suggested that the two can in fact exist inde-

pendently of each other, and in Chapter 4 discussed instances in which

this occurs. Since I have claimed that ethnic self-conception and

community membership are distinct phenomena, it is now my job to analyze

the nature of the relationship between them. How does "ethnic" member-

ship affect one's self-conception? and vice versa, how does one's

self-conception influence his membership choice? Both of these questions

are of great significance to the topic of this research, the factors

which encourage the maintenance of the ethnic group.

The way in which one's group membership influences his self-concep-

tion is fairly obvious and does not require extensive discussion. Just

being a member of the Greek community is bound to have a great impact

on an individual's self-conception and undoubtedly plays an important role in the way he defines himself. It is within the context of the group that "Greekness" develops as a significant element of one's self-conception. Of central importance to anyone's self-conception is its confirmation through community recognition of its validity. Thus in the local Greek community the individual learns that he is Greek, what it means to be Greek, and how to be Greek; and his emerging Greekness and "Greek" self-conception are confirmed in interaction with other community members.

How one's self-conception affects his choice of community membership (which defines his membership in the ethnic group, i.e., whether he is "assimilated") is less easily determined. The information presented in this chapter suggests several leads, however. If Greekness is a central element of the individual's conception, of who he is, it is logical that he would want to interact with other Greeks and to participate in a Greek community. An important aspect of a "Greek" self-conception involves special feelings aroused by being with other Greeks--dancing, eating and drinking, and speaking Greek. These unique Greek activities which give rise to "this tremendous exhilarating feeling, the kefi", are group activities which the individual cannot do on his own. Thus the person to whom "the kefi" is important needs other Greeks to help him get that feeling. A second factor is the equating of Greekness with Greek Orthodoxy. Since these two phenomena are so closely related in the minds of the Greek people, a "Greek" self-conception will usually predispose that individual to conceive of himself as Greek Orthodox as well. This religious self-conception will result in some sort of relationship, however tenuous, with the

Greek community and its members, since even nominal Greek Orthodox
will be married and have their children baptized in the church, and will
also attend a couple of services a year. The component of racial
superiority and the invidious comparisons with other groups which play an
important role in the self-conceptions of many Greeks may also influence
the individual to remain in the community. Because of these aspects of
his self-conception, he may view Greeks as people who are in some way
special, and desire to socialize within the group almost exclusively.
If non-Greeks are seen as cold, inhospitable, unfeeling, dirty, or lower-
class, why should one go outside the group to form relationships?

The effect of one's "ethnic" self-conception on his group membership, as expressed by participation in the local Greek community, was
noted by a 2nd generation man who discussed Greeks who have "married
out" and attend the church only once or twice a year.

> There's a certain peculiar spirit I guess with any person, and
> I can speak for the Greek I guess more than anyone else. For
> example, if I were to go in China, and I were to become involved
> with the Chinese community altogether, and married and had
> children, so on and so forth, and adopt that country, uhh--as
> a Greek, I will miss my identity, I would yearn for it. I would
> never--and then when I had the opportunity, I would come back to
> it. Although I may be completely a Chinaman, or completely
> engulfed in this society, I think whenever I have a chance,
> I will probably look for a chance to go back to my church,
> at least two or three times a year. ... So I think those who
> more or less go that route uhh have that feeling and yearning
> to come back again, and this is when you see them.

Thus one's self-conception does play a significant role in his group
membership. Other forces which encourage the individual to remain
within the Greek community will be considered in Chapter 6.

HOLY FRIDAY

Great Royal Hours--Christ crucified

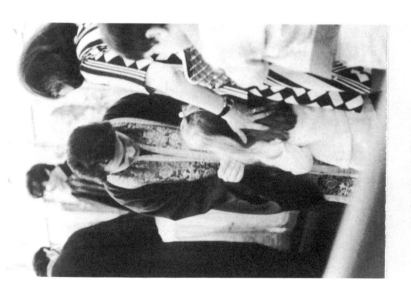

HOLY WEDNESDAY

Holy Unction

HOLY FRIDAY

Service of the Descent from the Cross

Crawling under the tomb

Reverencing the body of Christ

HOLY FRIDAY

Lamentations service--Procession of the epitafios

EASTER

"The kindling of the new fire"

Cracking Easter eggs, after Easter service

HOLY WEEK--EASTER

CHAPTER 6

MAINTAINING THE COMMUNITY

Although the salience of ethnicity in one's self-conception is a
significant feature of ethnicity in America, a more important issue is
his membership in the ethnic community, for this is the crucial element
determining the continuation of an ethnic group as a group. Of course
a strong "Greek" self-conception is often a factor in determining
whether an individual will continue to identify himself with the Greek
community, and in the previous chapter several forces which encourage
such a self-conception were noted. Nevertheless, there are also other
factors within the community which directly act to encourage the individual to remain within the Greek community, and these forces are the
subject of this chapter. I will first examine the significance of
community membership--what the individual gains and loses by choosing
to identify himself as a member of the Greek group--and then discuss
the several factors which encourage one to remain associated with the
community, concentrating particularly on courtship and marriage as a
vehicle for maintaining the group.

I. Significance of Community Membership

This section will consider the significance of membership in the
Greek community for those who claim it, why it is important to Greek
Americans to identify themselves with the Greek community. Several
ways in which one's community membership is beneficial--in giving the
individual a sense of "community", a source of identity and security,

and something "different" which sets him out from a crowd--will be
discussed, as well as one way in which such an identity may be detrimental, by proving too limiting and confining. The individual's
personal response to these implications of ethnic membership no doubt
affects the extent to which he chooses to identify himself as a member
of the Greek group.

A. A sense of "community"

> You come from a--Greece, you know, and you want to preserve
> what you brought with you, you don't want to just dispense it
> and let it go. I am Greek, and they're [parents] proud of it,
> they're glad we're Greek, they thought it was good, they wanted
> to pass it on, and they want to keep the group together. Golly,
> you know?

These comments from a 2nd generation girl demonstrate one of the central
reasons for maintaining membership in the community--"to keep the group
together". Chapter 4 noted that the special feeling of "community" which
is shared by those who have a common Greek identity and background is
the central meaning of Greekness for members. Those who identify themselves with the Greek community share this very gratifying sense of
community, which is to a large extent lost for many individuals who live
in modern urban society. It is a little bit of Gemeinschaft in a great
big confusing Gesellschaft world, as a 2-3 generation girl noted:

> It's part of an identity thing too, people wanting to relate
> themselves with a smaller sphere instead of just--there's so
> many--the wide world out there--it gives you a chance to
> associate with a smaller closed-in group.

The classical view that Gemeinschaft is on the way out in our rational-
istic urbanized and bureaucratized society simply does not hold in the
case of individuals such as members of Houston's Greek community, who
have tenaciously clung to their small ethnic group. Despite the numerous,

frequently-cited disadvantages of such associations (impediments to individual social mobility, e.g.), there must be an advantage to retaining these pre-rationalistic ties, and I believe that this is the sense of "community" which they offer. Being ethnic gives one a ready-made "community" with which to associate, and facilitates close ties with family, friends and church. This fact was noted by an American woman who married a Greek:

> I'm the one who pushes. Because I think that it's good to have an identity like that, I think that you're really privileged to have a heritage that you can keep that close with and keep in contact with, and identify with. I think it's great. I think it makes you feel just a little bit closer sometimes to your community, to your church, and family. And a lot of people don't have that heritage to hold on to. We all know Christopher Columbus and rah-rah-rah, and our American heritage. But this is relatively new, and I think it's nice to have an ethnic heritage too.

B. A source of security

Participation in an ethnic community also gives the individual a sense of belonging and of roots. Being a part of such a community is a very powerful source of security.

> It helps you know who you are! Because like I said you feel like an individual. Really, I go away to school at UT and ... I think all the time, "What am I?" But like the first Sunday you're back in church, it's like a home--it's a secure little haven. And it's not just the building--it's the whole thing-- you're back, you're safe--kinda a protective thing.

This 2nd generation girl's comment demonstrates a significant result of identifying with the Greek community: by tying him to a small, ethnic community, Greek membership gives the individual a strong feeling of security. The community is a "secure little haven". A young woman who became engaged to a Greek boy and joined the Greek church commented:

> I don't know, it's hard to explain, it's just a feeling--you

> know, of security. It's something different; and you're not
> alone. ... I'm recognized by everybody I know as a Greek,
> which gives me a good feeling. This is something I've needed,
> I've been looking for...I feel more "family" here than I do at
> home.

Extensive family ties and intense loyalty have acted to keep Greeks closer to "home" in general than many of their "American" counterparts. Rather than seeking employment elsewhere, Greeks tend to remain in their hometown, near their friends and family. This pattern of geographic stability is gradually declining as younger Greeks become more mobile; nevertheless, when a Greek moves to an unfamiliar city he finds a ready-made "community", centered around the local Greek church, waiting for him. This does not mean that there are no adjustment problems, but they are minimized by the presence of familiar Greek clubs, dances, church services, activities, and probably contacts with friends of relatives, relatives of friends, or friends of friends--or even people he met at a national convention.

This firm sense of security available to "ethnics" is lost to many other people in America's highly mobile, urban society. Again one comes up against a facet of urban industrial society which supposedly causes great psychic hardship on urban dwellers, which Greeks find to be little problem at all. An American who dated a Greek girl made several interesting observations on this feeling of security:

> Part of it I envy. Like I said, I'm a loner and yet every now
> and then, I do really feel insecure. I've always got me, you
> know; it's nice to have a lot of other people. And like G said
> to me one time, "One thing that's always nice about it is that
> it is never changing, it's always the same, it's a secure thing
> you know, like I can always go back to that." ... That is a
> good point about it, there's nothing wrong with having something
> secure to be able to go back to. I think in this case with some
> people that secureness has become an obsession, you know,

>"Don't change it, don't destroy it whatever you do." ...
>They're afraid by changing it they'll destroy it, which is
>true. It's easy for me to sit here and say that cause I
>have never had anything secure--I'm a loner, I'm pretty much
>by myself, do things by myself so I can easily say that. I've
>been alone, you know, so I know what that's like. Maybe if I
>hadn't, if I was just the opposite, I would be saying "No, no,
>let's don't change it." It's interesting to know why I am the
>way I am, maybe if I were born in the Greek, probably so,
>probably definitely if I were born in the Greek world I would
>probably be that way. It's a conditioning thing from the year
>zero right on up, you know. ... Maybe there was twenty some
>odd Greek people in high school, you know, you look through
>the year book and they are just regular people, and I'm sure
>they feel just like regular people. But they have that security
>thing, you know, they do have that, that "one place of birth
>I can go to and go 'ah, security'," you know. And in a way,
>I am envious of them.

In his comments one hears a common complaint of urban man: "I'm a loner,
and yet...I do really feel insecure." He recognizes the fact that Greeks
are "just regular people", and yet "they have that security thing" which
he envies. All is not rosy for members, however, for by protecting the
security they value so highly they can cause the community to stagnate.
There is little room for innovation, for any change may threaten the
community as they know it, and consequently threaten their security as
well.

C. A source of identity: Having "something different"

Perhaps the most notable aspect of being a member of the Greek
community is the fact that it makes the individual feel special, because
he has "something different" that many Americans cannot claim. Being
Greek provides the individual with the basis for a rather unique identity,
which sets him apart from the crowd. From the following statements we
can see that this aspect of Greek membership is very significant to
many Greek Americans. The group of 2nd, 2-3, and 3rd generation men

and women:

> C: Now it's nice to be different, because you don't want to
> be a number like everyone else.
> M: That's right.
> C: Really, it helps you to be an individual. It makes you feel
> --it gives you an individuality, and you know, you're something
> different, you're something neat now.
> S: At least you're not just anybody.
> M: I think it's cool, because I can just be myself, I'm differ-
> ent. I don't have to try to be anybody.
> C: I think that's one thing that wants us to kinda try to marry
> Greek people, you know, because we want to stay different, and
> stay neat.

A young 3rd generation man:

> To me, the only thing about--this seems a little egotistical or
> something, but--to me, the majority--the reason I would want to
> keep the tradition in the home would be to make myself different
> from the person that lives next-door to me.

"Greek" membership is significant for those who hold it by providing

them with a sense of "community" as well as a source of security and

identity in a large metropolis. Thus community membership is generally

beneficial; on the other hand, it also has drawbacks.

D. Limitations

There are several possible points of difficulty associated with

membership in the Greek community, but each is related to the fact that

it can prove too limiting to the individual. These problems are not

necessarily inevitable, but can develop when the individual is very

closely associated with the community--raised in a very Greek home,

deeply involved with Greek social affairs, and so on. This sense of

limitation was expressed by a 3rd generation girl.

> I think people do tend after a while if they've always been
> brought up in a really Greek home environment they want--they
> get to a point where they really want out of it because they
> don't like feeling limited.

Deep involvement with the Greek community limits the individual in

several ways. First, it restricts him socially and culturally. Those
who spend a large majority of their time in Greek activities--church and
Sunday school, GOYA, AHEPA, GAPA, Philoptochos, Annunciation school--and
whose friends and associates are mostly Greek have little time for
associating with others. An American woman mentioned an incident which
demonstrates the extent to which the social world of community members
can become tightly circumscribed:

> It happened last Sunday. We didn't go to church, and we were
> watching the TV services. And my four-year-old came in and
> asked the seven-year-old what he was doing and he said, "I'm
> watching the Greek Methodist church." And I said, "A,
> it's not the Greek Methodist church, it's just the Methodist
> church, 'cause there's only one Greek church." And it got me
> to thinking, he goes to Sunday school, he goes to school, and
> most of his entertainment stems from the same place, so why
> shouldn't the rest of the world be Greek? It's--his whole
> world is. And then also another thought occurred to me, A does
> not realize that I'm not Greek, you know, it has never occurred
> to any of us to explain, and the subject has never come up.
> It's just something that struck me, after he mentioned that--
> his whole world is so much this that it has never occurred to
> him that his other grandparents are not, and that all these
> other people around him are something else. And it's because
> of the church, because really we are--their school and every-
> thing is so church-oriented.

By confining themselves to Greek circles, many people do not experience
first hand what American culture and society have to offer. Their
association with non-Greeks is rather narrowly circumscribed, and generally confined to more formalized relationships--with co-workers, grocers,
or teachers--rather than informal relationships between friends. A
2-3 generation man and his American wife discussed this problem.

> H: The one good thing about it is you have some place to go,
> you know people and you have friends. But then again that's
> just one part of everything. When you go out of it, the people
> that you deal with are not going to be Greek, if you want to
> tell them something and they don't understand it because "That's
> the way we do it in Greece," you know, they're not there,

they're here.
W: And really a lot it's kinda like a crutch. But like you
said, it's something you can belong to, you can fall back on
it if you need a group to belong to.

This social restriction has another effect, however, in that it can also

give the individual a feeling of being boxed-in, a sense that many

possible alternatives which are available to non-Greeks are not open

to him as a Greek; he is being limited by being Greek, by identifying

himself with the Greek community. This feeling was stated very emotion-

ally by a young 3rd generation woman:

That's one reason I started resenting it, because like all the
friends that come over are Greek, and you go out, and the people
they take you to are all Greek, and you start resenting that
they're stifling my--you try to analyze what it is you don't
like about them, and the reason I don't like them is I think of
them as a hindrance to--the Greeks, you know--I think of them
as a hindrance to me.

It is precisely this feeling of restriction and limitation to which

many people who have left the Greek community object. It is possible

to avoid these confining aspects of being Greek by participating only

marginally in the Greek community, but in so doing one misses out to a

large extent on the beneficial aspects--the sense of security and inti-

macy that comes from belonging to a community as well as the sense of

being someone different and special. Thus it is rather difficult for

many Greeks to establish their membership and participation in the

community at a happy medium between these two points. There are of

course some Greeks who are quite content to throw themselves completely

into their Greekness and spend their whole lives within narrow Greek

social circles, and others who completely rebel against this restric-

tiveness and essentially become "Americans". Many people manage to

establish a satisfactory level of participation which successfully
works out the problem, and others may phase in and out of the community
periodically. A 2nd generation woman implied that this was her solution
to the problem.

> We've been very active in the community, in PTA work, the
> schools. And I've tried to be active at the church, but
> sometimes I get upset and just quit and resign. So--
> [What kinda participation do you have in the community right
> now?]
> In the Greek community? Right now? Nil, nothing.

For all of these solutions, the individual is still considered a member
of the group as long as he fulfills the basic requirements of Greek
blood, Greek Orthodoxy, and a modicum of social participation.

This discussion makes it appear that identifying with the community
is purely a matter of personal preference, that one is free to stay in
the community or leave it, as he will. This is not the case, for the
matter is much more complex than that. Pressures--some subtle, others
blatant--from parents, friends, the community, the church, and even
oneself act on the individual and greatly influence his final decision.
A 2nd generation man who left the community discussed his hopes for
his son, and mentioned such pressures.

> [Back to your son. Do you want him to be Greek?]
> I guess I'd like for him to know about it, and if I can tell
> him any of the good things about it, I'd like him to know that
> part, and he can participate if he wanted to. But I wouldn't
> want him to feel like he had to do it. Or I wouldn't want him
> to feel the same pressures that I felt.

These forces toward membership and participation provide the next topic.

II. Forces in Community Membership

A. What's being saved?

From the previous section one understands to an extent what is at stake for the individual who chooses to stay in or to leave the community. But what is the reason for the existence of pressures that work to keep the individual involved in the community? The obvious answer is that the Greek community, the local expression of the Greek ethnic group, will cease to exist if its members leave. Community members fully understand this and, in response to this problem, have developed numerous ways of encouraging the maintenance of membership. E.g., a 2nd generation girl in discussing the fact that community members are cold toward outsiders who might marry Greeks (and take them away from the community) hit the nail on the head by saying, "It's just as a protective measure. You just don't want your group to fall apart, that's all."

The community embodies all that is significant in being Greek—a sense of intimacy and togetherness with those who share one's religion, blood, culture, and social patterns—and this sense of togetherness is what is being maintained as long as the community survives. Among many Greeks there is a great sense of the seriousness of "losing" members. A 2nd generation man voiced a common fear when he said,

> I'm looking at this now—we're 2nd generation. All right, my
> children—I see a trend of drifting away. I really see this.
> It's scarey. Because we want our children to hang on to being
> Greek Orthodox. We're pointing in that direction in our home
> life and activity with the church and this and that. But I'm
> just wondering—tomorrow, their children—will they have a
> little bit, will they sit back and say, "Well, yes, I'm of
> Greek extraction, I'm proud of it."?

Those who no longer participate in the community, who no longer partake of the intimacy and togetherness it offers, are "lost", even though they may still have some ties to community members (in particular, relatives).

The sense of loss is particularly acute if it is one's own child who is lost, as the story told by an American woman of the community demonstrates:

> One [woman] in particular whose son did not marry a Greek girl and who left his church, and--well, I can't say left his family because she still sees them, but left his church community. ... She feels that she lost her son. She lost him to someone who's not Greek. And this is where she puts the blame. ... But she has said so many times when she sees me down there working, she'll come up and say, "Oh, I wish my son had married a girl like you." Meaning that she would liked to have seen her daughter-in-law down there. It's pretty sad. ... But I know she feels this way. She says, "If my son had married someone like you, I wouldn't have lost him."

Thus, since the community is so important to its members, and since they get so much out of it, they want to keep the group together and pass on the religion, cultural traditions, and friendships that are such an integral part of their lives, of them_selves_. The following sections will very briefly examine the ways in which community members act to develop and preserve one's attachment to Greek friends and the Greek church, and then consider in some detail the area of the most pervasive pressure--in dating and marriage.

B. Friends and church

Several ways in which parents encourage Greek friendships were examined in Chapter 3, so I will only cite the comments of two individuals, a 3rd generation boy and a 2nd generation woman, to demonstrate how and why parents do this.

> They'd always take us to church, picnics, and GOYA. They'd always take you even though you didn't want to go. That always took top priority. If there was something going on, a meeting or a dance, you were going whether you liked it or not. They wanted you to be social, so maybe you wouldn't pull away from the group. "Maybe he'll develop friendships that'll keep him close." And I guess it has worked.

[Do you feel that you should try to keep your kids around other Greek kids as much as possible? Or does it matter to you?] Very much. It matters to me very much, and I'm very--I mean, these parents that don't get their children involved in Sunday school, in Junior GOYA--now you cannot tell me that our church does not furnish the youth with enough activities and enough guidance, to keep them in church. ... I think that if you open your house, once your children are old enough, and entertain, and have Junior GOYA over here, have little parties --keep your children together. And they'll stay together, they are less apt to wander, and to get involved with other groups. Let's face it, we're all selfish in that respect. I want my children to stay in the church, and I'll do my darndest to keep them in the church. It's an effort for me to try to take J down to basketball practice once a week, and to run him to basketball games, and to give up our Saturday mornings to see him play basketball, but yet, for him, he knows all the boys. You see them after fellowship coffee, they cling you know, they start talking. Well, that to me is--if you keep the children involved, in the church, they'll stay there. There's one bad egg that's gonna leave no matter what you do, but I think that if you show all effort and really keep your children in, they'll stay there.

In other words, parents very actively encourage Greek activities, friendships, and church to "keep the children together". It is hoped that by doing so, they will insure their children's continued association with the church and with the group. Those parents who fail to do so may feel the sting of community criticism. A 2nd generation woman discussed the pressures she felt from other Greeks about allowing her children to participate in American activities and to draw away from the community.

I let them be very active in school, and tried to join the community. Now it may have not worked where they are as popular or as--do a lot in the Greek community. ... I wanted to bring my children up where they--I feel that I can associate with the Greeks as well as the--American friends. But I have through the years realized a lot of the Greeks have not accepted this. They look at me in a you know, think I'm making a--

There is great social pressure on the individual to stay in the church. It begins with one's parents pushing him into church participation, as a 2nd generation man implied in talking about a certain family.

> They're quite regular as far as the church is concerned, and I
> think the girls will be good Greek Orthodox. I think they had
> a good upbringing, their parents brainwashing them as far as
> being good Greek Orthodox--and Greek too.

Despite such "brainwashing", some individuals leave the church--perhaps

because of the problems discussed in Chapter 2. Those who choose to

leave the church of course experience intense social pressure from their

families and the community, frequently because they will be "lost" to

the community rather than for true religious reasons. A 2nd generation

man commented on the pressures he encountered on leaving the church.

> Their attitude is that if you don't pay your dues--they feel
> like you're deserting them, that you're rejecting your parents
> and all this stuff, you're denying your heritage, that you're
> just turning on them and your heritage and everything if you
> don't stay a member of the Greek church and pay your dues. Even
> though you disagree with everything, you don't believe anything
> in it, it's better to be a hypocrite and still pay your dues,
> then you're O.K. Which is really a crazy mixed-up value system.
> [What have people said that has given you this impression?]
> Well mainly "How can you do that?" Although they tell you
> stories of other people. They don't confront you directly. ...
> It's like "Well, you remember so-and-so, such a nice lady, well
> she had a son that married an American girl--an Americanida
> they say--and they didn't do this." It parallels your situation.
> "It broke her heart poor lady--now she sits around you know--"
> [Staring at the walls.]
> Yeh, that's it, and they make you feel like you're gonna kill
> somebody if you don't do that. It's not very subtle, but that's
> the type of feeling they try to create.

Such pressure on those who have strayed may seem overdone, but it is

necessary if the group is to be kept together. A central element of

Greekness, of the Greek group, is Orthodoxy, and it must survive so

that the group will have a religious, as well as a social basis for

existence. The comment of a 2nd generation woman demonstrates the

significance of staying close to the church:

> I don't think the Greeks that come over from Greece are
> inclined to stay close to the church like we are. They don't

> realize yet--they're still new, they don't realize that if we
> do not keep our church alive, that we will lose our children.

Again one sees that the central issue in keeping close to the church is
not really religion per se, but maintaining the group, keeping it
together.

Although the individual no doubt feels constrained by these forces
to have Greek friends and to remain in the church, the greatest pressures
probably occur when he begins to date and to seriously consider marriage.
The processes of courtship and marriage will now be considered in some
detail, since the future of the Greek group is greatly affected by
whether the individual chooses to marry a Greek or an American.

C. Dating and marriage--"Marry Greek"

The easiest way to maintain Greek culture, and society, and identity
in the United States is by keeping the Greek community separate, if not
geographically or socially, at least maritally. As long as Greeks do not
marry non-Greeks, a main bastion of Greek culture and identity--the
family--is kept "pure". Tinker has commented on the significance of
intermarriage:

> Marriage involves not only relations among the husband, wife,
> and children, but also relations with the extended family.
> The marriage is one knot in a broad and complicated net of
> social relations--long-lasting, important, and, above all,
> intimate social relations (1973:50-1).

Intermarriage is rightly viewed by community members as a threat, for in
the chain of relationships between individuals and families that makes
the community close the intermarried couple can form a very weak link.
Children whose parents are both Greek are more likely to cling to
Greek identity and customs than are those who have a non-Greek parent.

The children of such a marriage are likely to be less "Greek" than they would have been if the Greek parent had married another Greek, and less likely to remain associated with the community. Furthermore, a "mixed" marriage directly introduces American influences into the Greek community by the presence of the non-Greek spouse in the church, in Greek organizations, and in Greek social circles. These Americans have the influence of slowly eroding the Greekness of the Greek community by bringing in their "American" ideas and ways of doing things. Thus the Americanizing effect of mixed marriages is both delayed--through the one-half Greek/one-half American children--and immediate--through the influence of the American spouses on the Greek community. The Greek group will therefore be best able to survive if Greeks do not marry non-Greeks, and it is for this reason that community members discourage dating and marriage to non-Greeks.

1. Marriage preferences

It is not difficult to determine a general hierarchy ranking the possible spouses that a Greek might marry. Several clues about this hierarchy can be obtained from the following excerpts. The first is a 2nd generation couple whose comments came in answer to my question about whether it mattered if one's children married a Patmian, Chiotis, or so on.

> W: I think nowadays they want them to marry Greek Americans.
> They don't like to have their daughters marry fellows from
> Greece because they're over here with no security, no job, no
> education. Even though they're Greek. That they're Greek
> doesn't carry that much weight if they're not employed and
> they're not educated.
> H: I'm not too sure though that if they had their preferences
> that they would probably--
> W: Have them marry an unemployed Greek from Greece.

H: Right; than someone who's American who's well off unless they're rich--doctor, lawyer--then you forget all about your Greek heritage I think.
W: That makes a difference too.
H: I think definitely they would rather have their daughters marry an unemployed Greek than just someone outside the church that's better off.
W: I've heard that, "She married at 40, but he was a doctor" - and that was O.K. - "He's gonna take care of her," so it all has its--

The second example is a comment from a single 2nd generation girl:

To marry an American, a non-Greek, it has to be a really super non-Greek to be equivalent to a lower Greek--and a lot of times they'd rather see you marry a Greek that was kinda lower, just the fact that you're marrying a Greek. I know one lady that has two son-in-laws, and one's Greek and one's non-Greek, and in my opinion, if you look at it objectively, I think the non-Greek is a nicer boy, if I had to pick I'd take him before the Greek one. But see, she's more excited about her Greek one because he's Greek, see. That's kinda bad.

From these two comments one can construct a hierarchy which would probably

agree with that held by most Greeks:

1. Well-off Greek American;

2. Average Greek American;

3. Really rich Greek Greek or American;

4. Average Greek Greek or inadequate Greek American;

5. Inadequate Greek Greek or average American; and

6. Inadequate American,

where "inadequate" means unskilled, uneducated, unemployed, or having a

poor job. However, when discussing their marriage hopes, Greek kids

invariably begin by saying, "I will marry the person I love, whether

he (or she) is Greek or American or whatever!" The American emphasis

on "love" as the basis for marriage has not surprisingly had an important

effect on these young people's conceptions of courtship and marriage.

They may also be reacting to an extent to their grandparents' (and even parents') marriages, in which "love" was frequently not the foremost issue.

All other things being equal, however, if the young Greek were given the choice between an American and a Greek spouse, it appears he or she would generally choose the Greek. The reasons for wanting to "marry Greek" are much more vital and pressing than just feeling he would get along better with someone who understood his religious and cultural background. Many people really enjoy their Greekness and feel that it would be difficult to maintain if they married outside the group. The inconveniences which arise while one is dating an American might develop into major problems during marriage; these sorts of problems are described by a 2nd generation girl:

> Like a friend of mine was dating this boy. ... The main problem
> is that she has a lot of that Greek culture in her--and the boy
> that she's dating doesn't accept Greek ways very much, and it
> hurts her because she kinda feels like she's losing her identi-
> ty by trying not to--she's been brought up so--not extreme
> Greek, but a lot of Greek culture in her, and it causes problems.
> Because when she's with him, he doesn't like the Greek dancing
> and music and a lot of that, and she kinda enjoys listening
> to Greek records. She can't do what she likes to do, because
> he doesn't like it, and it hurts you when he doesn't like to
> do things that you like.

Experiences like this one make young people realize that "marrying Greek" is the best way to retain one's Greekness, and the sense of closeness to the community which comes from sharing cultural, religious, and social Greekness with its members.

2. Problems in "marrying Greek"

But "marrying Greek" is not easily accomplished. A 3rd generation girl's response to my question about what sort of person she hoped to marry expressed the difficulty of "marrying Greek":

> You really have to _try_ to marry somebody Greek and if you really
> don't have that real big urge to stay Greek, then it's real
> easy just to marry someone who's not Greek, because you meet
> someone that you like and everything like that. And otherwise
> you just have to go looking around for somebody that's Greek
> and you like, and that's another thing to try and find, you
> know.

Why is it so difficult to find someone who meets the two requirements,

"that's Greek and you like"? There are several factors which contribute

to this difficulty.

First, the number of Greeks in each age group is relatively small,

as a pool from which to pick a mate. One woman expressed this problem

very succinctly:

> Let's face it, my son has approximately twenty girls from which
> he might choose to date and to marry, within this local area
> in Houston. I'm going to tell him, "You've got to pick a wife
> from those twenty girls." I might as well line them up and say,
> "Take your choice."

This difficulty is accentuated by the fact that, because Greeks form such

a small percentage of Houston's population, most Greeks work or go to

school with very few if any other Greeks. Thus some of their main

possible channels for socializing are essentially non-Greek. This is an

especially acute problem for those who go away to college, because only

the larger cities have Greek Orthodox churches, and most "college" towns

have neither a sizeable Greek population, nor a church. This is a far

cry from the situation in which most "Americans" find themselves, in

which a large percentage of the persons with whom they work, go to

school, church, or clubs are marital possibilities. The small number of

possible mates among Houston's Greeks is further reduced by two other

factors.

Many of Houston's Greek families are related to one another "by blood"; when one considers relationships "by marriage" (symbetheri) and by religious sponsorship (kumbari) in addition to "blood" relationships, a very large number of the community's members are related to one another. Many of these relationships prohibit marriage according to Orthodox canon law. Chapter 3 noted such prohibitions in the case of kumbaria; there are also restrictions against marriage to symbetheri. Although some of the more distant of these relationships may not be a barrier to marriage according to canon law, the sense of a relationship is in itself a barrier to the individual's interest in someone as a prospective mate. A 3rd generation girl made this observation.

> In Houston, because there's not that many Greeks around--I
> mean there's a lot of kids, but we're all--of course, it
> wouldn't make that big a deal, that you're kumbari, but then
> it would make you like close friends, almost like a relative.
> So you've always had that relative idea, of relationship,
> with sons of your godparents and stuff like that.

Furthermore, among the young adults of the Greek community there is a strong feeling of "we've been raised together so close, we're like brothers and sisters, so we're not interested in dating each other." This feeling, of being "like" relatives is similar to having "that relative idea", in that the sense of being very close to an individual precludes any sexual interest in him. A 3rd generation boy provided a detailed description of the "brother and sister" feelings which work to keep Houston's Greeks from being romantically interested in one another.

> People say they wouldn't marry a Greek from Houston. Do you
> know what they are saying? A, the guy who moved here from
> G-----, we were talking about all the girls we think are good
> looking in his city and he's going "Ohh, what? Oh, man!" And
> then he came here and he's dating like C and to me like she
> is very attractive, I've thought about taking her out but I
> never did because we were brought up kind of together, the same
> city and all that, and it's kind of difficult to go out with

her. He came here and went out with her right away. So I
think maybe since we were brought up so much together you
just consider them too close. E--there's this girl that really
cares for him. And she's young but she really likes him. I
asked "What don't you like about her?" He said "I don't know,
she's really nice but like she lived down the street from us
for so long ya know she's like a sister." But then like
we'll go to another city and we'll start dancing with the
girls there and the guys that are from there are thinking,
"Ah man, they don't know what they're getting!" And we're
saying the same thing about them.

From this quotation one senses that what keeps these kids from dating

each other is not so much that they feel "related" as that they just

know each other too well. This effect is not quite as problematic as

it first appears, however, for young Greeks sometimes do marry others

who live in Houston. For one thing, there has been a large influx of

new Greek families into the Houston area within the past ten-fifteen

years, and consequently there are "new faces" who did not grow up

locally. In addition, those Greeks who are several years older or

younger than an individaul did not necessarily grow up in close associa-

tion with him; the age difference which separated them as children is

not so great when one is considering a possible spouse. When one

becomes old enough to seriously consider marriage, he or she may begin

to see the local girls or boys in a different light. For example, the

same boy who said that the boys from other cities didn't know "what

they were getting" in the Houston girls continued by saying,

I think I've started to accept Greek girls more than I used
to. Before, I look at 'em and ya know, "God, they're all
queer," ya know? They were all the same. And within the
last two years I've really changed. They have personalities
and they aren't all the same.

Despite these exceptions, the sense of "being like brothers and sisters"

is still a very important factor in determining whom a young Greek will marry, in that such feelings act to exclude many local Greeks from consideration.

3. How to "marry Greek"

Thus these several factors make it somewhat difficult to marry another Greek, at least one from Houston. If someone wants to "marry Greek"--as many do--and yet there is a very limited number of eligible people within his community--as there usually is--what happens? What are the methods which have been developed within the American Greek community to help people to "marry Greek"?

Many people who wish to "marry Greek"--either because of parental pressures or because they themselves are set on marrying only a Greek-- do not marry at all. This response was probably more common several years ago than it is today, and also more in the 2nd generation than in the 3rd; nevertheless, it is not at all unusual to see "lovely men and women" in their 30's and 40's who have not married, and probably will not marry. A 2nd generation girl made this comment in response to my question about marriage in the Greek community:

> I can think of a lot of nonmarried Greek girls that still
> live with their mothers. And they're like 40 years old.
> That's bad. I feel sorry for them. There are plenty of girls,
> like 35 or 40, even 45. But they've been kinda picky too,
> waiting for their little Prince Charming to come along. But
> I guess it was a little bit of both, wanting a Greek only,
> plus wanting a Greek only that was super-duper Prince Charming
> type. They may have found their Prince Charming non-Greek,
> but since he wasn't Greek, he wasn't the--being Greek adds to
> the--it completes the whole picture.

Marriage to a Greek Greek, as discussed in Chapter 3, is a possibility. Another is marrying a Greek from another town. There are two main ways in which young people meet and marry Greeks from other towns.

The first is by accident. This possibility for "marrying Greek" is pretty obvious. A 3rd generation boy's response to my question about what he thought would happen to the Houston Greek kids when they were interested in marrying describes this sort of "accidental" marriage:

> What will happen then? Eventually they're going to marry someone that's not Greek, or they might accidentally get lucky and find someone, maybe in their own town, that they do get along with, or someone who moved, and the thing worked out.

Other situations in which the individual might meet out-of-town Greeks include his visiting friends or relatives in another town, or other people's visiting their friends or relatives in Houston, people coming into Houston for weddings and baptisms, and so on.

The second way to meet a Greek from out-of-town is through the conventions sponsored by Greek organizations such as AHEPA and GOYA. "Oh, they met at a convention", is a standard way of explaining how two people came to be married. Of course, some of the activities sponsored by these organizations are not really "conventions". E.g, the GOYA chapters in Texas invite each other when they have banquets or other activities. A 3rd generation boy said:

> All I know about my parents, about how they met, was that they were at an AHEPA convention in Houston, my father was an Ahepan, and he went to Houston, and someone introduced my parents together, and Love! So from then they wrote. ... This is still true today, and like that's also why--when you were at the last GOYA meeting, and they were saying, "Well, how about inviting some others?" Well, we do that whenever we get a chance, whenever we have a GOYA weekend, or something, we'll invite the others. Well, out of courtesy, but also to get some new faces.

For the sake of simplicity, however, all of these activities will be considered under the title of "conventions".

The major attractions of a convention are the social events. There are also business meetings--for example, in the conventions of the AHEPA organizations, delegates choose the site for the convention two years later, elect their national officers for the year, and so on--but it seems that convention business takes a back seat to socializing as far as most people are concerned. In fact, one 3rd generation girl went so far as to say,

> Conventions are a big deal because everybody gets dressed up and sees who they can meet. And then there's people who're doing the businesses--you get to the stage where you're more into the business meetings you know, and then it gets to be a pain.

While discussing marriage within the Greek community, many if not most young people voluntarily mentioned the conventions as good places to "meet somebody". E.g., a 3rd generation girl commented:

> [How does this problem, of wanting to stay Greek, but not wanting to date Houston Greeks, affect people's lives?]
> See, we have these conventions. ... They're always in the summer and you can go there and meet all kinds of people. If you have to rely on that, it's pretty bad--I'd like to marry a Greek guy--I don't know if I will or not, but I really would.
> [What else do you have to rely on?]
> Nothing really, I guess.
> [Do a lot of people meet someone there, and end up marrying them?]
> Definitely. It's not the rule, but I have seen it happen several times. A lot of people get together at these conventions and a year later turn up married. I go to have fun, but I don't rule that out.

A 2-3 generation boy said:

> [It seems to be a problem--not caring for the Greeks you grew up with, but still wanting to marry a Greek.]
> There's an answer for that--there's the good old organization of AHEPA, and they have conventions expressly designed for that purpose. Sons of Pericles and Maids of Athena--that's the true purpose of that, to provide an excuse to get them all together to meet each other.
> [Do things come out of it?]
> Quite often they do. That's when the Greeks let it all hang out.

Thus young people are very aware of the possibilities for "meeting someone" at conventions; that parents also realize their "courtship" significance can be seen from the following excerpts. A 2nd generation girl made an interesting observation about parents' "selective protectiveness".

> My mother, when I was little, you know, about spending the night with other people? "Oh, you can't go here, you can't go there," but when I was sixteen years old I went by myself to New Orleans, without much chaperoning or anything. What I'm trying to say, the point is that they encourage you to go meet Greek boys in other cities, they let you go by your-self. Like when I was sixteen years old I went to New Orleans by myself, but I couldn't spend the night at a friend's house. It doesn't make sense. They'll pay the money to send you there, but if you want to go anywhere else...

Conventions provide an excellent opportunity for parents to encourage their children through positive reinforcement to meet and perhaps marry a Greek. The young people are given a week of parties and other social events, and an opportunity to meet other Greeks from around the country. Some families, especially those with "eligible" children, make the convention their annual vacation trip. A 2-3 generation girl explained her mother's attitude toward the conventions:

> I remember like when I went to [the convention in] Miami, it was a time when I was dating somebody that wasn't Greek, and we were kinda serious--and I went to Miami, and she said, "Well, why am I taking you for, if you're gonna marry him? And waste all my money." She looked at it like that, and I looked at it like going just for the good time. ... My mother's idea was that she was wasting her money.

This quotation is indicative of the attitudes of many parents toward conventions: the foremost reason to attend is to help your children find mates. They are quite willing to spend the large amounts of money required if the expense might lead to a "Greek" marriage, but they become much more reluctant if the chance of a match is slim.

The discussion so far has emphasized the "courtship" function of conventions, and might lead one to believe that everyone who attends conventions has marriage in mind; this is an exaggeration, of course. Many people go just to have fun and get together with friends they have made at previous conventions, or to meet new friends. Most young people who are not ready to "get serious" fit into this latter category, as a young 2-3 generation man pointed out.

> Girls really seriously go with the intention of meeting some-
> one, but boys go for different reasons, to see what they can
> get away with. It's a convention, and they realize they're only
> going to be there for three to seven days at the most--and
> they're going to go there just to have a good time, and to see
> what they can get away with. ... There's some girls that realize
> --the smarter ones know it's just going to be for a weekend,
> and they might just go there to have fun, but then there really
> are those who really believe.

Although many young people, especially boys, go to the conventions primarily to have a good time, most add, "of course, if I were to meet someone..." Thus many young people probably fall into the categogy of "those who really believe", even though most would not admit it.

Because of these different attitudes toward the conventions--with some people going "just for fun" and others seriously "looking for somebody"--there is a large chance for misunderstandings and disappoint-ment. Apparently this is an unavoidable outcome of the well-known "courtship" atmosphere of the conventions. This problem was mentioned by a 2-3 generation boy while talking about marriage in the Greek community:

> The hardest thing is when girls go to a convention, most
> every girl in Houston goes through this--they go to find a boy,

and they find one, for one night. And maybe the first night
he'll be with them, and the second night he'll find some other
girl and be with her. And they're just really crushed, and
it takes them months to get over it, especially when they're
young. Or a guy may go with them at a convention, and then
they'll be writing all this time, and at the next convention,
they'll go back thinking they'll be with the same person, and
to the guys, it's nothing. You see someone else who interests
you, and you're with them. You don't want to be with this other
person. I've seen it through like my sister, and also the girls
here. They're writing letters for a long time, and oh, they're
so happy!! with so and so in New Orleans or Shreveport, and
you say, "Oh, it's just puppy love," but they're dead serious.
I know what guys think--they care about the girl, and they
think she's nice, but they're not out to get a girlfriend or
definitely not to get married. Not like the girl wants a
boyfriend.

His experience was that girls were often hurt by being more "serious"
than the boys at the conventions; this situation could also be true
in reverse, of course.

Many young singles upon reaching an age between about 25 and 30
become more interested in meeting someone to marry. It seems that
some decide in advance that it is the "right" time to settle down and
get married, and they go to the conventions with exactly that in mind.
Almost everyone has at least one friend or acquaintance who met someone at a convention and was married within a few months. It is very
easy to meet people because in the atmosphere of the convention most
people are less inhibited about introducing themselves, for two reasons.
First, everyone at the convention is Greek, so they are not really
"strangers", and second, if one is to begin a relationship in less
than a week, he cannot be shy. These two reasons are expressed in the
following quotations from 2nd generation girls:

See, the thing is, the reason that people like to go to them
is that they're all Greeks there. You're kinda--you don't
restrict yourself. I don't know how to explain this, but when

you're at a convention with all Greeks, it's like they're all
connected there. They go there for a big time, plus if they
find anybody they like. Your parents might say, "Well, I know
somebody, meet so and so." And people who know people might
introduce you to somebody, of just people you meet on your own.
But you'd be surprised how many Greeks meet somebody at conventions.

A: It's a strange kind of an atmosphere.
B: It is, it's trying to pack--oh, I don't know, it's trying to
get to know somebody really well in a short space. And like
the ones that are district are so short--they're a weekend, that's
it! Or maybe four days, the long ones. The national ones are a
week long and at least you know if you're with someone for the
whole week, you can get to know 'em...
A: But you have such a short time, and you have to pack a relationship so quickly.
B: You can't be shy. If you're shy, you'll drown, absolutely.
You just won't last.
A: And you kinda do things that you would've done spread over
a month or something with someone that you see all the time,
in a weekend or a week.
B: Exactly--it's like when you date somebody for a month--that,
meaning once a weekend for four weeks in a row. O.K., but this
is four times, but four days in succession, so that you really
get to know the person faster. But you lose this security of
the length of time that you've known 'em, and you feel more
secure--like after four weeks you can do this, after four weeks
you can do that--but after four days, what?

Once two people have met, maintaining the new relationship is a

problem; this is frequently difficult because of the distance which

usually separates the two. The general solution is to write one

another through the year, and then meet again at the next convention,

or perhaps visit each other during vacations. Just about every young

Greek has had several of these relationships; as one young man jokingly

said, "I've had a lot of penpals!" A 3rd generation boy explained

his experience with trying to maintain a long-distance relationship:

I met a girl in New Orleans that I liked pretty well, but there's
that distance, and it kind of destroys things, but then again
there's so many things planned so often--if you're concerned
with that, you can work something out. You've got your summer
conventions, you've got your national conventions, mid-winter
conferences, basketball tournaments in the middle of all that,

and you can see each other about eight times a year--let's say
it that way. Plus trips that you might make on your own.

In many cases, these "long-distance" problems are too difficult to over-
come, and the relationship eventually fizzles out. Nevertheless, some of
these relationships do indeed result in marriage, as the reader has seen.
Furthermore, regardless of the actual number of relationships beginning
at conventions which result in marriage, the conventions as a courtship
arena are still an important facet of Greek life in the United States.

D. Marriage to Non-Greeks

I have now discussed the reasons that community members encourage
"marrying Greek", several problems associated with marrying Greek, and
some of the ways in which members act to facilitate endogamy. The final
option open to the individual--marriage to a non-Greek--will now be considered. Saloutos comments that intermarriage is increasing among Greeks,
despite the official position of the Greek Orthodox Church:

> The wish of our Church is that Greek Orthodox Christians be
> joined in wedlock only with Greek Orthodox. It is the only
> way possible to secure the perpetuation of our religious and
> national traditions and also peace and harmony in the Christian
> family (1973:403).

He reports the following figures on intermarriages performed within the
church:[1]

Year	Total Marriages	Mixed Marriages	Percent Mixed
1963	4025	1132	28 %
1964	4075	1190	29 %
1965	4383	1259	29 %
1966	4393	1405	32 %
1967	4332	1640	38 %
1968-69	5500	1755	32 %
1969-70	5101	2358	46 %
1970-71	5136	2473	48 %

The figures speak for themselves: intermarriage is on the increase. Chapter 4 discussed the fact that a number of those non-Greeks who marry Greeks may join the community, raising their children as Greeks and essentially "becoming Greek" themselves. Nevertheless, other non-Greeks may act to draw their Greek spouse away from the community, or the reactions of community members to the marriage in general and the non-Greek in particular may also drive them away.[2] The surest way to maintain the community is to discourage exogamy. How do community members, particularly parents, discourage dating and marriage outside the group? This question is of primary interest in the following sections.

1. Greek activities

One way in which parents act to encourage Greek friends is by placing their children in activities such as Greek school and Greek organizations. This is a way to push dating Greeks as well. The Greek organizations such as Sons and Maids (junior auxilliaries of AHEPA) and Junior GOYA all accept members beginning at about the age when young people develop an interest in the opposite sex, about twelve to fourteen. Children are encouraged to take part in many of these activities, and some parents also actively discourage other (American) activities. One day I overheard a woman say, "I don't let my kids participate in anything but the activities here at the church [this includes Sons and Maids] because it just takes too much gas!" In this case, the real issue was not gasoline, but keeping her kids in Greek rather than American groups and activities. The more Greeks one's child is acquainted with through such organizations, the higher are the chances that he will know available Greeks for dating. These organizations of course have parties and other social functions, to enable all the Greek kids to get together. They also provide contact not only with local Greeks, but with those from other surrounding areas as well; e.g., the Houston organizations have many functions in conjunction with organizations from other areas, such as Dallas, Ft. Worth, San Antonio, New Orleans and Shreveport. The discussion of the previous section indicated the importance of meeting Greeks from out-of-town.

2. Girls not allowed to date until older

In Chapter 3 it was noted that dating in the 1st and 2nd generations was influenced by a double standard. Boys were allowed to date whomever they cared to, but many girls were not allowed to date at all, and others were permitted to date only Greeks. The same influence is felt to some extent today in that (1) many young people--both boys and girls--are expected to date only Greeks, at least until they are out of high school, and (2) many girls are not allowed to date until they are fairly old, perhaps about seventeen.

One reason that parents may not want their daughters to date too much is probably the influence of the traditional Greek idea that women who go out a lot are loose; to keep a daughter from developing such a reputation, they would prevent her dating as long as possible. This explanation seems to be suggested by a 2nd generation girl's discussion of her dating experience:

> I read the Scarlet Letter, you know, the A for adulteress.
> And we used to make fun of our parents, you know, because
> people who used to go out, you know, were branded people,
> like they had a D on their forehead, for Dated. I mean,
> that's how bad it got. We had that little joke when we

> were growing up. We used to say like that among ourselves,
> "It's a contest of the mothers to see who can keep their
> daughters in the longest."

Another factor which may be of equal importance for "keeping daughters in" is to keep them from dating non-Greeks, however. As long as a girl is not dating anyone, she's not going out with "Americans". Apparently this is not an unusual solution. E.g., when I asked a 3rd generation boy about marriage to Americans, his response was:

> Girls' parents hassle them more than the guy's parents do
> about "marrying Greek"--I see it around, I know. A lot of
> people's parents do that. One girl--I wanted to take her out,
> and they were using the excuse that she was too young to date,
> not because they didn't want her to date me--they would like
> her to date me--but because they couldn't draw the exception
> on only me, because if she dated me, she'd also date non-Greeks.

A 3rd generation boy was discussing the attitude that "Greek is best", and said:

> A lot of the Greek people are like that. Like once I called a
> Greek girl I liked. Her mother answered the phone and said
> "What do you want?" And I told her. And "Who's this?" And
> I told her. Then she called the girl to the phone and you
> could hear in the background, "It's so-and-so, who's he?" I
> talked to her for a while and finally got around to asking
> her out. And she said "I can't--I can't date yet." I felt
> like a fool, two inches tall. I called her back a few times
> and I finally just forgot about it. ... This was when I was
> a senior, and she still couldn't date.

Again one sees that parents often will not let their girls date until fairly late; but in this excerpt we also find another factor at work. The fact that the mother answered the phone and demanded to know who was calling (the implication being, "Is this a Greek boy?") was not a unique occurrence. Rather, this is a standard way--more indirect than not permitting a child to date Americans, but just as real--in which parents can discourage dating Americans and thereby encourage going out with Greeks. I will call this the hassling technique.

3. The hassling technique

The reason for hassling is probably a home-grown practicing of the
principles of behavior modification. If unfavored behavior patterns are
punished and preferred ones rewarded, the subject will tend to act out
the preferred patterns; if a parent hassles his kids while they are dating
Americans and cooperates while they are dating Greeks, they will go out
with Greeks instead of Americans.

Of course there are many ways of hassling. Some of them are rather
mild but others practically border on violence. The method which is
probably the least direct is demonstrated in this excerpt from a 3rd
generation boy:

> I don't know if they're aware of what they're doing, but my
> mother, if she knows I'm taking out a certain Greek, well
> "Enjoy yourself!" and all this enthusiasm, you know. If they
> know I'm not, then it's kinda "Well, goodbye."...I feel that if
> anything the parents are more--I'd say they're prejudiced,
> like if you were going to take out, or bring over a girl that
> wasn't Greek. You sense it's there, a hostility. But then if
> you brought someone Greek, it's beautiful! They won't admit
> it, but it's there. This is part of their heredity. You
> can't erase it.

Another boy--who is not spared this sort of hassling despite the fact
that his mother is American--jokingly commented on the sort of problems
encountered in dating. "If you're taking out someone named Sophia
Poulos, it's 'here's $5, and take the car!', but if it's someone named
Shelley Rubenstein, it's more like 'there's a quarter, and take the bus!'"
There are also several other hassling tactics which can be included in
this category. One is related to general "dating rules" like taking the
car, curfew, where one is allowed to go, and what one can do. Each of

these points is more likely to present problems when one is dating an American than when dating Greeks. E.g., taking the family car seems to be a routine enough request until a boy wants to take out an American instead of a Greek. As one 2-3 generation boy said,

> In high school, there was some pressure "date Greek" and they had some say-so, because they had the car.

Curfews also cause trouble for the young Greek who dates an American. In going on a similar date, to a dance or movie, e.g., a Greek girl may be permitted to stay out until midnight or later if she's going with a Greek, but must be in by 11:00 if she happens to be going with an American boy. The same "rule" may apply to some boys as well, judging by the comment of this 3rd generation boy:

> And since I'm staying at home, I'll tell them what time I'll be in, and if I'm late I'll catch all kinds of hell--it depends on who I'm with, of course.

Although these types of hassling are annoying, they are probably the least harmful in that they generally involve only the Greek, and not the Americans he or she dates. The next hassling tactics to be discussed are not so harmless, however, for they affect the American girlfriend or boyfriend as well. The reader has already seen one example of these advanced hassling tactics, when the girl's mother said, "It's so-and-so--who's he?", probably as much for the benefit of the boy at the other end as for her daughter. Apparently the telephone hassle is not at all unusual. A 3rd generation boy discussed the pressures his parents put on him about dating an American girl:

> I'd be talking on the phone to this one and Mom comes storming in, "Who are you talking to?" and she knows darn good and well. And the girl can hear it, and she kind of feels bad about it.

Another way of hassling which is particularly hard on the American involved is the cold shoulder he or she may receive from the Greek parents when visiting in their home. This poor treatment of an American date sometimes acts to destroy the relationship between the Greek and American who have been dating, even if they were "serious" about each other. A 3rd generation boy describes what happened when his American girlfriend came over:

> D was really feeling the pressures, and the first time she came over to the house--I was pretty good in science, so I was going to be tutoring her, and she and a friend of mine came over right before a final. My mother just looked at her, and she was crying by the time she got over to the table in the living room. It was bad.
> [Do you resent that?]
> Yeah, we have it out quite often.

One should not think that all parents use all of these hassling techniques on their children who are dating Americans. Many parents do not mind if their kids date non-Greeks, but the phrase "as long as they don't get serious" is usually added when someone makes such a statement. If one begins to date the same non-Greek too often and it appears they may be "getting serious", even those parents who were not opposed before this point may begin to resort to hassling tactics in the hope that the child might--with a little encouragement--change his mind.

4. Effects of parental pressure

Parental hassling sometimes has a serious and destructive effect on the relationship between a Greek kid and his or her American date. In the following rather lengthy quotation, a 3rd generation boy describes how his mother's reaction to his American girlfriend helped precipitate their breakup, and how he came to be married to a girl from Greece.

> I mean, I could date her as long as I didn't get serious. At
> first it was great you know, we were in love and all this stuff
> you know, and then about the second--after the first year uhh,
> my mom griping at me, it didn't bother me that much. Then
> towards the second year it started getting to me, but I kept
> thinking that things were going to get better. ... I dated
> her for almost three years, and then I really got tired of it,
> I couldn't take any more. ... Right after the first year I
> noticed my mom and me not getting along affected my girlfriend.
> She got real upset because she didn't feel accepted. And that
> started affecting our relationship. For the next year I kept
> trying to make things better but they didn't get much better
> because she was getting more resentful toward the Greeks. And
> it wasn't her fault--she really felt like an outsider. My mom
> made her feel like that. Some Greeks were real nice to her
> but others didn't know how to accept her because of my mom.
> I thought maybe things would get better but then I started
> feeling different too. Maybe because she made me notice how
> they made her feel bad. Not wanted. And it started bothering
> me a whole lot more. I just got tired of it. ... And I saw
> that the situation with my mother wasn't going to change or
> anything, my mom thought she was nice, but that was as far as
> it went. And I don't know, and then after that, it was so
> much, I couldn't take it any more. ... I was corresponding with
> this Greek girl, so I decided I was just going to go see her.
> I broke up with this other girl right before I left. ... The
> Greek stuff brought on all the stuff but it wasn't mentioned
> during the break up. It just depressed me and her and we just
> didn't get along in other things. She was willing to be accepted
> at first. She couldn't understand why she couldn't come to
> church with me or come to church functions. I got kicked out
> of the house once for taking a non-Greek girl to a dance they
> had at the church. I got kicked out because I think I embar-
> rassed by mother in front of all the relatives by taking a
> non-Greek. Σκατά [skata, shit]! Then I went to Greece and
> hit it off with this other girl pretty good.

Thus, the mother's reaction was one--if not the most deciding--of the

factors which led this young man to forget about marrying the American

girl, and to finally marry a Greek from Greece. It was not his mother's

disapproval per se which led to his breaking up with the American; it was

not a case in which she said, "I don't want you going out with this

American," and he obediently began dating only Greeks. Instead, his mother's reactions--which also influenced how the rest of the community reacted toward the girl--put such a strain on the relationship that it was eventually destroyed. This was not an overnight development, but a long process which finally resulted in his not being able to "take it any more". He learned the lesson--"marry Greek!"--the hard way, and married a Greek girl.

In a sort of "crisis" situation he learned that life is much easier all the way around if one does not "get serious" about an American; there were hurt feelings and uneasy relationships within his family after this incident. Many young people learn this lesson more easily, on a day-to-day basis, however, before the situation develops into such a crisis. Brief episodes of parental hassling while casually dating different Americans soon get across the point that it is very difficult to carry on a good relationship with an American while being subjected to hassling from parents and the community. Here a group of young 2nd, 2-3, and 3rd generation men and women discuss dating:

> C: You know, it makes it so much easier to like someone if your parents like them too, I mean, you can bring them over to the house, it's just such a more--
> S: Yeah, it's more comfortable.
> C: The atmosphere is so much better.
> S: Yeah, there's so much pressure like--I take her places or like over to my house or something, and you just feel all this pressure. I just couldn't stand it. And I'm sure she couldn't either.
> D: Like us, living at home and still hanging around with your parents, you know, American kids don't care if their parents care or not, you know, and they're already out and they're not going to have to live around their parents, and we're still going to be hanging around them. You know, not that I dislike it either. I've had a lot more freedom and I--
> C: Your parents don't give you pressure, but you felt it, I know, because--
> D: Well, yeah, it was bad enough with me. ... I don't feel like guilty, but O.K., like at the beginning. But if you start

carrying on a longer relationship, you know, you start looking
at things in a broader viewpoint, in the future, and you start
seeing that it's not going to work out. As long as you want
to stay Greeky, sort of, it's hard.

It is obvious that these young people have learned from their parents'

"conditioning" that it is "easier" to like someone your parents like,

i.e., another Greek. Of course this is the case in almost any family,

but the pressures are felt very strongly by the young Greek, because he

(or she) generally remains in his parents' home until marriage. By

virtue of the expectation of "closeness" and "respect" in the family,

even those who may not live at home are still subject to, and intensely

influenced by, parental pressures. Should the individual continue

dating someone of whom his family disapproves, he encounters many

problems if, in conformance with his "Greek" values, he still "hangs

around" his family. If one does not want to comply with his parents'

wishes, the only alternative is to keep them in the dark by not telling

them whom he is dating. Several people have used this tactic of avoid-

ance successfully, thereby greatly reducing their own and their parents'

anxiety.

5. Threats and pleading

Hassling is not the only method parents use to get their children

to marry Greeks, however. Many "teach" their children that they should

marry Greek in various ways, which even include threats. E.g., a 3rd

generation boy said,

> Like my parents always say to me, "Marry a Greek, marry a
> Greek," you know, "the rest aren't."--   In a Greek wedding,
> there's a chalice that's usually given to the bride. Well,
> my mother has one that'll probably be used in my sister's
> wedding. And then there's another one that's smaller, that's
> engraved, I think it was my grandfather's, that will be used

in my wedding. But my mother said, "You're not going to get
it unless you marry a Greek!" And to me, well, that was so
long ago that I was saying, "What's a chalice?"

A 2-3 generation girl reported an interesting event.

"You should marry a Greek boy," because--I get that pressure
all the time. Not so much from my parents, but from my uncle
and aunt, which is terrible. The time I was going with J, an
N.G. [non-Greek], she wanted me to promise to her that I was
going to marry a Greek. Can you believe? She actually--because
she trusted my promise, she knew that if I promised her, that I
would never break my promise. I never promised her because I
knew that if I would, and if I broke it, it would just crush
her. ... Just--I get it every once in a while, you know! "He
should be a nice boy--as long as he's Greek," always "Yeah,
yeah, as long as he's Greek." This is what always follows every
sentence.

There are also other, more subtle ways of teaching the lesson, "marry

Greek." A 2nd generation college girl observed that her mother always

makes sure to mention any marriage in which the Greek and American part-

ners are not getting along or are breaking up. "Even though the American

was such a nice boy!," she comments. The lesson--that a marriage between

a Greek and an American is doomed to failure--is obvious.

6. Pressure on oneself

Aside from all this teaching of the "marry Greek" lesson, there is

another important factor which acts to discourage marriage to non-Greeks.

This is the pressure one puts on himself, resulting from the honest

unwillingness to hurt his family. E.g., a 3rd generation boy discussed

his chances for marrying a Greek, and commented:

My grandmother's idea of course would be--she would be hurt
maybe especially felt with my grandmother, as a sort of failure,
if--even if I married a non-Greek who converted.

Then he discussed a relative's marriage to a non-Greek, and her parents'

strong negative reaction, and continued:

> I don't think my parents would take it the way her parents did.
> But I know that they would be very hurt. That's the thing
> that's crossed my mind. ... Well, let's just say if I did, it
> would be after a lot of thought. There are great social pres-
> sures, there really are, but not as much as there used to be.

His comments suggest that the "great social pressures" against exogamy

are declining, but another pressure still exists. This is the pressure

exerted by one's conscience. Throughout his life, he has been told

"marry Greek!", and he realizes that this is his parents' expectation

of him, and that they will be sorely disappointed and hurt if he marries

outside the group.

7. Community pressure

The members of the Greek community can also exert pressure on an

individual to "marry Greek" by making him and his "intended" uncomfortable

when they are around other Greeks. The reader may recall the young man

who broke up with an American girl he intended to marry partly as a result

of community pressure; she felt unwanted and rejected by the Greeks, which

put a strain on their relationship. A 3rd generation boy also mentioned

the community reaction toward non-Greeks--"outsiders"--who come to com-

munity affairs or church services.

> I see it all the time, just a certain air, not being too
> friendly with them. Some people are able to do it, but then
> again others--it's something, I guess, barriers, that can't
> be overcome.

Such a cold shoulder often continues after marriage as well.

8. Reactions to intermarriage

In most cases of intermarriage today, the family's reaction is less

one of violent opposition than was previously the case. There is an

increased incidence of marriage to non-Greeks, and because of this increase, people are more accustomed to the idea of intermarriage.

Furthermore, they have also noticed the cases of "successful" marriage

between Greek and non-Greek, those in which the non-Greek partner has

joined the Greek church and community, and almost become "Greek". A

3rd generation college boy commented on intermarriage.

> Marriage to non-Greeks is getting more and more common every
> day.
> [What's the community reaction when somebody marries a non-Greek?]
> It used to be very strong against it, very strong. And in fact,
> I've seen many instances when people marry Americans sort of
> like—not exactly kicked out of their family—but apart. And
> their fathers sort of would push them to the side. I've noticed
> that very much in fact. You know, I've seen it happen where a
> father would disown his son and send him out for marrying an
> American. However, in this day and time, it wouldn't happen
> that way of course. It would be much more loose. I've seen
> the same person get accepted back into his family later on.
> They are not accepting him in the fashion that they would if
> say he had married a Greek; however, they are turning over and
> accepting them more and more.

Despite the increased acceptance of marriage to non-Greeks, one should

not underestimate the possible negative reactions to intermarriage by

the family involved. Fear of his family's reaction caused one fellow

who had married a non-Greek to keep it a secret, not living with his

wife for several years. One of his relatives mentioned this case while

discussing marriage to non-Greeks:

> [You said that people never really accept someone marrying
> a non-Greek?]
> I'll stick by that statement. I've got a relative who married
> a non-Greek—that was the one that was living with us and he
> was so uptight about marrying a non-Greek that he didn't tell
> anybody until five years after he was married, it slipped out.
> [How did he do it?]
> He had a house on J St. He had his family there—you know, it
> was his house. He gambles a lot—he plays poker all the time,
> so if he wouldn't come in at night, we knew he was playing cards.
> Which most of the time he was.
> [You mean he was living with y'all?]
> He was actually living with us... He maintained a whole 'nother

household. He even had some kids.
[Do you know other cases too?]
Like M's oldest son eloped. With a white. The family just
about severed all connections with him. It's only within
the last say four years that things have started getting
back together--but it'll never be like the family was.
[Do people usually get back together?]
I don't know, I doubt if it happens too often. That's a pretty
strong thing. When you do that sort of thing, you're going
against everything.
[Would your family do that?]
I don't know if they would or not. That's a pretty serious
thing, but you'd have to be prepared for it.

After all else has failed and the individual remains adamant about

marrying a non-Greek, his family may still exercise severe sanctions

against him. In some cases, the parents refuse to go to the wedding.

E.g., a young 3rd generation man expressed the hurt and anger he felt

when this happened to him.

They didn't even come to our wedding, and I'm going to hold
that against them for a long time. I would never want my
children to go through what I have had to put up with. Not
even to go to your child's wedding! Even if I disagreed with
the person my child picked, I'd never do that to him.

Moreover, the pressures sometimes do not stop even after the wedding.

One American woman described her experience.

His brother wrote to him but his mother and dad didn't have
anything to do with us for several months, say from November
until about the time he was ready to graduate from college.
What hurt most was seeing him hurt, because I don't think if
they hadn't accepted me that he would ever be happy because
it just hurt him that much. ... They tried to just get him to
leave after we were married through the letters from the brother.
It all hurt--you think about it even now and it still hurts--
but it was just something that had to work itself out I guess--
it wasn't easy.

Similarly, another American woman discussed the pressure she felt:

At first, I wanted to please. Mrs. B came over and would cry
on my shoulder because her son married me. Can you beat that?
"He marries you, and not even in the Greek church! ... I want
my son to be in love and all that, but with all the lovely

> Greek girls around all his life, why couldn't he have fallen in love with just one of them? Why not just one?"

In general, however, I think eventual acceptance of the couple back into the family is the most common course of action, but relationships are probably never "like they were", or like they would have been if the individual had married a Greek instead. It is not hard to understand how relationships are damaged by going through such a familial crisis: the couple who were rejected and hassled, and the parents and other relatives who so hoped for a "Greek" marriage, are likely to retain some feelings of resentment toward one another.

The increased occurrence of intermarriage has also softened extreme public opposition, to an extent. In fact, there is some feeling that intermarriage is just about inevitable. Nevertheless, the reactions within Houston's Greek community to marriage to a non-Greek are generally unfavorable. A 3rd generation boy made this observation:

> Usually the first reaction would be emotional, and they're not thinking really and piecing it, "Well, what is the objection really?" Well, more or less, it's just a standard thing, "Well, intermarriage--oh, no!!" It's a reaction, and then of course later on, it dies down, practically in every case now.

A 2-3 generation boy commented that even younger people "notice" inter-marriages:

> [What do you think the general community reaction is to inter-marriage?]
> The older ones point you out--they don't like it. The younger ones tolerate it, but they notice it. Earlier I would--I wouldn't call it "hold it against", that's too strong, but I would take notice of it, someone marrying outside the Greek.

An important element of the community's "noticing" is gossipping about it. To a 3rd generation college girl, this is the most prominent feature of the community reaction:

> [Is there a general community reaction to intermarriage?]
> Gossip, gossip, gossip. I'm serious. It's pretty bad. Like
> the older ones will walk around saying, "Look what that kid is
> doing to his parents--tearing his parents to shreds." They
> really believe in this complete obedience to parents--I mean,
> what they say, you do. They don't understand the kids now,
> going off and dating quote-unquote American boys and girls,
> or whatever.

Family and community reactions to an intermarriage are to some extent

related. In just about any case, an individual member of a family which

is facing marriage to a non-Greek is very likely to feel pressure from

the general community attitude, "Intermarriage--oh, no!!" For example,

a 3rd generation boy commented on a case of intermarriage in his family.

> Well, it's really kind of--I mean, it's not something that
> happened, that used to happen quite frequently. Now, it's
> getting more. Probably it wouldn't have been as bad if he
> converted over to the faith. It wouldn't seem as bad, because
> she would be married inside the church. But here, she had a
> Catholic wedding--
> [What about her father?]
> He's thinking more of what other people will think than of the
> real--like saying, "Your daughter, she married out of the faith,
> you're a failure in raising your own kid--what did you do wrong?"

This sort of community influence on personal attitudes is not at all

unusual in the Houston Greek community. A very common phrase is "What

would people think?", which is not surprising in view of the smallness

and extreme "togetherness" of the community. This fact will be discussed

in the next chapter.

In general, then, members of the Houston Greek community react

unfavorably toward marriage to non-Greeks. This is an understandable

reaction, for intermarriage is quite rightly viewed as a threat to the

community's existence. The Greek partner may adjust in such a marriage in

several ways, the extremes of which are almost totally leaving the Greek community to enter into the spouse's social circles, or having the American spouse enter the Greek community almost one hundred percent. Either extreme--as well as the choices which lie in between them--is harmful to the Greek community. In the case of the former extreme, it loses members; in the latter, the non-Greek spouses influence the Greekness of the community with their "American" ways. Thus marriage to non-Greeks is not looked upon with favor in the community, even if some intermarriage is considered "just about inevitable" because of the problems involved in trying to "marry Greek". Thus to preserve the Greek group, pressure is exerted on the individual--by the community, his parents, his peers, and even himself--to discourage him from marrying a non-Greek.

III. Discussion

Membership in the Greek community means many things to the individual. It gives him a sense of security, of belonging. It fosters a warm feeling of affinity and "community" with other members. It gives him "something special" that non-Greeks do not have, which differentiates him from the non-Greeks who surround him in his life "outside" the group--in school, work, and his neighborhood. He is not "one of the crowd", he is "different" and "special". But it also limits him in many ways: his friends are Greek, his church is Greek, his family is Greek, his _life_ is Greek, and he may begin to feel closed-in. The warm and comfortable Greek world which surrounds him can become stifling, and it is sometimes difficult to balance the positive and negative aspects of community membership.

The central meaning of belonging to the Greek community is belonging

to a group whose members share a sense of closeness based on biological,
religious, social, and cultural Greekness. Individuals who leave the
community, who are "lost", threaten this togetherness. Much effort is
expended to keep the group together by keeping members within the community, and this chapter has discussed several mechanisms by which this
is accomplished. E.g., one's family encourages him in various ways to
remain within the Greek Orthodox church, and to establish relationships
with Greek friends. Of the decisions the individual makes which affect
the future of the Greek group, the most momentous is his choice of mate.
Young people are coerced by family and community to "marry Greek", and
this is one of the strongest and most persistent of the pressures they
face.

Those individuals who have left the community, or who appear to be
on the way out, are subject to rather severe sanctions. This is most
obvious in the case of intermarriage. The family threatens disinheritance, refuses to attend the wedding, and ignores the couple; the community may give them a cold shoulder; parents may even try to persuade
the Greek partner to desert his (or her) non-Greek spouse. Despite
these pressures and sanctions against intermarriage, it appears to be on
the increase. The American emphasis on romantic love is of increasing
significance in later generations of Greek Americans, and this, combined
with the decreasing emphasis on blind obedience to parental authority,
has no doubt led to the greater rates of intermarriage. The important
question, however, is what significance intermarriage has for the future
of the ethnic group. Earlier chapters have indicated that intermarriage
does not necessarily imply the death of the group, for a number of

non-Greeks are incorporated into the community through marriage. As
community members become less hostile toward intermarriage, more couples
may exercise this option. Of course, if the many sanctions against
exogamy were to be removed, the intermarriage rates might increase
greatly, thereby cancelling any gains of non-Greek members by the loss
of more Greeks. The role of intermarriage in the community will be
further discussed in the concluding chapter.

The purpose of the sanctions discussed in this chapter is to "keep
the group together" by insuring that individual members maintain their
identification with the community. Once one has firmly established himself as a bona fide member, however, the pressures are not over, for
there are certain rules of performance which one must observe in his
"Greek" role. These are the topic of the next chapter.

Making trigones

Preparing spanakopites

Making bread

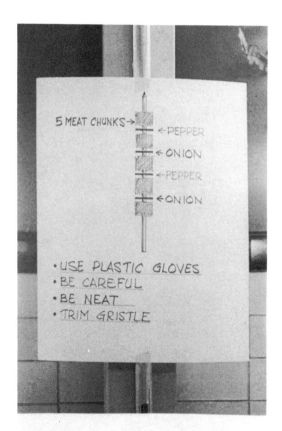

5 MEAT CHUNKS → ←PEPPER
←ONION
←PEPPER
←ONION

• USE PLASTIC GLOVES
• BE CAREFUL
• BE NEAT
• TRIM GRISTLE

Directions for making souflakia

Making <u>souflakia</u>

<u>Baklava</u> from the oven

Dancing and singing practice

GREEK FESTIVAL PREPARATIONS

CHAPTER 7

BEING GREEK--THE SOCIAL ACTIONS OF GREEKNESS

Membership in the Greek community implies that the individual is willing to be judged by Greek values and standards of behavior. There are several key rules which are applied to the performance of those who take on a "Greek" role, and in the first section of this chapter these rather strict standards will be examined. I will then consider the forces which compel members to abide by these rules of performance, and the ways in which they alter their behavior to do so. The third section will discuss ways in which individuals demonstrate their Greekness for Greek and American audiences, and the final section will examine several differing types of community participation.

I. Rules of Performance

Two impQrtant rules of performance--participation and being "socially Greek"--have already been discussed in some detail, and will also be considered later in this chapter, so I will only mention them at this point. However, there are two other significant standards of behavior-- propriety and success.

A. Propriety

Within the Greek community there is a strong emphasis on propriety, not in the sense of being very formal and strait-laced (far from it!), but in conducting oneself in certain prescribed ways. This includes apparel, deportment, conversation, and so on. The discussion of two 2nd generation girls demonstrates the significance of propriety.

N: I used to act very conservative around Greeks. [Like at this party the other night] T put his arm around me, and my mother said, "You shouldn't have done that in front of your father." ... I really used to watch myself. I would never do anything you know bold or anything.

C: But going to church sometimes, now that I've been away to college--I know that those people think I'm real goody-goody. You know the old--not people my age--well, even people my age maybe. But the older ones. And it comes to my mind "If they only knew what I do at school, they would be so shocked!"

N: They expect us to be pillars of virtue, you know. Just like their mothers. [laughter] It's like the American girls, well, they're the easy ones, you can do whatever you want with them because they're no good anyway. But the Greek girls, you know, ohh--beyond reproach!

B. Success

A second standard is success. Within the Houston Greek community one senses strong encouragement of achievement, competition, and success. A 3rd generation boy noted the pressure for achievement which Greeks feel:

They expect excellence, you know, in all things, the pressure as far as scholastic achievement. Maybe not so much athletic achievement, but I think it's just achievement. "You're Greek, you're something special." You're supposed to play that up. We've gotten that. I know, when I played on the church softball team, the coaches'd tell us that "You'd let this bunch of WASPs beat you!?" and like that.

Feelings of racial superiority, as discussed in Chapter 5, again come into play. One is expected to succeed in competition with non-Greeks because he is Greek and therefore "something special". But the expectation of success is not limited to competition with non-Greeks, for one must also be successful when his competitors are fellow Greeks. E.g., the group of young people mentioned the strong sense of competition and success which play such an important role in Houston's Greek community. M mentioned that a friend had done some research on Greek Americans, and continued:

M: He was doing some statistics on like Greek Americans, and he said we were the most affluent of all the cultures, or something like that.
D: Yeah, the unemployment rate for Greeks is like nothing, as far as our minority group into you know the unemployment.
M: The income is the highest of all.
S: Is that true?
D: Yeah, this is true. I heard that too.
S: Shoot, to me Greeks don't help Greeks that much.
M: That's not what we're talking about.
D: We're talking about how many Greeks are on welfare. They get out and work.
S: Oh, oh. And the ones that don't are too proud to go down to the welfare office.
D: Yeah, but everybody's got a job. They make up almost no-- maybe one percent...
S: The older Greeks don't help the Greeks as much as--like Jewish people really help Jewish people. They don't help the Greeks as much as much as they do.
D: Well, look, don't the Greek food deliveries go to the Greek places of business? Doesn't T have a lot--doesn't he go to M's? Doesn't he deliver food?
M: Yeah, but M turns around and opens up his own, that's what we're talking about. You got a hot dog stand, you're making a million dollars, a Greek will go across the street and open up his own hot dog stand. [laughter]
S: He'll stab you in the back.

It is probably this expectation of success which most effectively negates the community ideal of "closeness", for the individual is often willing to "stab you in the back" to achieve success. Thus one finds friends, business partners, or even brothers refusing to speak to each other, or even suing one another, over a business deal. In such cases, the expectation of "success" rather than that of "closeness" is of foremost importance.

Frequently Greeks characterize their group as "hard-working", and point out all that Greeks have accomplished since coming to the United States; this will to achieve they attribute to Greekness. The "American dream" is very real among Greeks, for most of them began with nothing and have worked their way far up the economic scale. E.g., a 2nd generation girl said of her father:

> He came in the early 20's. He was encouraged by my grandfather
> to come, to see what he could make of himself here, because in
> Greece, there isn't that much opportunity to better themselves.
> I think he had about a dollar in his pocket, you know.

Most Greeks can recount similar stories of relatives who came to the

United States with virtually nothing, and many of Houston's Greeks have

indeed accomplished a great deal. Some of the 1st generation individuals

developed very profitable businesses and made fortunes; a large percentage

of the 2nd generation attended college, and many have become professionals

or entered their own successful businesses. There is another element in

the group's background which causes Greeks to stress success—the rather

extreme class differences in Greece. A 2nd generation couple pointed

this out.

> H: They have a caste system there you know.
> W: After the war, this young man came in. ... When my father
> was a young man, he worked for his father, at his father's
> restaurant for a short period of time, and during the war we
> couldn't buy any automobiles—the automobile that we had had
> to last throughout the duration of the war, the 1939 car.
> The first car we got since the war was a 1946 Ford, and I
> heard this man—young man—told some other people, "Can you
> imagine that? A worker of my father driving around in a
> limousine?"

Thus some Greeks, particularly those who have arrived rather recently,

are anxious to prove that they are not of the lower class, that they

have fine possessions and plenty of money, that they are really somebody;

in short, they must prove that they are successful. Such proof often

takes the form of consumption which is not so much conspicuous as flashy

—jewelry, furs, fancy cars, and huge houses.

The emphasis on success in the community has had several implica-

tions. There is a feeling among some Greeks that success is the plumb line by which all people are measured, and the way in which an individual

accomplished his success is unimportant, at least so long as it benefits

the Greek community. E.g., an American who married a Greek man made

this comment.

> I met a man, and my husband told me he had been in the prison
> for smuggling in dope in his olive oil cans in his restaurant
> business. Mr. N [her father-in-law] saw him and said, "He's
> good man, gave pews to the church." I met another, who made
> his million by selling pornography in the back of his shoe
> shine stand years ago, my husband says. Then his father says,
> "He's good man, gave $5,000 to church." If my husband hadn't
> told me about those men, I'd never have known, by the way people
> talk about them. They're not good men! They made their money
> illegally. Now I'm not quite so harsh as I was then in my
> judgment of people, but the Greeks are really hypocritical in
> the way they judge people. Someone can be a total crook, and
> give something to the church, and they're automatically a saint.

The group of young people also made this observation.

> S: Like Mr. R [laugh], you know, he's a nice old man, you
> know, and he donated all this money to the church, but I've
> heard that he made a lot of his money by--
> D: Probably if they didn't have the money, they'd just be
> some old man.
> S: --Like during Prohibition and stuff, they made some money
> on some shady deals. And now they're donating it all to the
> church, and everybody thinks, "Oh, the great..." but it's
> the way he made his money, actually, when you think about it--
> D: But they really don't care.
> S: Yeah, no one cares, it's just that he's donating the money.
> How did he make it? He used to show skin flicks [everybody
> really laughs], back then, Mr. R. Then it was really wild,
> against the law. So you know, I hear about all these people,
> "Oh, he's so great," you know. Ahh, sure he's nice enough to
> donate all the money, but he's got it.

Furthermore, since everyone is measured by his "success", there is a

great emphasis on the appearance of success, on the material accoutre-

ments of financial security; houses, cars, clothes, etc. An American

woman who married a Greek man discussed one reason for his marrying a

non-Greek; this emphasis on material success played an important role.

> He has made the remark to me that for some time he knew that
> he would not marry a girl of Greek descent, even before we
> met. He felt that many of the girls that he was dating among
> the Greek girls were looking for something in a little bit
> more--materially rewarding, than what he had to offer at that
> time. ... They weren't knocking themselves out trying to
> catch him for a husband. And he was aware of it. He felt I
> think that they just expected him to have a little bit more
> to offer in financial security, you know. And this was
> apparently conveyed to him by more than one, so he sorta had a
> mental block, you know. So I think he'd more or less decided
> that was what they were all looking for, was financial security.
> And he was nowhere near financial security. And perhaps he had
> dated girls other than the Greek girls who did not convey this
> to him.

A third result of the concern with success is that young people are
strongly encouraged to enter respectable and profitable occupations.
E.g., a young man closely associated with the Greek community told this
story about an acquaintance:

> He came over from Greece, and was going to school to get some
> super degree cause he's really got the brains, but he really
> wants to be a singer. ... He was almost like the black mark
> of the family. He was really doing something wrong because
> he didn't come and get an education, and get a degree, and he
> was doing something wrong because he went to college for awhile
> and found out that he really didn't like what he was doing.

Thus one can see that achievement and success are significant elements of Houston's Greek community, and result in an atmosphere in which
the appearance of success, a respectable job, and contributing to the
community are of great importance. Several people who have divorced
themselves from the community--as well as many remaining in it--commented
very unfavorably on this aspect, noting that the community's values are
mixed up; people are judged not by their worth, but by their "success",
or their appearance of success.

II. Compliance

These standards of behavior are rather strict, almost ironclad, and not always easy to live up to. It is difficult for the individual to remain "goody-goody", or to at least always maintain the impression of being a "pillar of virtue". Real success and achievement are not easily accomplished either; frequently the individual must put aside his own wishes, even his own life's ambition, to accomplish what is expected of him by the community. If these "rules" are so rigid and require so much of the individual, why do people comply with them?

A. Forces

The first force which encourages compliance is the ever-present pressure of "What would people think...?" In such an intimate community in which most people know so much about each other, the weight of public opinion is a serious force in the way people choose to run their lives. A 2nd generation girl commented on her mother's preoccupation with the judgment of community members:

> She worries too much about "What are the other Greeks going to think?" My mother would keep us from doing something just for the sake of "What would people say?"

Two 2nd generation girls discussed their problems with community opinion.

> J: Once I made this dress that was really lowcut, and I wore it to a wedding, and I could tell that there was some comments made. ... It didn't bother me any, it didn't bother my father, but it bothered my mother, because she thought that someone would make a comment to the effect that "Did you see A's daughter in that dress?" You know, or something like that.
> L: You always have to worry about "what people will say."
> J: I know, that's a curse on us.
> L: You always have to be so careful.
> J: Yeah, and you have to keep up the image of being a good Greek girl. ... If some of the people knew some of the things I have done, I mean, not that they were so terrible, but they would be so terrible in their eyes, just so low down that they can make you feel like half an inch tall. You know, it's really a weight.

A second force which encourages the individual to "follow the rules" is a strong sense of obligation to his family. He does not want to hurt his family members by disappointing them or making them "look bad" in the eyes of the community. A 2nd generation girl commented:

> There's always a question of--you know, I think I owe something to my parents. ... You know, some people will say, "Look, your parents do what they do out of love of whatever, because they're your parents. As soon as you're old enough, go your way, live your life--and that's it, you don't owe them anything." But still, I feel like the only right thing--and I _really_ _feel_ like I have an obligation--but the question is, how far does that obligation go? You know, when does the point come when you say, "I've got to live by myself, I'm sorry, I'm leaving," or "I'm gonna marry so-and-so," or "I'm gonna just go out with so-and-so because it makes me happy." or "I cannot do this for you, I'm sorry." You know, just where do you draw the line?

These forces put a profound pressure on an individual because both the community and his family are such an important part of his life. One finds a great deal of security in his relationship with them, and the threat of ostracism from the community or being cut off from his family's love is for most individuals a rather frightening prospect. Thus many people are willing to alter their behavior to comply with community standards of performance.

B. Changing one's behavior

I will rather briefly examine ways in which Greeks modify their behavior to suit community standards, and then consider in more detail the adjustments of non-Greeks in the community. Since they are not as readily accepted as fellow Greeks, and their adjustment to fit the "rules" is in most cases more radical, they present a very interesting case.

1. Greeks

In section IV several responses of Greeks to the rule of community

participation will be considered; at this point I will discuss the way

in which the rules of propriety and success alter their behavior. The

comments of two girls, one 2nd and the other 3rd generation, demonstrate

that community pressure does indeed make them behave more "properly".

> I still, when I'm around Greek people, I still want to keep
> an image of--I want to be attractive to the guys, and feminine
> and all that, but I still--I wouldn't want them to think that
> I do a lot.
> [That you're "loose"?]
> Yeah! I really wouldn't want them to think that. I try to
> keep up the image. Whereas if I went to an American party,
> I really wouldn't care that much, because they wouldn't look
> down on me, and I'm afraid the Greek guys would.

> Greeks are conservative, you know--ideally. And there's--I
> mean, if we had a church dance, everybody would know the degree
> to which you could let loose in front of everybody else. At
> the Athens Bar, when I'm with all the group of kids, we can
> be more--in fact, with us, we could probably do whatever we
> wanted to, but like if there were adults involved there would
> be a comfortable stopping-point to where you'd know that this
> is what you're allowed to do.

The force of community opinion therefore causes people to "keep up the

image" when they are in front of a Greek audience. This is particularly

true if the audience is composed of the older generation. But the indi-

vidual must also be careful around his (or her) peers, who might "look

down on" him if he strays too far from the Greek rule of propriety.

The pressure to succeed also influences the lives of Greeks in

many ways; e.g., they may marry later than they otherwise would have.

The ideal is to be "secure" before one is married, to be out of college

and established in a profession. In response to a question about the

differences between his American and Greek friends, a 3rd generation

boy replied,

> Like people the same age, I find that a lot of my American

        friends are married, but that Greek kids the same age are single.
        "Wait a few years." With the Greeks, I guess the big thing for
        them is the stereotyped pattern, go to high school, get out of
        college, get a degree, settle down and get married.

A 2nd generation man was even more explicit about security in his reply

to my question about Houston Greek boys and girls not being interested

in one another.

        [A lot of people have said to me things like, "I've grown up
        with all these people, I've known them for so long, I'm just
        not interested in them." They are like brothers and sisters.
        Do you have that sort of feeling?]
        I am of the feeling that most Greek men don't marry before
        they're 25 or 26. I would speculate the general population--
        say, men--married sooner than that. ... I know that I was
        taught this, and a lot of my friends that are Greek Orthodox
        were taught to get your own life settled before you get out
        and marry. Get out of school, get a job, start making money
        and after you've accumulated some sort of security--you've
        gotten started--then it's time if you're looking in that
        direction to get married.

There are of course other ways in which pressure to succeed affects

the individual's life, and late marriage was given here as one example

of many. One may be influenced in his school performance, choice of his

major field in college, or his occupational choice, as well as in many

other decisions he may face throughout life.

  2. Americans

     The main reason that non-Greeks who want to fit into the group con-

form very strictly to the community's rules of performance is probably

that expressed by the woman who said,

        I was so determined to prove to them that I was just as good
        as any Greek girl and that I could be a good wife.

Non-Greeks have in most cases felt hostility from Greeks and are there-

fore anxious to prove that they indeed _can_ perform as well as any Greek.

Furthermore, if they have chosen to become a member of the group, they of course must satisfy its standards of performance. In fact, the reader

has seen that non-Greeks often must outshine the Greeks if they are to

become a part of the community.

In Chapter 5 it was noted that active participation is a requirement

for any non-Greek who seeks to belong to the community. Frequently this

means taking on jobs that the individual would not ordinarily have done.

> [You said that there were things you did when you were being
> a "good Greek wife". What kinda stuff was that?]
> I guess my immediate--was trying to please his family, not
> stepping on anybody's toes, agreeing to everything they said,
> doing things this way, and everything. Visiting this one, and
> then--participating in some activities that I really didn't
> care to do, but just to work myself in so I'd get to know these
> people and so they'd like me. And like I was chairman of the
> _____ for three years, and that was three terrible years.
> I hated it. ... I was there all the time for this Festival
> thing, and I was pregnant, and it was really a hardship to
> do this, and really, I had no business pushing that far, but
> I wanted them to see that I wanted to cooperate.

This woman--who is in no way an unusual case--felt it was very important

for her acceptance that she go all out in her work for the community, even

to the extent of doing a job for several years that she literally hated.

She and others like her realize that participation is a community "rule"

of performance which is particularly important for their membership and

acceptance as non-Greeks.

A second way in which a non-Greek accomodates herself to the commun-

ity's standards is by becoming "socially Greek", and one of the first

prerequisites for doing this is being married in the Greek church, even

if that would not have been her choice. Members of the community feel

very strongly about marrying in the church, as the remarks of a 2nd

generation woman whose son married outside the church demonstrate:

> I still want my kids to marry--even if they don't marry

> Greeks--that they would convert to our religion. I just
> believe in this. Like P marrying T, I like her, I really
> think he's got a good girl, really sweet, very thoughtful,
> very considerate of P and I'm just praying that someday P
> will see that he needs to get married in our church and
> maybe she'll convert, too.

The main theological reason for this attitude is the fact that the

Orthodox church does not recognize marriages which are performed in

other churches, and denies sacraments to its members who marry outside

the church.[1] Non-Greeks who marry Greeks are thus faced with strong

pressure to be married in the Orthodox church. One American woman

commented:

> The only way the church would recognize our marriage was
> for us to be married in a Greek Orthodox church. And at
> the time I felt like it had to be done that way.

In fact, many couples are married twice in order to conform to community

expectations. Sometimes circumstances force a delay in the church

ceremony, and the couple is married for the interim in a civil ceremony.

> We were married in a civil service first, and then in the
> church.
> [Why was that?]
> Well, K was married previously, and when we decided to get
> married, it was discovered that his wife never got an ecumenical
> divorce, you have to get it to--and for him to remarry in the
> church-- We went ahead and got married, which was a big shock
> to me--K never told me, but his family and all the Greeks would
> consider us not married until we were married in the church. I
> had a very rude awakening about four months after we were
> married, someone made a comment to us that we were not really
> married. I mean, as far as I was concerned I was married, but
> it--it was rather--I don't know, it surprised me that somebody
> would think that, you know.

In other cases, the non-Greek partner may not feel it necessary to marry

in the Orthodox church at first. After children are born and if the

family begins to take a more active role in the community, however, it

becomes more important that the non-Greek partner join the church, and

even be remarried in an Orthodox ceremony. Realizing that a church
marriage is expected of community members, the non-Greek may later comply
and arrange an Orthodox ceremony. Again, there are many ways in which
the non-Greek must conform to the expectation that he (or she) become
"socially Greek"--sending one's children to Sunday school, Greek language school, or participating in Greek social circles, attending church
functions--but marrying in the church has been given as an example of
one of the things which is expected of community members.

A third rule one must observe is "propriety". This is sometimes
difficult for non-Greeks, who have not been raised in the community, and
are therefore not familiar with the exact standards of propriety which
must be followed. Learning these standards can be a long process of
trial-and-error, and the individual may become very wary after having
made a few mistakes. In trying not to offend anyone's sense of propriety,
she (or he) must be very careful of her actions around Greeks. This
causes her to behave in an unnatural way, as one woman pointed out.

> I really want to be approved of, and I probably don't always
> act myself, as casual or carefree around women that are Greek,
> and I'm probably much more uptight, and polite and nice and
> what have you around like M--this Greek girl that I know--
> last year told O, "You're really married to a fine Christian
> girl." Well, that is not something that one of my friends
> would ordinarily ever think of, it would never cross their
> minds to say, you know? But it's probably because I have
> this very austere, uptight, quiet attitude, and she thinks
> it's just grand that I switched churches and am trying to do
> all this and everything, but the impression I made on her--
> when she made that statement, I knew I really wasn't my real
> self around her, and she's probably not her real self around
> me.

Furthermore, if she should momentarily forget that she should behave
"properly", or not realize that she is inadvertantly overstepping the

bounds of propriety, the results can be unfortunate.

> We were at a party Sunday night, and I have a divorced friend
> from college days that may be moving here, and C was talking
> to this guy that he's known for years--who's also divorced--
> and I said to him, "I want to be sure to get your phone number
> because I have a friend that's moving here, and I would like
> you to meet her." Well, C said, "You'll have to excuse my
> wife," which just infuriated me that he would apologize for
> me in public. But anyway C said as we left the party--he was
> incensed that I would be brazen enough to ask this man for his
> phone number! Probably if I had been Greek, and been raised
> like C, I would never have said that. His sister would never
> have said that, a lot of the Greek girls that I know would
> never have said that, 'cause they're much more--got this idea
> of "a woman's place", a woman's place.

In this situation, the woman's "improper" behavior toward a man was a

source of tension between her husband and herself. There are also

several other aspects of "propriety" such as conversation and other types

of behavior, which may cause trouble. An important element of propriety

is clothing, and several American women mentioned that they must be

very careful about their appearance when they are around Greeks.

> If S was real involved with being around the Greeks and really
> wanted me to carry off this business, and we had a lotta Greek
> friends, then it would really be hard for me. See, because
> then I would really have to act, or do things in a way that
> I don't--it doesn't seem natural, or something. I could see
> where I would be frustrated. I always get that feeling, because
> he always wants me to dress just so-so, and have my hair done
> just so for any Greek thing.

This woman's remarks reflect the importance of having a proper

appearance, but they also demonstrate the frustrations which face the

non-Greek who attempts to become a community member. She is expected to

conform to standards of behavior which may differ vastly from those

by which she was raised, and thus she frequently finds herself "acting"

in a way which does not seem "natural" to her. Until she has been

adequately socialized and fully incorporated into the group, taking on

its values as her own, she will continue to experience frustration.
One woman expressed occasional feelings of rebellion against the
community's expectations in this way:

> [Do you consider yourself Greek?]
> No.
> [What are you?]
> You know, there's a joke that "I'm a white one," which is
> what Greeks refer to Americans. Uhh, that's a very difficult
> --it's a difficult position to be in, because you really--
> you're orientated that way, but there are times that I feel
> like rebelling, and saying, "I don't want to!" And I really
> don't know how to answer that, I really don't know what I am.

Her feelings are not unusual.

"Success", the fourth standard of performance, does not generally
apply to non-Greek community members, for in most cases they are women.
Men are expected to be successful, but "a woman's place" is definitely in
the home, and thus the standard of success is not used to measure the
behavior of American wives. However, as the section has demonstrated,
the other rules--participation, social Greekness, and propriety--are
major forces in the lives of non-Greek members of the Greek community.

C. When the rules don't apply

These "rules" with which this chapter is concerned are not applied
to everyone, but only to those individuals who are associated with the
community. Those who have decided not to identity themselves as members
are not subject to judgment by Greek values, since they have not taken
on a "Greek" role. E.g., a non-Greek woman who did not commit herself
to community membership immediately after her marriage to a Greek told
this story.

> I lived with L's aunt and uncle for about nine months while
> he was in the Army. Every night when I got home from work,
> she had dinner on the table, and a little bit afterwards, she

would serve us coffee. Then Uncle T would say, "Let's go out!"
and we'd go to this restaurant where everybody in town went
at night for fun. We'd drink some brandy and listen to the
music and visit with everyone. At first I thought that his
aunt would be going with us, too, but when Uncle T said, "Well,
of course she isn't going," I realized that they both felt that
it was a Greek woman's place to stay at home at night, and maybe
watch a few TV programs, and have everything ready when the
others got back.

In this case one sees that the rule of propriety, of "a woman's place",
did not apply to her, since she had not yet taken on the role of a Greek
woman, and in particular because she had not yet tried to take on the
fundamental role of "Greek wife". Similarly, those who cease to identify
with the community no longer have to obey its strict rules of behavior.
A variation on this theme of changing one's behavior to satisfy community
expectations is consciously doing "Greek things" to demonstrate one's
ethnicity and identification as a community member.

III. "Being" Greek

How individuals express their "Greekness" publicly, i.e., techniques
of "being" Greek, will now be considered. This section will be concerned
with the means by which one presents himself as "Greek" to other Greeks
and to non-Greeks. A 2nd generation girl gave a hint that there may be
special ways of "being Greek" when she said:

To be Greek, is kinda neat now...And so you're not embarrassed
anymore. You've come to be proud of it and then you begin to
show it off more, so you do Greek things and stick around with
Greek friends and let people kid you and call you "Greek".

The question I will try to answer in this section is "How do you 'do
Greek things'?"

First, how does one present himself as Greek to a non-Greek? His

name will sometimes provide a clue, but many non-Greeks are not that
familiar with Greek names; a Greek name sounds "foreign", but the non-
Greek cannot readily identify it as Greek. Usually reference to one's
Greekness is somehow made in conversation with a non-Greek. E.g., the
individual may explain his behavior as "typically Greek", or make mention of how strict his parents are, "since they're Greek". Two young
2nd generation women mentioned this technique.

> G: My mother does that when people come to our house that
> aren't Greek--she'll say, "Well, we're Greek and we do these
> things," like that. She'll actually say something like that.
> "Well, that's because we're Greek."
> R: Or even the other night, that J was over...I'm sure we
> made comments you know--
> G: About being Greek--
> R: Yeah, to make sure he knew, to point it out. Or if some-
> body makes a comment, you know, "You're so 'blank'." "Well,
> it's the Greek in us!" You know, you might say that, where
> it would have nothing to do with it. Or you can tell jokes,
> you know, you can say "Well my mother did this today," and
> the Greeks will get it you know, and that forms a closeness,
> you know, you feel it in the air.
> G: "If my mother makes one more koulourakia, I'm gonna stuff
> it up her nose!"

This is all pretty obvious, but necessary with those who are not familiar
enough with "Greekness" to recognize more subtle clues. E.g., a 3rd
generation boy mentioned the blatant way in which some Greeks call
attention to the fact of their Greekness.

> If anybody says, "Are you Greek?" I'll say yeah, and if anybody
> wants to talk about it, of course I'm Greek--but to just go out
> and say, "Have you heard I'm Greek?", I don't think I'd do that.
> And some kids do take it very far to a point. And I don't think
> I'd ever do that.
> [What do they do?]
> They'd just have--GO GREEK or wear a T shirt or wear just any-
> thing to school to attract attention.

Expressing one's Greek identity to a Greek audience is a more subtle
procedure. One may let a few Greek words or phrases drop occasionally.

E.g., most Greeks upon entering a room will greet each other with a standard Greek routine--"Κάλη μέρα. Τί κάνεις?" "Καλά." ("Kali mera. Ti kanis?" "Kala.")--and then continue the rest of the conversation in English. Once the common "Greek" bonds have been established, it is all right for the conversation to switch to English.

> R: I think going to a party, where there's mixed--you'll
> walk in, and you might throw out a Greek word, you know.
> G: I've noticed that.
> R: It forms a circle around the Greek people--like a dotted
> circle.
> G: They all turn around and look, and you can see who's Greek.

There are other "Greek" things which one may do to express his Greekness. When he is with a group of Greeks the individual may talk louder than he normally would, in keeping with the "Greek" trait of being vivacious, emotional, and loud. Another way in which Greeks may project their identity with "Greekness" is by treating one another very warmly and touching one another.

> R: I might go up to a Greek guy or something, I'll just be
> warmer. A big kiss and a slap you know or something. Or a
> Greek girl--I can kiss a Greek girl, but you can't kiss an
> American girl, so if there's a--if it's mixed, you know, you
> really might. I'd go up to G and kiss her or something.
> G: A great big hug you know 'cause you just don't feel
> inhibited about it like you would with someone else.

Upon greeting one another, Greeks frequently embrace, and an American who was closely involved with the community at one time made the following observation about this behavior:

> It's like, there is from the year one this thing, this close-
> ness, and it gets to the point almost like its a symbol. It's
> always like "Oh, hi!" hug, hug. It's almost like that's the
> thing to do, you know? On the outside the real huggy-hugginess
> and kissy-kissiness of friends is like if you were to write
> down in a book, you know, "If two people hug and kiss each other,
> this means that they're really good friends." And on the outside,
> it looks that way. But is it that way at all? I don't think so.

> It gives the appearance that that is what's happening and
> I wonder if sometimes they do that because it does give the
> appearance, and that's what they want to give. For themselves,
> for the whole thing. It's another throwback to the closeness.
> It's another thing to show, "Hey look at us Greeks." That
> hugging thing, that's also something that's true in Negroes,
> "Hey, right on, brother! Hey, baby! Black power, black is
> beautiful." That thing of "Look at us, we're close." You
> know. It's like it's a symbol, and almost a false symbol.
> I think with all of them at different times, a lot of it is
> just show.

This is not to say that those who hug one another do not feel close,
but that an element of this behavior may be to give a "Greek" cue, to
express one's "Greekness" and to demonstrate one's feeling of solidarity
with Greek society and culture. I sense a similar phenomenon in another
behavior. When several Greeks get together, conversation sometimes
turns to self-consciously "Greek" topics in which those conversing actually seem to have little interest. It seems that this is done to stress
the Greek ties which unite them. E.g., I was at a Greek gathering one
evening and the conversation revolved around how hot it was in Greece
this summer, Greek soap operas, where people stayed when they visited
Greece, and anecdotes about things that happened to them while in Greece,
rather than politics or current events or how their kids were doing in
school, or "Have you heard the latest on so-and-so?"

One also presents himself as Greek to both Greeks and non-Greeks
through his surroundings, as well as through his behavior. Virtually
all Greek households have Greek knick-knacks sitting around the house
--Greek vases, ornamental koloumboloi (worry beads), sculpture, or
painted plates--which serve as a cue to the visitor that he is in a
Greek household. This practice was mentioned by an American who is
married to a 2nd generation man:

> At home I have Greek vases, we have Greek records that we play.
> It's just a part of his heritage that we have accepted and
> that we like....I have Greek things because I like them and
> because you can identify a little bit with them. People coming
> into your home other than Greeks see these things and they
> admire them, and ask about them.

Thus there are several ways in which an individual can present him-

self to others as "Greek". Perhaps the arena in which "being Greek" is

most frequently carried out is at the Greek Festival. Many people show

up during these three days to be Greek publicly, and then return to their

American lives until the next Festival. As a young 2nd generation woman

commented,

> There's some kids who don't come around a lot. But when they
> find out it's kind of neat, they come to the Festival. I've
> seen a lot of these people bring their friends to the Festival.
> So once a year, they're Greek, because it's neat then. And
> other times it's not.

These "Festival Greeks" will be discussed more fully in the next section.

Of course there are also many other situations in which people play at

at "being Greek".

> R: If you go to like the Festival or something and you kinda
> want to show off, if it's a situation where you want to show off
> that you're Greek, then you'll start the Greek dancing, and you'll
> put a good Greek dancer out in front, and you'll really--and then
> you know, the others, you'll kinda help them along. But with the
> Greeks!! You'll just start dancing it up!!
> G: Oh yeah.
> R: And you feel together, en masse, this pride coming up. And
> it's strengthened by knowing each other.
> C: Like that night over at Mrs. M's, when C and M and I just
> started dancing, and T and J [American friends] were watching
> and stuff. We were Greek dancing, and that was kinda our thing,
> you know, separate from what y'all know, and all this kinda stuff.
> It's kinda clique-y, but...

Thus there are several signals with which one can show his "Greek"

membership and self-conception. These signals serve to demonstrate to

himself and to others that he is indeed a "Greek". Such signs are particularly important to a group of people who will be discussed in the next section.

IV. Styles of "Doing Greek"

There are many types of Greeks, both outside and within the community. For example, in Chapter 4 differences were noted between those Greek Greeks who are considered community members and those who are not; community participation is the key to membership for such people. The same is true of Greek Americans. I will now examine styles of Greekness as they are expressed through various ways of participating. First those who are not considered true community members will be briefly considered.

A. Non-members

There are two types of non-members, "imports" and Greek Americans who have left the community and become "socially American". Both of these have periodic contact with the community by attending Easter services and by coming to the Greek Festival. Since Greek Greeks have already been discussed at great length in Chapter 4, only "American" Greeks will be considered at this point.

For Greeks who have dissociated themselves from the community, occasional contact reaffirms the Greekness in their self-conceptions. Many attend Easter services for just this reason, as a 3rd generation woman noted.

> [How about the Easter Greeks? Why do they just come once or twice a year?]
> It's more like a renewing the fact that you're Greek. For the people that don't attend church very much, this kinda helps say, "I'm still in things!!" Not so much maybe to other people, but just to themselves, too. ... The reason they go is just because --it's like because their parents went and so, it's kinda just

something--this is Easter time, so that's what you do. And
if you have that degree of Greekness, just that one little
bit--this kind of thing reminds you, each year you're gonna
go to the church on Easter.

Taking part in the Festival serves the same purpose, but there is also

another reason for Festival participation. The Festival provides an

opportunity for these people (as well as community members) to publicly

proclaim themselves as Greeks. As one woman said, "That's show time!"

There is a feeling of resentment among more active Greeks toward "Festi-

val Greeks", for it is felt that they do not work throughout the year,

or even the last weeks before the Festival, and then come in at the last

minute to claim attention for themselves as "Greeks". This resentment

was expressed by a 2nd generation couple:

> W: --the type that is Greek only if it suits him, status-wise.
> H: Around Greek Festival time, that's when they'll come out
> and blossom. ... I know a family that you seldom see at church,
> all year round, and then all of a sudden, they're Greek Greek
> at the Festival. Just because their friends are coming, and
> they want to be shown that they're in there, pitching in with
> the rest of them, so they can show to their friends, "Oh, look,
> she's part of the community! Look what she's doing! She's
> behind there helping, she's doing this, and that." It's really
> just a show, I think, and then you don't see them anymore.
> [Do you think they have Greek friends during the rest of the
> year?]
> H: I think they socialize more with Americans. They have their
> clubs, and they go to American clubs, American activities. ...
> But when it comes to the general public, to be seen, "Yes, I
> must come down there for three days, do something. Stand pretty,
> look pretty or do something."

Community resentment was probably what prompted Annunciation's priest to

put the following announcement in the church bulletin:

> Our entire Church family is involved [in our annual festival]--
> men, women, and children. All are called to participate and
> work. Some of our family members have toiled for months in
> preparation for the three-day presentation, while others will
> come forward during the three days to offer their support.
> Every effort and each offering is complete in itself. As St.

> John Chrysostom reminds us in his Resurrection Sermon, "He
> that comes at the eleventh hour is as welcome as he that
> comes from the first." ... This is not a time for judgment
> of each other's participation, but a time for full unity
> and joy. Respect of one for the other must prevail if we
> are to receive the respect of our visitors.

There are also other people who are very marginal in their participation, and they are generally considered non-members. These are wealthy Greeks who contribute money to community projects, but do not participate themselves. A 2nd generation man discussed such a person and said:

> He climbs the ladder of success, material success, and alienates
> himself to some degree from the Greek community. ... They feel
> that--they go through a period of feeling that they're superior,
> to some extent--that they have come out of this small community
> status to the greater, American, more cosmopolitan status. So
> the church doesn't mean too much. ... But they do come around
> once in a while, but it's usually just to see what's going on,
> just to come back down again in this small community, but they
> don't come with the feeling of participation. ... Like J--he's
> got so involved with business. He was very much involved with
> the Greek community, and dancing and all this. But then he
> went into business, and boy, he just--more and more and more
> involved in it, and he slowly but surely completely drifted
> away, from the participation in it.

It is important to note that such people are admired for their success and wealth, but their values are questioned by those who have remained in the community. Sure, work is important, and there is absolutely nothing wrong with making money, but are these things so important, should they be so time-consuming, that the individual has no time or energy to give to his own community? The money which wealthy Greeks donate to the community is greatly appreciated, but those who give it are not really considered part of the community by many members, because of their lack of participation in, or identification with, the community.

B. Community members

Thus one must have a certain minimal level of participation to be considered a community member. In fulfilling this requirement, however, there is a wide range of possible types of participation. A 2nd generation woman commented on two types of participation:

> You have people that are active in the social life of the church, that may not take part too much in the services themselves. Or even know that much about it. And there might be others that are--take part more in the church, but they don't take part in the social life as much.

Since people who attend church but take little part in Greek activities have been discussed in Chapter 5, those who are socially active but seldom attend church will now be considered. Two 2nd generation girls discussed an extreme example of this:

> [What about the people you mentioned that go to the social things and not the church? Do you think people really do that a lot?]
> T: In other words, attending more social functions than the church? I do. ... Really, a lot of people just get dressed up to go to the fellowship coffee.
> M: I've had people tell me that they completely skipped church, and just came to the fellowship afterwards.

This is not to say that such individuals only come for "fun" affairs, for some are among the hardest workers in the community. Their distinguishing feature is their limited attendance in church.

A second type is the "night club Greek", whose entertainment revolves around Greek clubs. Some of these individuals are Greek Americans, but most are "imports". A 2nd generation man commented on one such fellow:

> He's a fun Greek. To him, everything is a ball--you know, he's not the religious type, he's not the--B just isn't--I couldn't classify him as a Greek Greek, because he doesn't fall into all this uhh--he's not for Greece, I mean, he's a fun Greek. He works hard, and likes his good time--his Greek good time. You know, like going to the Athens Bar.

Perhaps the most significant difference in styles of participation

is found between those who are active in Greek fraternal organizations
(such as AHEPA) and those who are not. Those who are Ahepans are generally the more nationalistic and culturally-Greek members of the community.
A 3rd generation girl (who is active in the Maids) discussed the attitudes
of church-oriented Greeks toward the fraternal organizations:

> They don't really consider AHEPA as being very worthwhile. I
> mean, they consider it as being more secular, and they're inter-
> ested more in the church and the workings that are really related
> to it, the things that are worthwhile. Like Philoptochos, GOYA,
> things like that. ... There is a definite distinction--people
> that are real active, the board members and things like this,
> are usually not Ahepans. The Ahepans are a separate set of people.

V. Discussion

Thus one can see that the Greek population of Houston is a very
diverse group whose members may or may not identify themselves as members
of the community. One may visualize Houston's Greek population as divided
into several categories, according to their community membership and
style of social participation. These are the categories which Greeks
themselves would recognize. The salience of Greekness in the self-
conceptions of each type varies, but certain categories (e.g., Ahepans,
"fun" Greeks, and "imports") are likely to be more Greek both culturally
and in self-conception; whereas others (religious and Americans) are
likely to be less so.

The Community
"Americans" who have joined the community
imports who have become Greek Americans
Ahepans, Gapans, etc.
"fun" Greeks
mixed participation (both social and religious)
social, not religious participation
religious, not social participation

Outsiders

"Easter" Greeks   imports
"Festival" Greeks   =   Americanized Greeks
                     wealthy Greeks

completely Americanized Greeks

Those who are not community members may still consider themselves

"Greeks", periodically reaffirming this self-conception by attending

Greek activities. Within the community there is a wide range of "Greek"

styles, but the uniting factor is a sense of togetherness and closeness,

a feeling of parea with other members.

GREEK FESTIVAL DANCERS

GREEK FESTIVAL DANCERS

A future dancer

Festival dancer

Entertainment from a local Greek restaurant

Gift shop

TWO CHILDREN'S DANCE GROUPS

Dinner serving line

Making dough for <u>loukoumades</u>

Broiling and selling souflakia

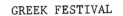

GREEK FESTIVAL

CHAPTER 8

CONCLUSIONS

The basic issue which the Greek American faces is not whether he
will continue to conceive of himself as a "Greek", but whether he will
remain a member of the Greek community. Within the community he finds
security and a gratifying sense of intimacy and closeness. His family
and friends are very warm and loving, and deeply concerned about him.
His religion is an integral part of his life and his identity. And yet
the community is also very limiting; if he becomes too deeply involved
in it, he may have no opportunity to be himself, to express his personhood in any way apart from being Greek. As long as he is a community
member, he feels the burden of playing his Greek role, according to Greek
rules.

Some people are so deeply involved in their church, family, and
community that leaving the ethnic group would never occur to them.
Because of the subtle entrapment of deep involvement within the community
there may be no real choices left by the time the individual is old
enough to choose. This was particularly true among the 1st and 2nd
generations, who lived in a geographical and social ghetto to a greater
extent than does today's 3rd generation in Houston. A young person of
this generation in many cases does not necessarily assume community
membership automatically--it becomes a more problematical thing than it
was for his parents, and often takes the form of a conscious decision.

The decision is not an easy one to make. If he opts for the freedom
of anonymity he sees in the world outside the Greek community, he must

inevitably sacrifice the rewards of ethnic membership, the "togetherness" he feels with his family, friends, and church. Nor does he make the decision alone. There are constant pressures from all sides encouraging him to "keep Greek". The community envelops him in a network of close relationships with others "of Greek blood"; the church is an ever-present force keeping him associated with the community; his family may threaten to stop loving him if he chooses to leave. The sense of shame and guilt at having disappointed people who have given him so much love and had such high expectations of him is a heavy burden, and unwillingness to bear it may keep the individual within the community. That family members--parents and children--are often willing to sacrifice their relationship with one another over someone's leaving the group is a particularly poignant element of American ethnicity which demonstrates the overwhelming significance of ethnic membership for many individuals and highlights the dynamic force of ethnicity in America.

If he decides to leave the community, he feels that he has "escaped" --from the narrowness and limitations of the community. Members of the community feel he has been "lost"--he has forsaken the love, warmth, and closeness they offered. And they are both right.

I. Two Lives

In the preceding chapters I have discussed the basic facts of being a Greek in Houston, and attempted to show the relationships between the social meanings of Greekness, community membership, the forces which encourage a Greek self-conception as well as continued membership in the community, and the social actions by which individuals demonstrate their

Greekness. But perhaps the most graphic way to show how people view

their alternatives, deal with the pressures they feel, and finally make

their choices, is to let them speak for themselves. Two women, one

"Greek" and the other "American", will be quoted. The 2nd generation

Greek woman is reassessing what being Greek means to her. The American

woman tells about marriage to her 2nd generation husband, joining the

Greek church, and eventually leaving the community altogether.

A. A Greek woman: "A great feeling to know that I don't have to be

Greek"

> This is funny, because these high school girls were writing some
> lunchroom cards for me and they came to S-----------, and they
> were trying to pronounce it and they couldn't, and I said,
> "It's S-----------," just real easily, and they just looked
> at me, and I started to say, "That's a Greek name," you know,
> I'm proud, it's a Greek name, and I stopped myself. And I
> thought that was real strange. All of a sudden I thought, "Why
> should I tell them it's a Greek name? It wouldn't mean anything
> to them." But any other time I would have been so proud to say,
> "That's a Greek name."
>   I noticed that two Greek kids in T's class got Good Citi-
> zens for the month--they choose three out of the class. And I
> thought, "Gee, T should have gotten it so it would be three
> Greeks!" And I thought, "Now, that is really thinking Greek,
> is that ever thinking Greek!"
> [How do you feel about your own being Greek? You told me that
> you weren't going to worry about being Greek any more, you were
> just going to be yourself. But still you have this pride thing.]
>   Well, it's just a habit, I don't think it's really.   I
> think it's something you have to grow out of, just like popping
> gum. I mean, after so many years--
> [Are you Greek any more?]
> I'm Greek, I just don't limit myself to being Greek, you know.
> That's what I've been trying to get away from. I hope that my
> children aren't just "Greek", you know, I hope they're broad-
> minded enough to--If I had had my way, I would have--I don't
> want to break away from the church itself, but I can't see where
> Greek fellowship is that important in our lives.
>   It's just a feeling of not wanting to be pinned down in the
> Greek, you know. And I can't get this across to my husband,
> that in this day and age--maybe it was O.K. when we were growing
> up, but our children are going to be traveling all over the
> country, meeting non-Orthodox, non-Greek friends. And we shouldn't

limit them in any way.
[Does he feel they should be encouraged in Greek activities?]
Oh yeah. You know, Junior GOYA, our son should be active in
Junior GOYA they ought to be going to Sunday school, all this,
and I'm not that excited about it.
[Was there a turning-point in your life when you said, "This
social Greek thing isn't satisfactory."?]
Yeah, well, it was more of a spiritual turning-point. I saw in
the Greek community--I didn't see the Christian fellowship that
I was looking for. I think if I hadn't've had this spiritual
awakening, that I would still be trying to fit into the Greek
community.
[So up till then it was like you were raised in that church so--]
It was where I was supposed to be, but afterwards, I realized
that maybe this wasn't where I was supposed to be, maybe I didn't
have to be in this church, and I didn't have to be Greek. Before
--at first I did really try in my own church, so I don't really
feel that I'm turning my back on the people there, or doing the
wrong thing. But it's one of those things that you just sorta
have to wait and see. You know. Who's going to be affected by
it? Your family? Or will it affect you later? Are you just
searching for something that's not there?
     But it's just a great feeling to know that I don't have to
be Greek if I don't want to be, that I don't have to go to Greek
church, whereas before I always felt that you're Greek, you know,
you go to the Greek church.
[Do you identify being Greek with being in the Greek church?]
It's hard for me to--I mean Greek is church to me--I mean, I
think of an Orthodox Greek.
[What about your Greekness apart from the church? What do you
mean when you say you're not gonna worry about being Greek any
more?]
Well, it hits both areas. I mean, I'm free to be a Christian,
and if I choose the Orthodox faith, you know, that's fine, but
I'm not committed to it.
[So your self identification would be primarily Christian--]
And second Orthodox, and last Greek. Greek to me is just down
on the bottom. It really is, I just don't put that much emphasis
on being Greek. Greek wasn't always far down the scale, it's
just been in the past two or three years that I can say that--
being Greek was always an important thing because you were
different and uhh--no, I don't think it's always been unimportant.
[But you still have ties with Greek people.]
Well, these are like--for instance, A [who left the church]. You
don't suddenly drop all your friends because you leave the church,
if you find out later on through the years that your interests
are not the same, that bond that you maybe possibly had with
someone isn't there anymore, you sorta drift away from one
another. But then, like I say, I'm still in the early stages
of this, and uhh--some people like A can just walk away, and I
think that takes a lot of courage. And a lot of understanding

from his wife, that must've been a tremendous thing for her
to accept, if she didn't feel the same way he did. But in
a case like mine, I can't just walk out.

This Greek woman is in the process of reexamining her Greekness.
It has become a relatively insignificant element of her self-conception,
and she is beginning to wonder if she might feel less limited outside
the community. But strong pressures--particularly from her family--are
keeping her within the community. This, then, is a case of continued
community membership without the encouraging factor of a strong "Greek"
self-conception. In an attempt to reconcile participation with her
self-conception, she has to an extent withdrawn from the normal prescribed
activities of members. She has fewer Greek (and more "American") friends
than most other Greeks of her age and generation, and participates little
in community social affairs. She feels it unnecessary to push her children into Greek activities, but her husband disagrees. They are certainly
less involved than most Greek children, but she will undoubtedly feel
more pressure from others to place them in Greek organizations and social
circles when they become older. Presently she is "only in the early
stages" of withdrawal, and it is uncertain whether she will be able to
completely leave the group, or if relationships with her Greek family,
friends, and church will keep her a community member indefinitely.

B. An American woman: "You have to live your own life."

I met J in high school and was completely unaware, never
having met any prejudice before, I was completely unaware, and
he hid it. He would date me, and I had no idea that he wasn't
supposed to be. I don't remember exactly how it came out,
eventually he would tell me that his parents wanted him to
date only Greek girls, seriously. It was O.K. if you dated
just once in a while, but they didn't want you to date over
and over again the same girl.
In that age period between thirteen and sixteen, he used

to go with them to other states, they used to go in groups
to these weddings and baptisms, and it would be like a whole
weekend vacation, which really sounds like a good fun time,
but at that time he was getting to know the girls that were
his age, because there was at that time not a large Greek
community in M, and not that many Greek girls were available
for him to date, and so he was introduced to a lot of them
from other places.

He never really told them too much about it, he would
just get by, and if they asked was he going to date P [the
speaker] tonight, I think sometimes he would say "Yes",
once in a while, and other times he would say "No". So they
didn't really know what was going on. I knew that he had
trouble coming to see me when we were dating a lot. They
would put restrictions on him, and wouldn't let him have the
car, so then he would just hitchhike up. It was a tension
there, but we were young enough that we just didn't pay that
much attention.

Once he went to college, there was no strong communication
between them. He would go home and they would pressure him to
go to a wedding or a baptism or something, and every once in a
while they would import girls for him to date. And this was a
source of problems between us.

...We had decided that we were going to get married that
summer, and were engaged and everything. So he at his gradua-
tion, after he'd gotten his diploma and everything, in his
robes, me on his arm--there we are! And we walk over together.
She [his mother] burst out in a barrage of Greek which I couldn't
understand, and I just stood there, tears streaming down my face,
because I knew that whatever she was saying, I knew she wasn't
happy. If you've ever seen two forlorn characters, you saw us
that day. Here we were, with no one to celebrate with. So we
celebrated with somebody else's family.

We decided we'd get married in the Greek church. For their
sake. 'Cause that's what the Greeks expect. Whether the marriage
is the girl or the boy, they expect that the other person, that
isn't Orthodox, will be married in their church. So we decided
to be married in the church, and they attended. They invited
very few people, which was unusual for Greeks.

We moved away, that helped a lot, there was no problems
because we were way away. And we would come visit and we would
stay at J's mother's house, and things sorta went very well.
And they began accepting me much better and became warm towards
me. We both tried to forget the problems and nasty words said.
And that's another thing, I never said anything. I don't know
if that was good or bad. When she would come out with these
things, I never really said anything, which I would now, were
I ever to be faced with that prejudice again. But I was young
then, and sorta not really outspoken. I sorta accepted these
things, and kept them inside. Now that caused a problem in our
marriage.

Especially when it came to joining the church. I refused to

join the church when I was married, which was the normal, the accepted thing. Anybody that married Greek Orthodox was then expected to become a member of the church. I just couldn't accept the stuff, and so I didn't join. And that was hard for them to take. So then we tried to become members of the church, and we'd go, and it was all in Greek. J was never that strong anyway, so we just ended up not going to church at all. That's what happened. And then we moved to R, and all of a sudden we started finding people we liked in this particular church. I started singing in the choir, all in Greek, and I really made a special effort to really become part of the congregation. That was about the closest I ever came, and then his mother came out one day and spoiled it all.

She came out to visit us. I was nine months pregnant with our first child, and she said, "Have you joined the church yet?" And I said "No." And I was so close to joining at this point. And she said, "Well, I can't hold my head up in the community any longer. If you don't join the church, I'll have to cut you and J off from the family. So if you come out at Christmas time, and you haven't joined the church, then don't come home to our house." And this really hurt—all of a sudden, it came down on my head again. This prejudice. I couldn't take it, I really couldn't. We'd had such good warm feelings with them, we'd become a part of them, we felt, and I just didn't feel like it meant that much to me. So I went to the church and I joined. I really didn't believe in it, but just to keep the peace I did it.

So we came to Houston. Father Nick came to see us, and we liked him, so we went to the church at first. But it didn't last very long. Because we didn't really feel that we were getting much from it that we really needed. First I stopped going to the church. I said that "I really can't go any more. I feel strongly enough that it's not for me, I feel like I've tried for eight years to fit in, I cannot do it any longer," and "If you want to, that's fine." So that lasted about four months, J would every once in a while go down to the church by himself. And after a while he would just come home and say, "P, it's not where it's at. I just can't stand it any longer, I'm not going to go there any more." And he stopped going. [Did you ever feel not accepted by the Greeks?] I never felt not accepted. If anything, they wanted me to become more a part of it. I'm a very outgoing person, though, and people that are more shy, that don't really get into the activities, could feel that way. And even in the M group, the real strong group there, I'm accepted. They don't treat me as an American. But they pressure you to be a part of their church, and I can't. Their church doesn't give me anything, so I really can't be a part of it. Now I have, I would say, gone out of my way to be a part of them.

Last Easter when J's mother came down to visit us, J told her that we were no longer going to be Greek Orthodox. And she did resent it, and she showed her resentment towards me in some ways. But she treated us as adults, evidently. Because this time she did not threaten not to see us again, and it makes me wonder--all these years I've been putting up with this, you see? Being sort of afraid to really tell her how we felt. ... We did one more thing to make her feel better. At Easter we had a huge celebration here, a Greek Easter. We roasted a lamb in the back yard, like the village, and she and I cooked for a week previous to it. We had about twenty-five people here, and we opened the whole house and had a regular Greek Easter. And she really just appreciated that. What I felt like we were telling her was, "We do not reject Greek tradition. It's a part of us, we love it." I love that part of J, I just do not accept the religion. And I think she got the message.

And when I went home that summertime, I felt that things were O.K. But there was no pressure to come to church on Sunday, or the children, to take them to church, like there used to be. And it was very nice. ... Some of the Greek people are very much against pants. There isn't anybody I don't wear cutoff shorts and halter tops around except them. Until this summer when I went home, and then decided that I was just going to be myself. Nobody said a word to me. They've either got to accept J and I as the people we are or--they already know that we are the renegades of the family, because for one thing, we don't live around them, which the rest of the families all do. We've always lived apart.
[What if you'd done it earlier?]
I think that what would have happened is that they would have cut us off. And there would have been a lot of hurt, but I think they wouldn't have kept that way. They love J so much, he's the only boy--I can't imagine them not seeing him forever. And their grandchildren? There's no way. But I didn't know that they were playing a game, and I feel that they were-- especially when she came out at that time that I was pregnant and said that she would cut us off, I don't believe she would have.
[Are your kids Greek?]
The question came up the other day. I said, "I wonder what T would say if we asked him, 'Are you Greek?'?" So we asked him. And he said, "Well, I think that I would tell them that I was half-Greek." And I don't know what B will say. Because I think that T had more of it than B did. T knows that he was named after his grandfather, who was Greek. B was not named after anybody. Because by then, I was really beginning to feel that I was not going to name all my children after Greek people. When I named her B, they just about died. One of the relatives says, "B? Is that Italian? What is it?" And I said, "It's Irish." That was about the first thing I ever did. That was real brave.

It took us long enough to realize that there were things that you just don't do--when you become a mature person, you don't continue doing things for you mother's sake. You have to

> live your own life. And some people I guess never really get
> out of that. That's what prejudice can do to you. I've often
> wondered why I haven't felt more strongly bitter about it. I
> don't really know why, except that they are loving people, and
> there are some beautiful things about them. And it's sad that
> they have to feel that way about people that are outsiders.

In this young woman's story one sees at work the pressures described
in earlier chapters--the way in which her husband's family tried to coerce
him to "marry Greek", and her to conform to "Greek" standards. Her
comments also relate to the central question of this dissertation: if
the continuation of the group depends on keeping people within it, how
is this accomplished? In the case of this couple, what went wrong? It
appears that the major point of difficulty was church membership--neither
of them felt that the Orthodox church satisfied his needs, and in leaving
the church by definition they left the ethnic group as well. Again one
can see that the church is the single most defining of the ethnic group's
social boundaries. It is interesting to note that the group's "rules"--
such as dress and participation--no longer applied when the couple declared that they were "no longer going to be Greek Orthodox", i.e., no
longer members.

And yet another factor was at work as well in their leaving the
group--"this prejudice" which P felt so strongly from her husband's
family and other Greeks. This was of course based on the community's
emphasis on the importance of "Greek blood". Although she insists that
she never felt "not accepted", the tenor of her other comments (as well
as discussion with her husband) indicate that she has indeed felt
rejection because of being non-Greek. Her remark that "they wanted me
to become more a part" reflects the Greek "rule" that non-Greeks who

marry into the group should become as "Greek" as possible by marrying

in the church, becoming Orthodox, and raising their children as Greeks.

Thus community members send out contradictory messages--both "We want

you to be one of us." and "You'll never be one of us." These messages

come on different levels. On the surface, it may appear that all is

well, that the American is quite welcome in the community, and yet just

beneath the surfaces he (or she) senses that she can never fit in

because he is not Greek. This double bind can be very disconcerting,

and combined with a lack of interest in the Orthodox church--as in this

case--it can cause the individual or couple to drift away from the

community. The impact of "blood" on the continued membership of non-

Greeks in the Greek group will be further discussed in a later section

of this chapter.

II. Re-examination of Theories

A. Social boundaries

Chapter 1 discussed ethnicity in America and proposed that tendencies

toward both assimilation and cultural pluralism are in fact occurring

simultaneously. Ethnic identification--the individual's identification

of himself as a member of, combined with his continued participation in,

the ethnic group--was seen as the primary feature affecting the future

of ethnic groups, since a group which loses all of its members ceases to

exist, and is therefore successfully assimilated. It is their mainte-

nance of social boundaries defining who is a group member which insures

the continued existence of ethnic groups; this research project examined

the elements of Greekness which are necessary attributes of group membership--Greek "blood", community participation, and Greek Orthodoxy --and the forces which keep individual members associated with the community. Of these three prerequisites, Orthodoxy most clearly defines one's membership--those who leave the church are no longer true community members. Being of Greek blood is also a significant aspect of membership, as the comments of non-Greek members so poignantly demonstrated. Community participation is the most flexible of the three, for a wide range of types and degrees of participation is acceptable. There are many ways of being Greek, and so long as the individual maintains a modicum of participation, he is accepted as a member. One may conclude that the boundaries of the ethnic group are in general well-defined, but still somewhat permeable. It is rather easy to leave the group by dropping one's Orthodoxy; although those who do so are often considered "still Greek" because of their "blood", it is generally recognized that they have effectively severed their ties with the group. It is more difficult for the non-Greek to become a true member, however, since he is not "of Greek blood". Those who become socially Greek and raise their half-Greek children as Greeks are usually accepted to some extent, and their children are considered true Greeks. Thus the boundaries of the group are cross-able.

Greek Americans were seen to be "assimilated"[1] in some respects, but also a pluralistic group whose members sharply distinguish themselves from "outsiders", i xeni. What is the nature of the compromises Greek Americans have made which allow them to "assimilate" and yet retain a distinctive identity? This section will briefly examine the aspects of Greek life which keep it in some sense distinguishable from other groups in American society.

1. Areas of assimilation

In general, it appears that the traditional "Greek" patterns which have been lost are those a group must inevitably lose in adjusting to life in a new land. Greek Americans have discarded those things which might interfere with their functioning in America; the loss of these social and cultural patterns will not appreciably affect the continued existence of the group. To reiterate a point made throughout this dissertation: Greek Americans have not maintained traditional "Greek" patterns intact in the United States, nor is it necessary that they do so to remain a distinguishable group. Rather, in response to their American experience, Greek Americans have developed a culture which takes elements from both Greek and American cultures, as well as having developed some patterns uniquely its own.

Naturally in this process some Greek traditions are becoming obsolete. Arranged marriages and dowries are now rare, and dating customs have become more liberal and Americanized. The spoken Greek language is also becoming a less important aspect of Greek American life as the community becomes predominantly composed of 2nd and 3rd generation members. Social relationships have been modified as well. Patrioti are not as significant for 3rd generation individuals as they were for their parents and particularly grandparents. Furthermore, patronage of Greek businesses has become less common as community members have been widely dispersed over metropolitan Houston. These areas of "assimilation" do not signal the ultimate disappearance of the ethnic group, however. Just as Greek Americans have discontinued some traditional Greek customs in the development of a Greek American culture without losing their group identity, certain current Greek American patterns may eventually fall by the way as well without threatening the group's continued existence. One ideal which seems to be of decreasing importance is the cultural ban on working wives. It appears that more Greek American women in recent years have begun working outside the home, and current developments in woman's rights in American society will no doubt contribute to the increase of this pattern. Such changes do not mean that the group is being assimilated, however, for the social boundaries which separate it from other American groups continue to operate.

2. Differences remaining

Furthermore, Greek Americans have maintained many cultural and social patterns which differentiate them from non-Greeks. Although the family characterized by "closeness" and "respect"--which Greeks often cite as a factor clearly differentiating them from "Americans"--is also character-istic of other ethnic groups, several aspects of this phenomenon seem uniquely Greek. These are the widening of kinship ties to include in-laws (symbetheri) and distant cousins, and the extension of kin-type relationships to include kumbari, friends, and even the Greek community in general. Of course the "festive" aspects of Greekness--Greek foods, music, and dancing--are very much alive in the Houston community.[2] Furthermore, the community "rules" of performance discussed in Chapter 7, particularly those concerning propriety and success, are somewhat differ-ent than those which might be found in non-Greek groups. These remain-ing elements act to give Greek Americans a feeling of distinctiveness which helps the group remain separate from other Americans.

3. How the community remains separate

What aspects of the community maintain the boundaries which keep Greeks in some sense "separate" from non-Greeks? The community organization, characterized by overlapping networks of kin, kumbari, and friends which bind members to one another in a complex web of relationships, acts to give members a significant and gratifying feeling of belonging to an intimate, family-like group. The round of Greek activities and organizations--religious, social, recreational, educational, and cultural-- provide an exclusively Greek world in which the individual can spend as much of his life as he wishes. Another aspect helping Greeks to maintain the boundaries separating them from non-Greeks is the ideology of differentness which stresses the importance of "Greek blood", and in some cases also includes attitudes of racial superiority and invidious comparisons with other American ethnic groups. Individuals who have throughout their lives been reminded that they are basically different from, and even superior to, non-Greeks because of their "blood" are likely to remain associated with other Greeks. Related to this ideology of differentness based on "blood" is the community's emphasis on endogamy, and the means of meeting other Greeks--such as the use of conventions-- which have developed in response to this pressure to "marry Greek".

Perhaps the most significant aspect of Greek American life maintaining the community's separateness, however, is its close association-- in fact, virtual identification--with the Greek Orthodox church. That Greeks have a religion which is theirs alone strengthens greatly the community's tendency to remain socially, if not geographically, isolated

from the surrounding American society and culture. Greek Orthodoxy is
the strongest and most clearly defining of the social boundaries which
separate Greek Americans from non-Greeks, and so long as the Greek
Orthodox Church survives, there will always be a Greek American ethnic
group. Thus the most serious threat to the group's continued existence
comes neither from the loss of the spoken Greek language nor from
intermarriage, but from the possibility of American Orthodoxy. Were
America's myriad Orthodox groups to unite into a common church, Greeks,
Syrians, Russians, etc., might become the fourth element in the theoretical "triple melting pot" of American society. Presently, Orthodox in
general do not intermarry with Catholics--to whom they are closest
religiously of America's three major faiths--because of the differences
which have historically separated the two churches,[3] as discussed in
Chapter 2. Thus Orthodox have not been assimilated into the general
"Catholic" melting-pot described by Kennedy (1944), or into a fourth,
Orthodox melting-pot. Nor will this occur so long as national Orthodox
churches are maintained.

Therefore, despite the fact that several cultural elements of the
Greek community are undergoing change, one should not conclude that the
ethnic group is being assimilated, and that these changes necessarily
foreshadow its disappearance. Many aspects of the community continue to
differentiate community members from non-Greeks, and will prevent total
assimilation as long as they are operative.

B. Ethnic identification

Chapter 1 also suggested that the term "ethnic identification" is
used to denote two interrelated, but separate phenomena. One is the

individual's conception of himself as a participating member of the ethnic group. As Chapter 5 demonstrated, these two aspects of ethnic identification are indeed closely related, and one often follows from the other. Nevertheless, the distinction between them is an important one which can be useful, since those cases in which the relationship between the two is problematic--individuals who have strong "Greek" self-conceptions but do not consider themselves members of the Greek American group, and vice versa--are of particular interest in the study of ethnic groups. For example, recent immigrants from Greece naturally think of themselves as "Greeks" but in many cases do not become a part of the Greek American community, whereas Americans who marry Greeks frequently join the community, despite their lack of a "Greek" self-conception. Of these two groups, American members obviously contribute more toward the continuation of the ethnic group than do Greek non-members. Furthermore, the distinction is also significant for Greek Americans who are born into the community; the forces which encourage one type of ethnic identification may still continue to work when those which influence the other are no longer effective. E.g., a number of individuals who consider themselves "Greek Orthodox" rather than "Greek" do not feel that Greekness is a significant aspect of their self-conceptions, but remain associated with the community through the church. Based on my research experience, I would suggest that in general Greekness becomes less central in the self-conception of an individual before he leaves the community; even though he may not consider Greekness important, his ties to his church, family and other community members act to keep him within the group for some time. Thus, in the "assimilating" individual, the decreased significance of one type of ethnic identification--the self-conception--apparently consistently precedes the loss of the other. For these reasons, the distinction between the two aspects of ethnic identification is a valuable one which should be more fully examined and utilized in the field of ethnic groups.

C. Other theories

Several current theories in the ethnic-group literature should be re-examined briefly at this point. The first of these is Hansen's "third-generation return". I found no evidence in Houston's Greek community to support Hansen's hypothesis that the 3rd generation "returns" in any way to the culture that its parents deserted. Apparently few of the 2nd generation ever "left", and the children of those who did have not "returned" to the community; these 3rd generation people could possibly have become somewhat interested in their Greekness, but they have not returned to join the community, and this is the real issue. As noted in Chapter 4, such individuals would probably be considered "outsiders" and face the same problems as Americans who marry into the community, since neither group was "raised Greek".

The very concept of "generation" itself has proven to be a difficult one to apply to the realities of the Houston community. The first problem which presented itself was the mistake of lumping recent immigrants with individuals who came to the United States fifty years ago under the title of "1st generation", for the two groups differ greatly. Another difficulty is the existence of a number of marriages of different generations. Most of these are 1st/2nd generation couples, and I have labeled their children "2-3" generation (which is accurate, but obviously awkward) but there are also marriages of imports and 3rd generation

individuals, 3rd and 2-3 generation individuals, and so on--how are their

children to be designated? Furthermore, using place of birth to determine

generation does not accurately describe many individuals, particularly

in two cases. Some were born in Greece but came to America as very

small children; they are 1st generation by birth, but 2nd generation by

experience. Other cases are even more confusing, because of travel

between Greece and America. E.g., I am acquainted with several individu-

als who were born in America and taken to live in Greece as very small

children, only to return to the United States as teenagers. Nor are

such intermediate-generation cases rare. Of the households contacted

in the telephone survey, 19% involved partners of intermediate or

different generations--marriages of 2-3 generation individuals, 3rd

and import, 1st and 2nd generations, and so on. Thus a theory which

discusses individuals only in terms of 1st, 2nd, and 3rd generations

oversimplifies the nature of ethnicity. Attention should be focused

on group membership and its social boundaries instead, for it is from

this perspective, rather than that of generations, that one can most

fully and accurately consider assimilation, the basic question of

American ethnicity.

An issue which has been of particular interest throughout this work

is intermarriage, and it has been dealt with in a rather ambivalent

manner, which reflects its role in the community. On the one hand, I

have stated that increased rates of intermarriage do not necessarily

signal the death of the group, for non-Greek spouses often enter the

community and raise their children as Greeks; on the other hand, I have also outlined in some detail the problems of adjustment which face the non-Greek who attempts to do this, because of the community's emphasis on "Greek blood" and its reluctance to accept "outsiders". Both of these statements are true, even though they appear to be somewhat contradictory. Intermarriage does not have to cause the group to disintegrate, but the emphasis on "blood" and the exclusion of strangers which serves as a basis for the restrictions against exogamy act as a "self fulfilling prophecy". Community members fear destruction of the group and in an attempt to prevent it, exercise severe sanctions on those Greeks and non-Greeks who try to intermarry. Unfortunately this behavior often backfires, resulting in the opposite result. The individuals marry, then may leave the group which caused them so much heartache; or they may try to remain in the community, but the non-Greek partner is so unhappy over his or her obvious non-acceptance that the couple gradually drifts away. The main problem here is that community members confuse the folk theory of "Greek blood" with those processes which are more fundamental to the community's existence. The fact is that the group's continuation is contingent not upon maintaining the purity of bloodlines, but on the transfer of Greek cultural, social, and identificational patterns from one generation to the next. This task can be performed by non-Greeks as well as by individuals "of Greek blood", and many Americans are more than willing to do so. Thus, intermarriage does not have to result in eventual assimilation, but the group's existence may be truly threatened so long as "Greek blood" is so strongly emphasized that those who are not biologically Greek are excluded from full-fledged community membership.

III. Generalizability of Findings

To what extent can the findings of this study of Houston's Greek community be generalized to other Greek communities, or to other ethnic groups? This is of course rather difficult to determine, but a comparison of the Houston community to other Greek communities and of Greeks to other ethnic groups should give a general idea of the applicability of this study to these more general categories.

Although each community no doubt has its own unique combination of size, age, generational composition, and socio-economic status of members, and extent of cultural Greekness and "institutional completeness", the Houston Greek community is probably fairly representative of many other Greek communities. For the purposes of this discussion, Greek communities may be placed along a continuum from very large (New York City, Chicago) to quite small (Waco, Colorado Springs). The communities on the one end have large Greek populations and a number of Greek Orthodox churches, whereas those on the other have a handful of families and no church at all. The Houston community falls somewhere toward the "large" end. It is not nearly so large as the communities in large cities on the East and West Coasts, but it is the largest in the southern and central United States.[4] It is of course less able than larger cities to maintain a strictly Greek community culturally, because it lacks the population and the resources to do so. Nevertheless, it has developed a degree of "institutional completeness" (Breton 1964) far beyond the reach of smaller communities. The Houston community can meet many of the social, educational, recreational, cultural, and religious needs of its members, who are therefore less likely to go outside the ethnic group to satisfy these needs. This is a significant aspect of the Houston community's ability to maintain itself, whereas smaller communities which may not even have a Greek Orthodox church are more likely to lose members to the non-Greek society and culture which must, by default, play such an important role in their lives. Perhaps the Houston community is of an ideal size for the maintenance of its group: it is large enough to have a good degree of institutional completeness, and yet small enough to provide the individual with a sense of parea with other members. Another important factor is the socio-economic status of Houston's Greeks, which is much higher than that of many Greeks in larger cities. As a result, the Greeks of Houston are much less subject to prejudice than are Greeks in New York City, for example. For this reason, Houston's Greeks are less apt to leave the community because of the external pressures of prejudice and discrimination. Thus the Houston community is representative of others which are moderately large (having one church) and fairly institutionally complete, whose members are fairly well-off, and not subject to extreme prejudice.[5] Those communities which are much smaller (and probably those which are much larger as well) may find it more difficult to keep members within the ethnic group.

Several conclusions of this research project may apply to other ethnic groups as well. E.g., "blood" and a sense of being a "special" people undoubtedly plays a significant role in the maintenance of many groups. Furthermore, the central role of the national Orthodox church in maintaining the ethnic group surely also holds in the case of other national Orthodox groups as well. One may wonder to what degree the church is actually necessary; in an ethnic ghetto, a central organization like the church may play a smaller role in organizing and defining the community, but in a metropolis like Houston where ethnic populations are widely scattered, such an institution is vital to the group's continuation. Nor is it likely that this defining role could be filled by another organization, for the church's traditions provide an important overarching link to the group's past which a secular organization cannot. Thus one would expect to find a similar boundary in other groups whose ethnic (perhaps national) churches keep members separate, preventing their being drawn into an American melting-pot. This would also include Jews, but important differences remain between Greeks and Jews in each group's "religious" boundary. American Judaism is flexible and varied in comparison to Eastern Orthodoxy. Those Jews who--as a result of "Americanization"--are not comfortable in Orthodoxy can become Conservative, and Conservatives who want a less "traditional" religion can turn to Reform Judaism; in each case, the individual remains within the social boundaries of Jewishness. Greeks and other Eastern Christians do not have such choices, for there are no divisions which represent degrees of "Americanization" within the Orthodox churches in America. This lack gives the Orthodox groups a brittleness not found in Judaism. The Orthodox is faced with a yes-or-no situation. He is either in or out; there are no degrees of "Orthodoxy" for those who are dissatisfied with the traditional church. Those ethnic groups to which the present analysis most directly applies are probably other national Orthodox groups--such as Russians, Syrians, Serbians, Armenians--and Jews, but the basic theoretical orientation of this work can be easily applied to other ethnic groups. The specific social boundaries of other ethnic groups will of course differ from those of Houston's Greek community, and the analysis of the boundaries will tell the researcher much about the group.

IV. Topics for Further Study

There are several questions raised by this project which I did not have the opportunity to examine in great detail. The Greek American kinship system and the relationships created by kumbaria are both fascinating. Those who are interested in networks would find the Greek community a rich source of data. I was also unable to examine the Greek fraternal organizations as extensively as I would have liked. However, the main topic which this dissertation introduces but cannot begin to discuss adequately is the Greek group which is not a part of the Greek American community.

Before beginning this study, my sights were set high--I intended to find out everything possible about being a Greek in Houston, Texas. After a few months of observation, however, I realized that Houston's Greek population is much too complex for one person to cover well, and that another Greek group, composed largely of recent immigrants, exists outside the context of the community. Thus there is not a single, united Greek community in Houston, but two groups which have a very tenuous relationship. These two groups come into contact on occasion, but generally move in different social circles and situations. I chose to concentrate on the "official" community, which is organized around the church, and to examine the other group only as the research brought me into contact with it. Consequently, this work is oriented toward the perspective of community members, and examines recent immigrants only as they affect the community. It would be very interesting to look at these "outsiders" to the Orthodox community and discover whether they are organized into a "community" themselves, and whether they have the same sense of "groupness" which is so characteristic of the Greek American community. Is their social organization composed of similar overlapping networks of kin, kumbari, and friends? I suspect that, although many of them know each other, they are not so closely tied through complex interrelations as Houston's Greek Americans are, and they do not form a "community" in the same sense. How do they feel about the Greek American community? What factors influence their choice to join the Greek American community, or to remain separate from it? What is gained or lost in making either choice? To what extent are they culturally different from members of the Greek American community? Is it likely that their group will continue to exist and grow until there are two parallel, yet distinct and equally developed, Greek communities in Houston? These questions are fascinating, and the research necessary to answer them would contribute much to the knowledge about Greek Americans, as well as about ethnic groups in general. No doubt other groups find themselves in an analogous situation, in which there is little contact between "new" immigrants and the "old" immigrants and their descendants.

V. Future of the Ethnic Group

The final, and I suppose obligatory, question is what I see as the future of the Greek American group, based upon my experience in the Houston community. As this dissertation has hopefully made obvious, I suspect that the group will continue to exist for the foreseeable future. An earlier section of this chapter summarized the features of Houston's community which act to deter assimilation, and most of these exist in other Greek American communities as well. The most significant of these is the Greek Orthodox Church--the center of Greek American life--but others include the close and intimate ties between family, kumbari, and friends which by their nature act to keep the individual at least marginally associated with the community, and the ideology of differentness which tells him he is a special person precisely because he is Greek.

Perhaps the greatest danger to the group's continuation, however, lies in this emphasis on "Greek blood", since it may cause the increasing number of intermarried couples to leave the group. This research experience has taught me at least one important fact about ethnicity in America, and that is that it can be--and perhaps for the good of ethnic groups and America should be--a very flexible thing. The ultimate significance of American ethnicity is not biological, but cultural, social, religious, and identificational. No group can claim that the "blood" of its members is "pure", undiluted by that of other peoples, and thus a fixation on the genetic aspects of group membership is misplaced. If the Greek American group disappears, Greek blood will continue to flow through the veins of many people, but of what significance is this "blood" if Greek American culture, social structure, religion, and identity have not survived? In the interest of maintaining "Greekness", group members should be willing to adopt a more flexible attitude toward non-Greeks who choose to enter the group and "become Greek". By doing so, the rich Greek cultural heritage which is so highly rewarding to many individuals will survive and be passed on to other generations.

Putting "scientific" detachment aside for a moment, I would like to make one further observation--that group members should also adopt a more flexible attitude toward Greeks who elect to leave the group. This may be a surprising assertion in view of this work's orientation, but I believe it is necessary if America is to be a democratic and culturally pluralistic society. Cultural pluralism is indeed democratic for groups in that it allows them to retain their traditional culture and society within the larger American society, but it must also be democratic for individuals (Berkson 1920). If individuals are to be free to reamin within their traditional ethnic group, they must also be free to choose to leave it. Berman best expressed this idea in his study of Jewish intermarriage:

> An open society where ethnic boundaries survive because they serve the individual's need for variety, for belongingness, for continuity, for identity, for authenticity--where ethnic boundaries are not prison walls--where those Jews who would rather be Gentiles and Gentiles who would rather be Jews are equally free to cross the boundary and find a more congenial ethnic home--that, in this writer's opinion, is a good society (1968:256).

FOOTNOTES

FOOTNOTES

CHAPTER 1

1. In his study of 2nd generation Italians in Boston, Gans (1962) found evidence to support this contention. He reported:

> Generally speaking, the Italian and Sicilian cultures that the immigrants brought with them to America have not been maintained by the second generation. Their over-all culture is that of Americans. ... Acculturation thus has almost completely eroded Italian culture patterns among the second generation, and is likely to erase the rest in the third generation. ... Assimilation, however--the disappearance of the Italian social system--has proceeded much more slowly. Indeed, the social structure of the West End... is still quite similar to that of the first generation. Social relationships are almost entirely limited to other Italians. ... Intermarriage with non-Italians is unusual among the second generation, and is not favored for the third (1962:33-5).

In response to this contention, Greeley commented:

> It is hard to imagine that a working class Irish community would be as politically unsophisticated as Gans' urban villagers. It may well be that the ethnic collectivities are losing all specific cultural content, but such a phenomenon must not be presumed without definite evidence. It is altogether possible that subtle differences in interpersonal behavior and role expectations may still persist both as a result of ethnic distinctiveness and as a cause of continued distinctiveness (1964:111).

2. Although many researchers use "more American" as one end of the continuum, I feel that "less ethnic" is the more appropriate phrase, for reasons discussed on pages 13-14. It is an easy trap to fall into, however, since ethnic people such as Houston's Greeks tend to view the antithesis of Greekness to be some vague and amorphous concept of "Americanness". E.g., in explaining his behavior, a 3rd generation man may say, "I'm more American than my parents," meaning that he is less traditionally Greek. This usage causes no problems until one talks about his self-conception, in which case the "more Greek-more American" terminology becomes very awkward and misleading. This is because all Greek Americans, with the possible exception of a few original immigrants, consider themselves Americans who are also Greek. The centrality of Greekness in their self-conceptions may vary, but their being American is a _fact_ which is so obvious that it need not be questioned or discussed in the way their Greekness sometimes is.

3. The 1970 federal census reports the following figures for the Houston metropolitan area.

POPULATION OF HOUSTON SMSA: U.S. Census[*]

total population	Greek population		
	total	foreign-born	foreign or mixed parentage
1,984,940	2102	723	1379

[*]1970 Census, General Social and Economic Characteristics, Texas, p. 481, Table 81.

This information is incomplete in that it does not include members of the 3rd generation, and because many Greeks are born in non-Greek areas such as Turkey and Egypt, and are thus not classified in the census as "Greeks". Therefore the total population of Greek extraction is probably somewhat larger than the 2102 reported. Even when the figures are adjusted to compensate for this, it is obvious that the Greek population is quite small. These figures may be complemented by the 1970 census of the population which was taken by the local Greek Orthodox church, the Annunciation.

HOUSTON'S GREEK POPULATION: Annunciation's Census

Total Greek population[*]	adults (18 and over)	children
1923	1322	601

[*]includes NASA area, Bellaire, and Pasadena

My estimate of 2500-3000 is based on the figures reported in these two sources, increased to compensate for the fact that each source by its methods tends to underestimate the total number of Greeks.

4. To obtain census information, church workers called each individual listed in the metropolitan Houston telephone directory whose name appeared to be Greek. This procedure has the obvious disadvantage of failing to include women who have married non-Greeks, Greeks who have changed their names, and individuals who are not listed in the directory. Nevertheless, this census supplies important information concerning Houston's Greek population.

5. 503.13 and 6954.94 square miles respectively, as reported by the Houston Chamber of Commerce.

6. Another group which is a classic exception to this view is of course the Jews.

7. "I am a student at Rice and I'm writing a dissertation on the Greek community here," satisfied many, but others wanted to know exactly what about the community I was studying and I replied, "My main interest is in ethnic identification--like, if someone's grandparents came from Greece many years ago, why would they continue to consider themselves Greek? What kinds of forces act on the individual, so that he would continue to identify with the Greek community?" (I have never been a good liar, and in a case like that, honesty is definitely the best policy.) The next question was usually "Why Greeks? Why not another group?" My answer again was the truth. "I am interested in ethnic groups, and I looked around for a while at the groups in Houston, but I really needed a group that concentrated around a church, because otherwise I'd spend most of my time trying to find the Irish or Italians or Poles in Houston. So that left the Orthodox, and the Greeks are the largest and most active Orthodox group in Houston. So, Greeks."

8. The Greek language was also used in many situations when English easily could have been; several non-Greek women who have married into the community expressed this feeling to me, and I could easily corroborate it with my own experience. Some people who agreed to interviews failed to show up, and others agreed to talk to me only at times when they were sure to be doing several other things, therefore totally destroying the possibility of an undisturbed interview; those who promised to put my name on mailing lists did not do so; others who were to call me so I could participate in certain events never called. I also ran into excessive red tape in several instances. In such a situation there was little chance of losing perspective by "going native", for there were constant reminders of my status as an outsider.

    Nevertheless, after I had participated extensively in the community, some individuals asked why I didn't join the church. "When are you getting baptized? We'd love to have you." Others frequently asked, "When you finish your project, you'll still be coming around, won't you? I'd hate not to see you again," or "You're not gonna leave us, are you?" This may have just represented a feeling on the part of some that it would be polite to make some such comment, but I believe that others genuinely meant what they said. In spite of the feeling that I did become quite an active participant, conducted very candid interviews with many people, and generally came to appreciate the meaning of being a community member, I have no illusions that I became an integral part of anything, or that my presence will be greatly missed by all.

CHAPTER 2

1. Ware 1963:chapter 1.

2. Ware 1963:chapters 1 and 2.

3. Ware 1963:50.

4. Ware 1963:82-3.

5. Ware 1963:chapter 3.

6. Ware 1963:81.

7. Sherrard 1959:99.

8. Rinvolucri 1966:136.

9. Sherrard 1959:101.

10. Schmemann 1963:273-4.

11. Schmemann 1963:283.

12. Ware 1963:100.

13. Ware 1963:98.

14. Runciman 1968:chapter 10.

15. Runciman 1968:406.

16. Ware 1963:13-4.

17. Ware 1963:203-4.

18. Orthodox Weekly Bulletin, Annunciation 7:28.

19. Ware 1963:40-2.

20. Benz 1963:6-7.

21. Kalokyris 1971:16.

22. Kalokyris 1971:40, 45, 50.

23. Kalokyris 1971:51-5.

24. Personal Welcome to the Orthodox Church :4, 9.

25. Ware 1963:271.

26. Saloutos 1964:chapter 6.

27. Saloutos 1964:chapters 6 and 14.

28. Hammond 1956:25.

29. The Consecration of Our Church :20.

CHAPTER 3

1. Of the households contacted in the telephone survey, 20% had such relatives living in them. Of these, 70% were mothers and 17% were fathers of the head of the household or spouse, and the other 13% were other relatives, such as unmarried sisters.

2. From a Greek Orthodox Archdiocese publication on baptism and sponsorship.

CHAPTER 5

1. Greece's immediate history is not too inspiring, as a young 2-3 generation man noted concerning the rule of the military since the coup of 1967.

> It gives you a feeling of a background of some kind. It's something to identify with. But then again I don't want to—sometimes—identify with the Greeks. Like the junk that goes on over there now. The country itself—you want to separate yourself from what goes on over there.

The return to civilian rule which followed the military leaders' abortive attempt to seize control of Cyprus by overthrowing Archbishop Makarios in 1974, however, has given Greek Americans a new sense of hope in the future of Greece.

2. "Hadji" is of course the Moslem term for "pilgrim". Because of their being ruled by Turks for hundreds of years, many Greek terms and even traditional "Greek" foods are actually Turkish in origin.

3. A more appropriate designation is "less Greek" or "fully non-Greek". Greeks who choose to leave the community, or whose Greekness plays little or no role in their personal self-conception have generally severed their connections with Greekness out of distaste for certain elements of Greekness—narrow-mindedness, feelings of racial superiority, etc.—rather than from admiration of American culture and society. As noted on pages 13-14, they do not become "American" so much as they cease to be "Greek". Nevertheless, Greeks themselves use the term "American" to refer to "non-Greek" things, and in this section I will remain consistent with their usage. See footnote 2, Chapter 1.

4. Kasperson 1966:8-23.

5. Eliot 1972:200.

CHAPTER 6

1. These figures do not reflect the number of people who have married outside the church. Thus the percentage of mixed marriages is larger than the 48% reported here.

2. Of the households contacted in the survey, 25% of the marriages involved a non-Greek partner. Assuming that the national figures reported by Saloutos hold true in Houston, about half of the couples of mixed marriages performed in the church remain in the community, and the other half leave.

CHAPTER 7

1. This is true technically, but to my knowledge no one has been denied the sacraments in the Houston church.

CHAPTER 8

1. Here "assimilation" is not used in the sense of the total disappearance of a group, but in the broader sense in which many sociologists use it, signifying an adjustment to American society in which certain "old world" patterns are modified or replaced by American ones.

2. Again, it is interesting to note the differences in Greek Greek and Greek American patterns. Greek dancing is a significant aspect of Greek American culture, but it is virtually dead in urban Greece. Two recent immigrants from Athens, for example, commented that they knew no traditional dances until coming to America; Western dancing was all they had learned in Greece.

3. In fact, a pamphlet published by the Greek Orthodox Archdiocese states that it is preferable for Orthodox to marry Protestants rather than Catholics, who are much more insistent on conversion and on raising the children of intermarriages in Catholicism.

4. E.g., the Eighth Archdiocesan District of the Greek Orthodox Church of North and South America, of which Houston is a part, covers 11 states with 43 local communities, and Houston is the largest.

5. Examples in this area might be Dallas, Fort Worth, San Antonio, New Orleans, Omaha, Denver, and Salt Lake City.

This survey was based on a random sample of 175 households chosen from Annunciation's most up-to-date list of Houston's Greek population. This list includes those contacted in the 1970 church census, with the exception of those who requested that their names be removed. Admittedly, it best represents those connected with the church in some way. Of the households contacted, 147 (84%) cooperated, 22 refused to cooperate, and 6 had moved and could not be traced.

When calling the household, I asked to speak to the head of the household or his wife ("May I please speak to Mr. or Mrs. X?"), except when it was obvious from the names that either the husband or wife was not Greek, in which case I specifically asked to speak to the Greek spouse ("May I please speak to Mr. X?"). I explained myself and what I wanted to know in the following way:

> My name is Donna Collins, and I'm a graduate student at Rice University. I'm doing a research project on Houston's Greek Americans and as part of this project I'm calling about 200 households to get some general information--like where the family was from in Greece. Would you mind answering a couple of questions?

1.   Are both you and your wife (husband) of Greek descent?

2.   Are you yourself from Greece? Is your wife (husband)?

3.   What area of Greece are you (your parents, grandparents) from? Same for spouse.

4.   When did you (your parents, grandparents) come to the United States? Same for spouse.

5.   How old were you (they) then? Same for spouse.

6.   Do you have any children?
     (If so) How old are they? Do they all live at home?
     (If not) Are they in college? married?

7.   Do any other people besides your wife (husband) and children live in the household with you?
     (If so) What is his (her) relationship to you?

8.   How old are you? How old is your wife (husband)?

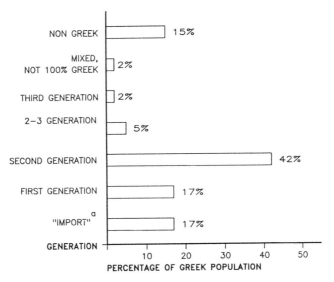

FIGURE 8
GENERATION OF ADULTS OF HOUSEHOLDS SURVEYED
N=256
a "IMPORT" DENOTES RECENT ARRIVAL FROM GREECE
—SINCE WORLD WAR II.

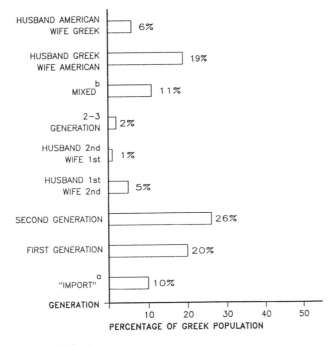

FIGURE 9
GENERATIONAL COMPOSITION OF MARRIAGES
N=147
a "IMPORT" DENOTES RECENT ARRIVAL FROM GREECE
—SINCE WORLD WAR II.
b INDIVIDUALS INVOLVED NOT FULL GREEK; OR
HUSBAND 3rd, WIFE 2-3 GENERATIONS; ETC.

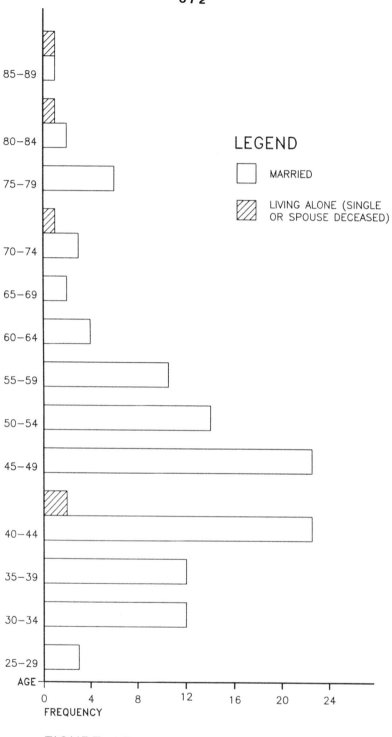

FIGURE 10a
MALES.

FIGURE 10
AGE OF ADULTS OF HOUSEHOLDS SURVEYED.

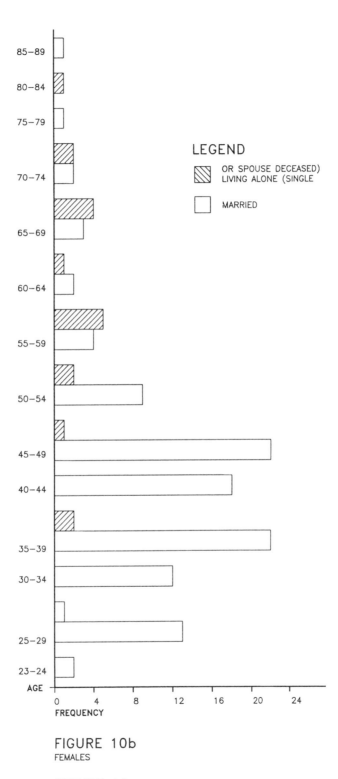

FIGURE 10b
FEMALES

FIGURE 10
AGE OF ADULTS OF HOUSEHOLDS SURVEYED.

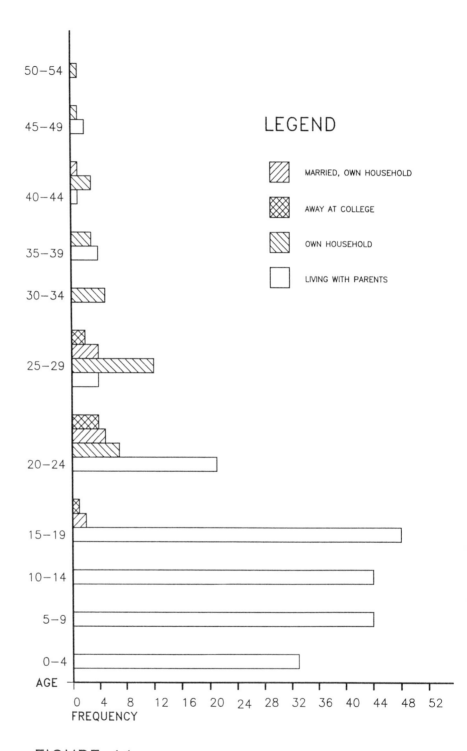

FIGURE 11

AGES OF CHILDREN'S GENERATION IN HOUSEHOLDS SURVEYED

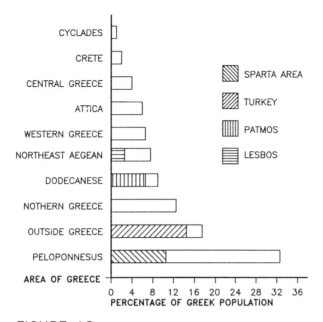

FIGURE 12a

IMMIGRANTS BEFORE WORLD WAR II
N=331

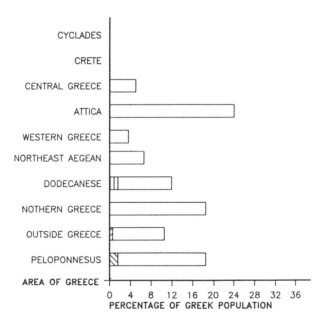

FIGURE 12b

IMMIGRANTS SINCE WORLD WAR II ("IMPORTS")
N=38

FIGURE 12

AREAS OF GREECE REPRESENTED iN HOUSTON'S POPULATION.

APPENDIX B: SEMISTRUCTURED INTERVIEWS

interview number	schedule number	name of interviewee	sex	generation	age	type	tape	hrs. in length
1.	#1	1	F	2-3	17	K	–	3
2.	#1	2	F	3	19	B	x	1 1/2
3.	#1	3	F	2	40	B	x	2
4.	#1	4	M	2	45	A	x	3
		5	F	2	40	D		
5.	#1	6	F	2-3	23	A	x	3
6.	special ?s	7	M	–	28	R	x	1 1/2
7.	#1	5					x	1
8.	#1	8	F	3	19	FE	x	1
9.	#1	9	F	3	24	A	x	1 1/2
10.	#1	10	M	3	16	B	x	4
11.	#2	2&8					x	1/2
12.	#1	2&8					x	2
	and just	11	M	2-3	24	JK		
	listened	12	M	2-3	30	JK		
13.	#1&#4	13	M	3	20	K	x	2
		14	F	–	20	Q		
14.	#6	15	M	2 (1/2 Gk)	40	–	x	1
15.	organizations	8					x	1 1/2
16.	#4	11					x	2 1/2
17.	#1	16	M	3	18	B	x	2
18.	special ?s	17	M	–	20	Q	x	3
19.	#1	18	M	2-3	21	F	x	3
20.	#1	19	F	2	19	B	x	2
		20	F	2	21	B		
21.	#1	21	M	2-3	26	E	x	1 1/2
22.	#1 & special ?s	22	M	3	20	D	x	2
23.	#1	23	F	3	19	D	x	2 1/2
24.	#4	24	F	–	35	N	x	1 1/4
25.	#4	25	F	–	30	N	x	3 1/4
26.	#4	26	M	2	30	IM	–	1/2
27.	#4	27	M	2-3	30	IM	x	1 1/4
		28	F	–	30	P		
28.	#4	29	F	–	45	N	x	1 1/2
29.	#4	30	F	–	35	O	x	3
30.	#4	31	F	–	45	N	–	1 1/2
31.	#4	32	F	2	45	EM	–	2
32.	conventions	33	M	3	25	FA	–	2
33.	#4	34	F	–	32	P	x	2
34.	#4	35	F	–	38	O	x	1
35.	#4	36	F	–	40	P	x	1 1/2
36.	special ?s	37	F	2	40	L	–	2
		38	F	2	40	L		
37.	#6	39	M	2	40	–	–	1
38.	#4	40	M	–	35	O	–	3
		41	F	2	35	AM		

interview number	schedule number	name of interviewee	sex	generation	age	type	tape	hrs. in length
39.	special ?s	42	F	3 (1/2 Gk)	19	K	-	1
40.	#4 & special ?s	43	M	3	24	KM	-	2
41.	special ?s	44	M	2	45	I	-	3
		45	F	2	40	I		
42.	#4 & special ?s	46	M	2	30	IM	x	3
		47	F	-	30	P		
43.	#4 & special ?s	48	F	3	28	LM	x	1 1/4
44.	#4	49	M	2	40	AM	-	4
		50	F	-	35	O		
		51	F	1/2 GK	30	H		
45.	#4	52	F	-	40	P	-	2 1/2
46.	#4	53	F	-	35	N	x	2
47.	#2	54	F	2	40	B	x	2
48.	#4	55	F	-	20	Q	x	1 1/4
49	conventions	2&56	F	2	22	A	x	3
50.	#2	57	M	2 (1/2 GK)	50	C	-	3
		58	F	2	45	C		
51.	special ?s	59	F	2	35	D	-	1
52.	#1	60	M	2	45	A	-	1/2
53.	#2	5					x	2
54.	#2	19&20,61	F	1	55	B	x	1
55.	special ?s	62	M	2	26	E	-	3/4
56.	#2	63	M	1	60	C	x	2 1/2
		64	F	2	55	A		
57.	#2	65	M	2	40	C	x	3 1/2
		66	F	3	35	E		
58.	#2	67	F	2	40	G	x	2 1/2
59.	#3&#5	5					x	2 1/2
60.	#3&#5	68	M	2	45	G	x	3
		69	F	2	42	G		
61.	#3&#5	32					x	2
62.	#3&#5	4					x	3
63.	#3&#5	8					x	2
64.	#3&#5	19&20					x	2
65.	#3&#5	5					x	2
		70	F	2	55	K		
		71	F	3	27	K		
66.	#3&#5	72	M	1	40	D	x	3
		73	F	1	32	D		
67.	#4 & special ?s	74	M	3 (1/2 GK)	21	C	x	1 1/2
68.	#6	75	M	3	25	-	x	1 1/2
69.	special ?s	76	M	1	80	G	x	2
70.	#3	2					x	1 1/2
71.	#1	19,20,77	F	2	21	B	x	1
72.	#4	78	M	-	55	N	-	3
		79	F	2	50	A		

Interviews have been classified into 18 main categories according to their type and degree of community participation.

A typical for sex
B typical for sex, with more church attendance
C typical for sex, with less church attendance
D participation in church only (or primarily)
E social activities, but little church participation
F fraternal organizations primarily (e.g., AHEPA)
G 100%
H left church
I left both church and community
J social life is independent of church
K marginal--little participation, but still a church member
L marginal--little participation, no longer church member
M married to non-Greek
N American married to Greek, who has "become Greek"
O American married to Greek, who has entered community
P American married to Greek, who is outside community
Q American who is dating or engaged to Greek
R American convert to Greek church, not married to Greek

A, "typical for sex", indicates that the individual attends a moderate number of church services, social activities, and is (or has been) involved to some extent in Greek fraternal organizations. In general women are more active in the church than men, and a man who is labelled B is about equivalent to a woman labelled A. G represents individuals who are very active in all facets of community membership--church, social affairs, and fraternal organizations. Those who are classified J may come to church occasionally, but their identifying characteristic is their involvement in social networks whose members are tenuously affiliated with the church and community; they may come to the Festival and attend church services two or three times a year. The other categories are self-explanatory. Some people could not be easily classified in one category, and they are given two designations. For example, an individual who is married to a non-Greek is classified first according to his participation, and then his marriage--e.g., AM. In calculating the number of each category interviewed, only the first letter--the individual's most defining characteristic--was used. Information about the participation, sex, age, and generation of respondents is reported below.

sex			age	
male	41%		16-19	10%
female	59%		20-24	18%
			25-29	9%
generation			30-34	13%
1st	6%		35-39	11%
2nd	38%		40-44	19%
3rd	15%		45-49	10%
2-3	10%		50-54	3%
1/2 Greek	7%		55-59	5%
non-Greek	24%		60-64	1%
			80-84	1%

average time of interviews
2 hours

group interviews
2 people 16
3 people   4
4 people _1_
        21 (29% of 72)

categories

A	11%
B	11%
C	6%
D	8%
E	5%
F	4%
G	5%
H	1%
I	6%
J	3%
K	8%
L	4%
N	8%
O	5%
P	6%
Q	4%
R	1%
clergy	4%

(M   N = 8)

summary of some categories

non-Greeks	19
dating or engaged to Greek	3
convert	1
married to Greek	15
entered community	10
outside community	5
Greeks	60
left church	3
left church and community	5
married non-Greek	5
left community	2
remained in community	3
other community members	47
Total	79

#1   1.   family
        different from American families?
        family roles and relationships
        are women expected to be "better" Greeks?
        others in household?
        effect of giagia in household?
        family history and background
        kinship terms and chart
        extended kin?   who is a relative?

     2.   marriage to non-Greeks
        extent?
        opinion of it?
        community opinion?
        family reactions
        effect on ethnicity--will the family be Greek?

     3.   godparenthood
        who are your godparents?
        where are they from?   (patrioti?)
        how chosen?
        religious and social significance
        obligations of godparent and godchild to each other
        who's considered a godrelative--how deep does it go?   rules of
          marriage
        kumbari--relationship and obligations

     4.   friends
        what percent Greek?
        who are they?   why are they such good friends?
        patrioti?
        stereotypes of people from different areas of Greece
        neighborhoods
        businesses

     5.   customs
        how different from Americans?   customs.
        what customs does family and individual follow:
              naming   name days   vasilopita
              fasting   iconostasion   etc.
        relationship with name-saint
        are certain customs particularly denotative of one's level of
          Greekness or Orthodoxy?   What questions would you ask to find
          out this information about somebody?

     6.   religion
        how central to being Greek?
        major aspects and problems;
          language

7. Greek identity
   how central to conception of self?
   situations in which Greek identity most important
   how transmitted? specific ways encouraged by:
       parents   school   relatives
       language   religion   newcomers
       friends   visits to Greece
   who is a Greek American? are there marginal cases?
   the term "Americans"--what does it mean? connotations. who
       uses it?
   part-time Greeks--Easter Greeks and Festival Greeks

8. Greek language
   in home, school, daily use?
   attended Greek school?

9. background history
   Houston, Texas, the United States, or Greece

10. are there any important things I've overlooked? things I'm too
    ignorant to know I should ask about?

11. favors
    I would appreciate it if you would help me on this project by
    letting me know when things are going on that I should parti-
    cipate in, or help me get to know more about Greek American
    life by:
            introducing to friends, relatives, etc.
            telling me about special church services, social events
            inviting me to family get-togethers, weddings, baptisms,
               or funerals.

#2 1. Kin
       chart
       range of kin known
       which know and associate with each other?
       what's a relative?

    2. kumbari
       chart
       rules and who's godrelative to whom?
       how godparents chosen, specifically?
       which has more honor the status, parent or godparent?
       are families or individuals kumbari? why?
       "can't return the oil"?
       special treatment of godparents?
       offer of kumbaria to settle feuds?

    3. marriage sponsor
       prestige relative to baptismal sponsor?
       who may be? how chosen? whose choice, bride or groom?
       duties? title? kumbaro to both bride and groom and families?
       when would nuno not be kumbaro, when kumbaro not nuno?

religious and social obligations? what does he buy?

4. <u>patrioti</u>
   societies
   who are your patrioti in town?

5. <u>dating and marriage</u>
   rules
   wrong for sexes to be alone?
   hopes for children: marry Greek? play with Greek kids, get in
     Greek activities
   hopes for self: marry Greek?
   conventions: how do people get together? cases
   preferential routes of marriage: past and present
   cases of proxenia

6. island vs. mainland people--differences?

7. Greek Greeks

8. <u>Orthodox church</u>
   attitudes toward
   kids turning to Protestant churches?

9. <u>"being Greek"</u>
   signs about being Greek, and about being a certain kind of Greek

10. attitudes toward other groups

11. entertainment--certain groups and places?

#3 1. what is "respect"? what are respectful and disrespectful
       activities? why do you call people thio and kumbaro who are
       not? what does respect have to do with this practice?

    2. what determines the cutoff points for symbetheri and kumbari?
       who does this, individual or family? why some relationships
       maintained and other not?

    3. what is "closeness"? in family? what are "close" and "distant"
       relatives, kumbari?

    4. what kinds of Greeks are there? Peloponnesians, Patmians, etc.
       what are the main geographical divisions in Houston community?

    5. how last names Americanized? stories about this.

    6. what is the significance of the <u>oil</u>?

    7. what's a friend? how do Greek and American friends differ?
       what can be imposed on a friend, relative, kumbaro? functions
       of friends. what are different kinds of friends? who's a
       friend, and a friend-that-counts?

#4 (for partners in intermarriages)

    1. how did you meet?

what was dating like?

2. family reactions to marriage, Greek and non-Greek
   pressures to marry "own kind"? be specific

3. what religion were you?
   did you convert to the Orthodox church? why? when?
   were the children baptized in the church?

4. how Greek is your family?
   friends
   godparents
   customs--names, namedays, saints, iconostasion, vasilopita, etc.
   language
   church attendance and activity
   parochial school

5. community attitudes toward marriage and non-Greek partner,
   children acceptance? attitudes toward community
   what about "blood"?
   what if spouse died or they were divorced? what would community
   reactions then be toward non-Greek spouse and children?

6. non-Greek's self-conception--Greek or American?
   children's identity
   how is behavior altered around Greeks to fit in? how do you
   "be Greek"? how do you "be American" when around non-Greek
   family?
   situations where you choose Greek or American behavior.
   If I were to marry a Greek, what advice would you have for me,
   based on your experience? how could I fit into the community?

7. how would you advise your children in their own marriages?
   should they marry Greek?

8. are there any other questions that you think I should ask others
   in your situation?

#5 1. tell me about your life, particularly as a Greek
       what was it like for you, growing up?
       neighborhood   social events   school
       friends   contact with Americans

    2. were your parents strict about the activities that you could
       participate in?

    3. dating experiences, college, marriage.

    4. was there ever a time that you questioned the value of being
       Greek? of belonging to the Orthodox church? of participating
       in Greek social circles?
       why? how was it resolved?

    5. what's your present level of participation in the Greek community?
       what's your present level of Greek identity now?

6. have you turned out like your family wanted? why or why not?

7. different routes of Greekness. are there different ways of
   of being Greek, different types of participation as a Greek?

8. what kinds of Greeks are there?

9. what do people do that makes them fall in these categories?
   specific individuals in each category
   could you tell by talking with them or watching them what
   category they are in?

10. what must people do to be a Greek? what if a person is not
    Greek in
    culturally   anything but personal identity?
    socially   is that person really Greek?
    religiously   if so, in what way?
    identificationally

11. (list of 40 individuals) how about _____? what
    category does he fall into? what does he do to be classified
    that way?

#6   (for priests, bishop)

1. could I come to weddings, baptisms, funerals, house-blessings?

2. Annunciation:
   programs and what they are trying to accomplish.
   position as cathedral? why Annunciation?
   list of members and those who aren't really members.
   people who've married out of the church and part-time Greeks
   church records--board minutes, parish publications, church
       directories, general assembly notes, records of Greek
       school and Sunday school, Goya records.

3. communion
   why do people take extra pieces of bread afterwards? what is
       this called? what's the significance of it?
   babies' communion--carrying candle

4. Easter
   why do people pick up rose petals on Holy Saturday service?
   why do children crawl under the tomb, and then later faithful
       walk under it on Good Friday?
   why do people shout in repetition of _anesti_ and _elave_ during
       sermon of St. John Chrysostom?
   significance of Easter eggs? what's done with them?
   meaning of Holy Unction
   special ceremonies with individuals--_efhi_, etc.

5. other services
   houseblessing and holy water. Epiphany service. why did so
       many people take communion?

soul's day--boiled wheat
ceremony 40 days after birth of child
baptism and marriage
vasiliko in Adoration of Cross
godparenthood--who can baptize, who can marry whom?
namedays

6. Liturgy
why do people kiss priests' and bishop's hands?
part of service where celebrants hug each other?
difference when bishop conducts liturgy?

7. Orthodoxy in the United States
changes in church from Greece
Greek language
why no American Orthodoxy?
how important is the "Greek" part of Greek Orthodoxy?
attitudes of young people towards church
future of church
is Annunciation changing now, becoming more Americanized?
what's being changed? what are the limits of change allowed
    by hierarchy? how much Greek is required in service? etc.

8. canonical law
who may and may not be godparents? marriage sponsor?
who may marry whom? kin, godrelatives

9. Houston community
comparison with other communities. similarities? differences?
how is the community organized? what groups are there?

The interviews were in most cases not as rigid as the "schedules"
might suggest. The order and wording of many questions were varied
according to the person with whom I was talking in any one situation.
When a respondent was in a hurry, interviews were shortened to include
the questions I felt most important at the time; the topics with which
the respondent seemed most comfortable; or the questions I felt the
respondent to be in a position to answer particularly well. Furthermore,
schedule #1 appears here in its most complete and developed form. I
began with only very general and vague questions, but the schedule
developed as my knowledge, based on observation and the responses I
received, increased. Thus in Appendix B a report that an interview
was based on schedule #1 may signify one of a range of #1s, from an
early and relatively undeveloped form to a later and much more specific
one.

APPENDIX D: COMPARISON OF RESPONDENTS IN TELEPHONE SURVEY AND INTERVIEWS

telephone survey		interviews	
age	N = 490		N = 79
under 15	25%		–
15-19	10%		10%
20-24	8%		18%
25-29	8%		9%
30-34	6%		13%
35-39	9%		11%
40-44	8%		19%
45-49	10%		10%
50-54	5%		3%
55-59	4%		5%
60-89	8%		2%
generation	N = 256		N = 79
import	17%		–
1st	17%		6%
2nd	42%		38%
3rd	2%		15%
2-3	5%		10%
"mixed blood"	2%		7%
non-Greek	15%		24%

Greek Americans in many cases do not speak "proper" Greek, and in this report I have remained consistent with their usage rather than trying to "correct" their Greek. For example, Houston's Greek Americans use the form οἱ πατριῶτοι as the plural of ὁ πατριώτης, rather than the proper οἱ πατριῶτες. They also combine English grammatical forms with Greek terms, as in "the old γιαγιάs" rather than "γιαγιάδες", and "He στεφανώσηed us." In this glossary of Greek terms commonly used in my report, I will continue to use their speech patterns.

transliteration / Greek / translation

Americanida / ἡ Ἀμερικανίδα / American woman

epitafios / ὁ ἐπιτάφιος / tomb of Christ

giagia (pronounced yaya) / ἡ γιαγιά / grandmother

kefi / τό κέφι / "the feeling"

kumbaro(m), - a(f), - i(pl) / ὁ κουμπάρος, ἡ - α, οἱ - οι / co-parent(s)

kumbariá / κουμπαριά / institution of co-parenthood

mavro(m), - i(pl) / ὁ μαῦρος, οἱ - οι / Negro(es)

nuno(m), - a(f), - i(pl) / ὁ νουνός ἡ - α, οἱ - οι / godfather, god-
    mother, godparents

pappou / ὁ παππού / grandfather

parea / παρέα / "the group", community, fellowship

patrioti (pl) / οἱ πατριῶτοι / people from one's local area of Greece
    (similar to Italian paesani)

stefanosi / στεφανώση / to crown, in a wedding service

symbethero(m), - a(f), - i(pl) / ὁ συμπέθερος, ἡ - α, οἱ - οι / in-law(s)

Theotokos / Θεοτόκος / Virgin Mary, Mother of God

thio / θεῖο / uncle

thia / θεία / aunt

xenos(m), - i(f), - i(pl) / ὁ ξένος, ἡ - η, οἱ - οι / stranger(s)

BIBLIOGRAPHY

BIBLIOGRAPHY

Abramson, Harold J.
    1973 Ethnic Diversity in Catholic America. New York: John Wiley.

Annunciation
    1959 The Consecration of Our Church. Hellenic Eastern Orthodox
          Church -- Annunciation, Houston

Attwater, Donald
    1962 Christian Churches of the East, Volume II. Milwaukee: Bruce
          Publishing.

Barth, Fredrik
    1969 Introduction. In Ethnic Groups and Boundaries. Boston:
          Little, Brown and Co. pp. 9-38.

    1969a Pathan Identity and Its Maintenance. In Ethnic Groups and
          Boundaries. pp. 117-34.

Bender, Eugene I. and George Kagiwada
    1968 Hansen's Law of "Third Generation Return" and the Study of
          American Religio-Ethnic Groups. Phylon 29:360-70.

Benz, Ernst
    1963 The Eastern Orthodox Church: Its Thought and Life. Garden
          City, New York: Doubleday Anchor Books.

Berkson, Isaac B.
    1920 Theories of Americanization: A Critical Study, with Special
          Reference to the Jewish Group. New York: Columbia University
          Press.

Berman, Louis A.
    1968 Jews and Intermarriage: Summary, Conclusions, and Discussion.
          In The Blending American: Patterns of Intermarriage. Milton
          L. Barron, Ed. Chicago: Quadrangle Books.

Berry, Brewton
    1951 Race Relations. Boston: Houghton Mifflin Co.

Breton, Raymond
    1964 Institutional Completeness of Ethnic Communities and the
          Personal Relations of Immigrants. American Journal of Sociolo-
          gy 70:193-205.

Burgess, Thomas
    1913 Greeks in America. Boston: Sherman, French and Co.

388

Cabasilas, Nicholas
    1960 A Commentary on the Divine Liturgy. London: S.P.C.K.

Calian, Carnegie Samuel
    1968 Icon and Pulpit. Philadelphia: Westminster Press.

Campbell, J. K.
    1964 Honor, Family, and Patronage. New York: Oxford University
          Press.

Campbell, John, and Philip Sherrard
    1968 Modern Greece. New York: F. A. Praeger.

Carlson, Stan W.
    1954 Faith of Our Fathers: The Eastern Orthodox Religion. Minnea-
          polis: Olympic Press.

Coniaris, Anthony M.
    1970 A Personal Welcome to the Orthodox Church. Minneapolis:
          Light and Life Publishing Co.

Eisenstadt, S. N.
    1955 The Absorption of Immigrants. Glencoe: Free Press.

Eliot, Alexander
    1972 The Horizon Concise History of Greece. New York: American
          Heritage Publishing Co.

Etzioni, Amitai
    1959 The Ghetto--A re-evaluation. Social Forces 37:255-62.

Fairchild, Henry Pratt
    1926 The Melting-Pot Mistake. Boston: Little, Brown and Co.

    1944 Dictionary of Sociology. New York: Philosophical Library.

Fishman, Joshua
    1961 Childhood Indoctrination for Minority Group Membership.
          Daedalus 90:329-49.

    1966 Language Loyalty in the United States. The Hague: Mouton
          and Co.

Foster, George M.
    1953 Cofradia and Compadrazgo in Spain and Spanish America.
          Southwestern Journal of Anthropology 9:1-28.

Frazee, Charles A.
    1969 The Orthodox Church and Independent Greece, 1821-1852.
          Cambridge: University Press.

Freidl, Ernestine
    1962 Vasilika: A Village in Modern Greece. New York: Holt,
          Rinehart, and Winston.

Gans, Herbert J.
    1958 The Origin and Growth of a Jewish Community in the Suburbs:
          A Study of the Jews of Forest Park. In The Jews. Marshall
          Sklare, Ed. Glencoe: Free Press.

    1962 The Urban Villagers. New York: Free Press.

Geismar, Ludwig
    1954 A Scale for the Measurement of Ethnic Identification. Jewish
          Social Studies 16:33-60.

Giannaris, George
    1972 Mikis Theodorakis: Music and Social Change. New York:
          Praeger Publishers.

Glaser, Barney G. and Anselm L. Strauss
    1967 The Discovery of Grounded Theory. Chicago: Aldine Publishing
          Co.

Glazer, Nathan
    1954 Ethnic Groups in America: From National Culture to Ideology.
          In Freedom and Control in Modern Society. Morroe Berger
          et al., Eds. New York: D. Van Nostrand and Co. pp. 158-173.

Glazer, Nathan, and Daniel P. Moynihan
    1963 Beyond the Melting Pot. Boston: MIT Press.

Goldlust, John and Anthony H. Richmond
    1974 A Multivariate Model of Immigrant Adaptation. International
          Migration Review 8:193-226.

Goldstein, Sidney, and Calvin Goldscheider
    1968 Jewish Americans. Englewood Cliffs, New Jersey: Prentice-Hall.

Gordon, Milton M.
    1964 Assimilation in American Life: The Role of Race, Religion,
          and National Origins. New York: Oxford University Press.

Greeley, Andrew
    1964 American Sociology and the Study of Ethnic Immigrant Groups.
          International Migration Digest 1(2):107-13.

    1971 Why Can't They Be Like Us? New York: E. P. Dutton and Co.

Hammel, Eugene A.
    1968 Alternative Social Structures and Ritual Relations in the
          Balkans. Englewood Cliffs, New Jersey: Prentice Hall.

Hammond, Peter
    1956 The Waters of Marah. London: Rockliff.

Hannerz, Ulf
    1969 Soulside. New York: Columbia University Press.

Hansen, Marcus L.
    1952 The Third Generation in America. Commentary 14:492-500.
        (First published in 1938).

Herberg, Will
    1955 Protestant-Catholic-Jew. New York: Doubleday and Co.

Holden, David
    1972 Greece without Columns. New York: J. B. Lippincott.

Humphrey, Craig R. and Helen Brock Louis
    1973 Assimilation and Voting Behavior: A Study of Greek Americans.
        International Migration Review 7:34-45

Hyman, Herbert H.
    1954 Interviewing in Social Research. Chicago: University of
        Chicago.

Jacopin, Armand
    1967 The Eastern Liturgy in the American Context. Diakonia 2(1):19.

Kallen, Horace M.
    1924 Culture and Democracy in the United States. New York: Boni
        and Liveright.

Kalokyris, Constantine
    1971 The Essence of Orthodox Iconography. Brookline, MA: Hellenic
        College, Holy Cross School of Theology.

Kasperson, Roger E.
    1966 The Dodecanese: Diversity and Unity in Island Politics.
        Chicago: University of Chicago Press.

Keeley, Edmund, and Philip Sherrard, Eds.
    1961 Six Poets of Modern Greece. New York: Alfred A. Knopf.

Kennedy, Ruby Jo Reeves
    1944 Single or Triple Melting Pot? Intermarriage Trends in New
        Haven, 1870-1940. American Journal of Sociolgoy 49:331-9.

Lazerwitz, Bernard
    1953 Some Factors in Jewish Identification. Jewish Social Studies
        15:3-24.

Lazerwitz, Bernard, and Louis Rowitz
    1964 The Three-Generation Hypothesis. American Journal of Sociology
          69:529-38.

Levi-Strauss, Claude
    1949 Elementary Structures of Kinship. London: Eyre and Spottis-
          woode.

Lieberson, Stanley
    1961 A Societal Theory of Race and Ethnic Relations. American
          Sociological Review 26:902-10.

Liebow, Elliot
    1967 Tally's Corner. Boston: Little, Brown, and Co.

Metzger, L. Paul
    1971 American Sociology and Black Assimilation: Conflicting
          Perspectives. American Journal of Sociology 76:627-47.

Mintz, Sidney W. and Eric R. Wolf
    1950 An Analysis of Ritual Co-Parenthood (Compadrazgo). Southwestern
          Journal of Anthropology 6.

Nagata, Judith A.
    1969 Adaptation and Integration of Greek Working Class Immigrants
          in the City of Toronto, Canada. International Migration
          Review 4(1):44-68.

Nahirny, Vladimir, and Joshua A. Fishman
    1965 American Immigrant Groups: Ethnic Identification and the
          Problem of Generations. Sociological Review 13:311-26.

Novak, Michael
    1971 The Rise of the Unmeltable Ethnics. New York: Macmillan.

Papadeas, F., and George L., comp.
    1973 Μεγάλη Εὐδόμας - Πάσχα (Holy Week Easter). New York.

Parenti, Michael
    1967 Ethnic Politics and the Persistence of Ethnic Identification.
          American Political Science Review 16:717-26.

Park, Robert E.
    1930 Assimilation, Social. In Encyclopedia of the Social Sciences,
          Vol. 2. Edwin R. A. Seligman, and Alvin Johnson, Eds. New
          York: Macmillan Co.

Park, Robert E., and Ernest W. Burgess
    1921 Introduction to the Science of Sociology. Chicago: University
          of Chicago Press.

Patrinicos, Nicon D.
　　1970　The Individual and His Orthodox Church. New York: Orthodox
　　　　　Observer Press.

Petrakis, Harry Mark
　　1965　Pericles on 31st Street. Chicago: Quadrangle Books.

　　1966　A Dream of Kings. New York: David McKay Co.

　　1969　The Waves of Night and Other Stories. New York: David McKay
　　　　　Co.

　　1970　Stelmark: A Family Recollection. New York: David McKay Co.

　　1973　In the Land of the Morning. New York: David McKay Co.

Plax, Martin
　　1972　On Studying Ethnicity. Public Opinion Quarterly 36(1):99-104.

Price, C. A.
　　1959　Immigration and Group Settlement. In The Cultural Integration
　　　　　of Immigrants. W. D. Borrie, Ed. France: UNESCO.

Redfield, Robert, Ralph Linton, and Melville J. Herskovits
　　1936　Memorandum for the Study of Acculturation. American Anthro-
　　　　　pologist 38:149-52.

Rinder, Irwin D.
　　1965　Minority Orientations: An Approach to Intergroup Relations
　　　　　Theory through Social Psychology. Phylon 26:5-17.

Rinvolucri, Mario
　　1966　Anatomy of a Church: Greek Orthodoxy. London: Burns and
　　　　　Oates.

Rossi, Peter and Alice
　　1961　Parochial School Education in America. Daedalus 90:300-28.

Runciman, Steven
　　1968　The Great Church in Captivity. Cambridge: Cambridge University
　　　　　Press.

Saloutos, Theodore
　　1956　They Remember America. Berkeley: University of California
　　　　　Press.

　　1964　The Greeks in the United States. Cambridge: Harvard University
　　　　　Press.

　　1973　The Greek Orthodox Church in the United States and Assimilation.
　　　　　International Migration Review 7:395-408.

Sandberg, Neil C.
　　1974　Ethnic Identity and Assimilation: The Polish-American Communi-
　　　　　ty. New York: Praeger Publishers.

Schmemann, Alexander
 1963 Historical Road of Eastern Orthodoxy. New York: Holt,
       Rinehart, and Winston.

 1971 A Meaningful Storm. In Autocephaly: The Orthodox Church
       in America. St. Vladimir's Seminary Press.

Schrag, Peter
 1972 The Decline of the WASP. In Nation of Nations. Peter I.
       Rose, Ed. New York: Random House.

Sengstock, Mary C.
 1969 Differential Rates of Assimilation in an Ethnic Group: In
       Ritual, Social Interaction, and Normative Culture. Inter-
       national Migration Review 3(2):18-28.

Sherman, C. Bezalel
 1961 The Jew within American Society: A Study of Ethnic Individual-
       ity. Detroit: Wayne State University Press.

Sherrard, Philip
 1959 The Greek East and the Latin West. London: Oxford University
       Press.

 1964 The Pursuit of Greece. Great Britain: Walker and Co.

Shuval, Judith
 1963 Immigrants on the Threshold. New York: Atherton Press.

Strauss, Anselm
 1959 Mirrors and Masks: The Search for Identity. Glencoe: Free
       Press.

Suchman, Edward A.
 1964 Sociomedical Variation Among Ethnic Groups. American Journal
       of Sociology 70:319-33.

Suttles, Gerald D.
 1968 The Social Order of the Slum. Chicago: University of Chicago
       Press.

Tinker, John N.
 1973 Intermarriage and Ethnic Boundaries: The Japanese American
       Case. Journal of Social Issues 29(2):49-66.

Treudley, Mary Bosworth
 1949 Formal Organization and the Americanization Process, with
       Special Reference to the Greeks of Boston. American Sociological
       Review 14:44-53.

Uyeki, Eugene S.
 1960 Correlates of Ethnic Identification. American Journal of
       Sociology 65:468-74.

Veidemanis, Juris
    1963 Neglected Areas in the Sociology of Immigrants and Ethnic
           Groups in North America. Sociological Quarterly 4:325-34.

Ware, Timothy
    1972 The Orthodox Church. Bungay, Suffolk, Great Britian: Penguin
           Books.

Warner, W. Lloyd and Leo Srole
    1945 The Social Systems of American Ethnic Groups. New Haven:
           Yale University Press.

Weinstock, S. Alexander
    1969 Acculturation and Occupation: A Study of the 1956 Hungarian
           Refugees in the United States. The Hague: Martinus Nijhoff.

Whyte, William Foote
    1943 Street Corner Society. Chicago: University of Chicago Press.

Wirth, Louis
    1928 The Ghetto. Chicago: University of Chicago Press.

Woodhouse, C. M.
    1968 The Story of Modern Greece. London: Faber and Faber.

Xenides, J. P.
    1922 The Greeks in America. New York: G. H. Doran.

Yinger, J. Milton
    1961 Group Identification or Withdrawal. Daedalus 90:247-62.

Zangwill, Isreal
    1909 The Melting Pot. New York: Macmillan.

Zborowski, Mark
    1969 People in Pain. San Francisco: Jossey-Bass.

INDEX